ANCIENT EGYPTIANS

ANCIENT EGYPTIANS

THE KINGDOM OF
THE PHARAOHS
BROUGHT TO LIFE

BY ANTON GILL

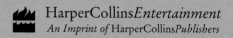
HarperCollins*Entertainment*
An Imprint of HarperCollins*Publishers*

Ancient Egyptians accompanies the
television series of the same name created
by Wall to Wall for Channel 4, TLC ®, and
Granada International in association with
Canal+, Norddeutscher Rundfunk/Germany,
RAI - Radiotelevisione Italiana,
Seven Network Australia and Warner Home
Video Inc., A Warner Bros. Entertainment
Company.
www.walltowall.co.uk

HarperCollins*Entertainment*
An imprint of HarperCollins*Publishers*
77–85 Fulham Palace Road
Hammersmith, London W6 8JB

www.harpercollins.co.uk

Published by
HarperCollins*Entertainment* 2003

9 8 7 6 5 4 3 2 1

Text © Anton Gill 2003

Photographs by Giles Keyte
© Wall to Wall (Egypt) Ltd 2003

ISBN 0 00 714399 0

Set in Adobe Garamond and Trajan

Printed and bound by
Scotprint

CONTENTS

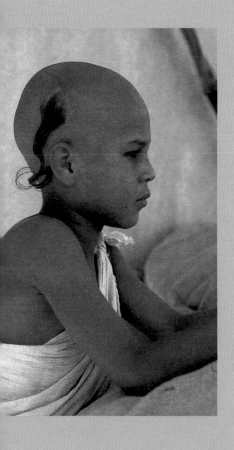

BE MERRY ALL YOUR LIFE;

TOIL NO MORE THAN IS REQUIRED,

NOR CUT SHORT THE TIME ALLOTTED FOR PLEASURE.

IT OFFENDS THE SPIRIT TO BE ROBBED OF ITS TIME,

SO WASTE NOT AN HOUR MORE THAN YOU MUST

TAKING CARE OF YOUR HOUSEHOLD.

WEALTH WILL COME EVEN IF YOU INDULGE YOUR OWN WISHES.

IT WILL BE USELESS IF YOU THWART THEM.

Instruction of Ptahhotep, *c.* 2350 BC

INTRODUCTION

Ancient Egyptians is inspired by the Channel 4 television series of the same name, produced by Wall to Wall. The series takes four stories from the lives of ordinary Egyptians living in ancient times and relates them in dramatic form. But the Egyptian empire lasted for 3500 years, and the events of each of the four episodes are separated by centuries. Ancient Egyptian civilization is famous for its relative changelessness; but changes did occur, in everything from perceptions of the gods to fashion, and there were great upheavals in the later stages of its history, when the closed world of the pharaohs became open to foreign influence. Thus, Part One of this book attempts the briefest survey of Ancient Egyptian history, so that the reader may be able to locate the stories in the context of the civilization in which they took place. An extensive bibliography provides information for those wishing to delve further.

This isn't a history book in the strict sense of the word, however, and the retelling of the key stories, which forms Part Two, follows the television series, to focus on what it was like to be an ordinary Egyptian at the time, and to glimpse a real North African world. There is a huge amount of material in the papyrus record concerning the 'official' history of Ancient Egypt, but relatively little that concerns the lives of the common people. In creating *Ancient Egyptians*, some assumptions have been made in interpreting the papyri and ostraca available to us, and gaps in stories have been filled by informed assumptions, for which there is academic precedent. What is presented both in the television series and in Part Two of the present work is authentic, with modern restoration and bridges.

Egyptology is still a relatively new academic discipline – it is barely 200 years old – and much disagreement exists between scholars over interpretation, dates, and individual people. One of the earliest kings, Narmer, for example, is sometimes also known as Menes. Another name by which he is sometimes known is Aha, though some scholars hold that Aha was Narmer's successor. The situation becomes less confusing the further we proceed through Egypt's history, but the precise and infallible

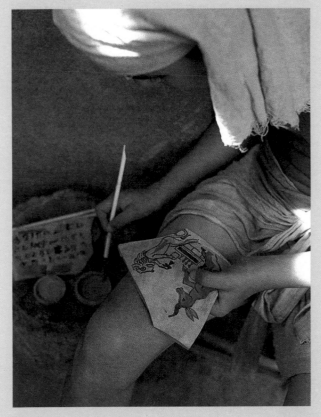

Ostraca, inscribed and painted pottery fragments, are a rich mine for Egyptologists reconstructing the lives of ordinary people in Ancient Egypt.

sorting and verification of such remote people and events, however well documented at the time, will always be difficult.

There is no standardized Roman Alphabet spelling of either Ancient Egyptian or Modern Arabic personal or place names. In this work, I have used the Ancient Egyptian names, rather than the old Greek or Roman ones, for most persons and places, e.g. Khufu rather than Cheops, and Psamtek rather than Psammetichus; but where a later name is more familiar than the Ancient Egyptian name, I have retained it, e.g. Memphis rather than Mennefer or any other variant. Where further explanation or clarification is necessary, it is provided in brackets immediately following the word in question, and this includes any modern Arab names. The use of the academic convention of transliteration of Ancient Egyptian language, with its complex system of diacritical

marks, has been avoided. In general, the convention of spelling followed is that used by Ian Shaw and Paul Nicholson in their *British Museum Dictionary of Ancient Egypt* (British Museum Publications, London, 1995).

I have used the convention BC (Before Christ) and AD (Anno Domini), which nowadays are sometimes given as BCE (Before Common Era) and CE (Common Era). I have stuck to the former convention because it is more familiar to the general reader and because it is adopted by the majority of writers on ancient history.

Among the many people who have helped and contributed to this book are the production team of *Ancient Egyptians*, especially the producer, Ben Goold, and the assistant producer, Alan Eyres. At HarperCollins I have to thank commissioning editor Val Hudson, editor Monica Chakraverty, Joanne Wilson, Juliet Davis and Martin Hendry. I also thank Marji Campi and Joanne Fletcher. The staffs of the British Library, the London Library and the British Museum have been as helpful as ever. The Egyptian Museums of Berlin, Cairo and Turin, and the Petrie Museum in London, have provided valuable information; and I owe a special debt of gratitude to all those scholarly Egyptologists whose works I have consulted, and which are listed in the bibliography.

LEFT: The fertile conditions of the land along-side the Nile were perfect for the flowering of a great civilization.

OVERLEAF: The magnificent Temple of Karnak in Thebes was the largest religious institution in Ancient Egypt.

PART ONE
CIVILIZATION
OF THE NILE

LAND AND PEOPLE

THE TWO LANDS

The civilization of what we know as Ancient Egypt was one of the earliest and certainly the longest-lived of any in recorded history. There were thirty-one royal dynasties, stretching from the accession of King Narmer in about 3100 BC to 30 BC, when the famous Queen Kleopatra VII committed suicide, all hope lost despite her magnificent political juggling, and power was ceded to Rome. During those three thousand years, Egypt enjoyed relative stability, and that was reflected in cultural forms that changed little in all that time, from clothing to temple architecture. Only in its dying centuries did the influence of Greece and Rome become apparent, and even then the immigrants from those cultures, who considered themselves superior, nevertheless adapted to the mores and cultural expression of Egypt.

A civilization that lasted three thousand years is hard to imagine today, and it is even harder to conceive of a culture that barely changed in all that time: a culture that neither wanted to change, nor was often influenced to change by outside elements. As we will see, there were changes, some profound, some short-lived, but none fundamental.

One reason for this extraordinary stasis may be found in the landscape and the climate of Ancient Egypt. These varied only slightly, almost negligibly. The Nile, the principal source of the country's strength, economic security and power would, from time to time, either fail to rise high enough in the season of Inundation, or rise too high. Either extreme – and the margin was a matter of a very few metres – would spell disaster for the harvest that

A view of Thebes clustered around the walls of the Temple of Karnak on the east bank of the Nile.

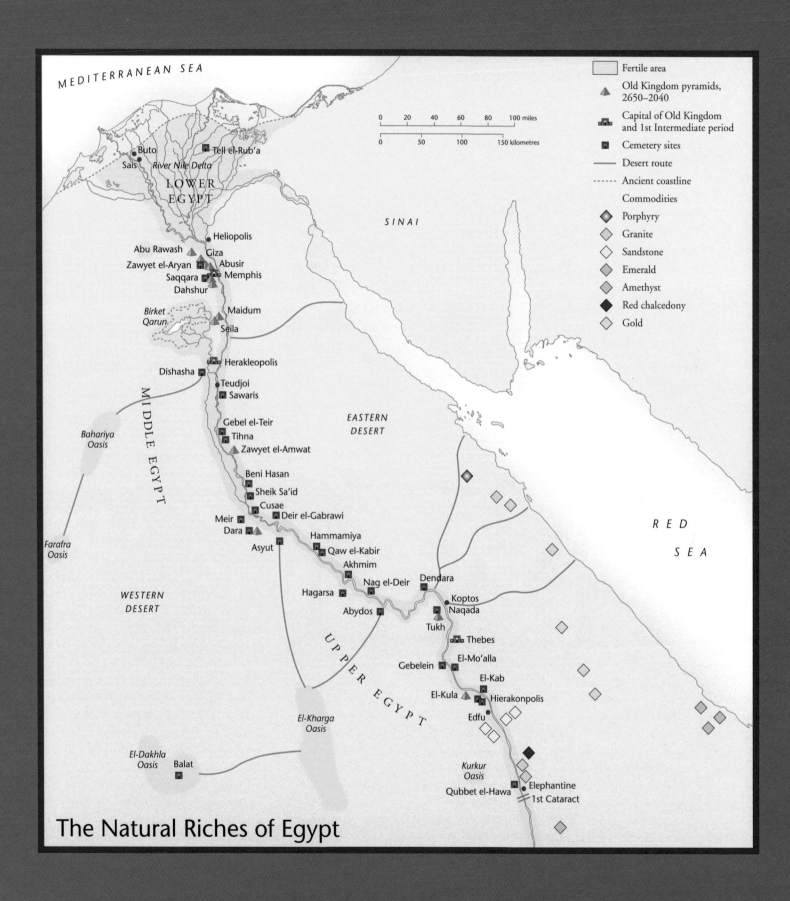

The Natural Riches of Egypt

Fertile area

Old Kingdom pyramids, 2650–2040

Capital of Old Kingdom and 1st Intermediate period

Cemetery sites

Desert route

Ancient coastline

Commodities

Porphyry

Granite

Sandstone

Emerald

Amethyst

Red chalcedony

Gold

MEDITERRANEAN SEA

SINAI

RED SEA

EASTERN DESERT

WESTERN DESERT

LOWER EGYPT

MIDDLE EGYPT

UPPER EGYPT

River Nile Delta

Buto
Sais
Tell el-Rub'a

Heliopolis
Abu Rawash
Giza
Zawyet el-Aryan
Abusir
Saqqara
Memphis
Dahshur

Birket Qarun
Maidum
Seila

Herakleopolis
Dishasha
Teudjoi
Sawaris

Gebel el-Teir
Tihna
Zawyet el-Amwat

Beni Hasan
Sheik Sa'id
Cusae
Deir el-Gabrawi
Meir
Dara
Hammamiya
Asyut
Qaw el-Kabir
Akhmim
Hagarsa
Nag el-Deir
Dendara
Abydos
Koptos
Naqada
Tukh
Thebes
Gebelein
El-Mo'alla
El-Kab
El-Kula
Hierakonpolis
Edfu

Bahariya Oasis
Farafra Oasis
El-Kharga Oasis
El-Dakhla Oasis
Balat
Kurkur Oasis
Qubbet el-Hawa
Elephantine
1st Cataract

0   20   40   60   80   100 miles
0   50   100   150 kilometres

THE EGYPTIAN YEAR

Ancient Egypt was basically an agrarian society and life there depended very much on following the seasons. Most peasants lived at subsistence level, but life was not uncomfortable. The year began as the dog-star, Sirius, known to the Egyptians as *Sothis*, reappeared from behind the sun after being eclipsed for seventy days. (It is perhaps no coincidence that in funeral arrangements a seventy-day period of embalming separated the death of an individual from his or her entombment or burial.) The first season of the year was *Akhet*, the Inundation, lasting from June to October. Heavy rainfall in the Sudan raised the level of the White Nile and a few

centuries passed, the height of a town would increase as new structures were raised on the rubble of the old.

When the waters began to recede, the agricultural year could begin, though the insects must have made work torture at times. Fields were repaired and demarcated anew, partly to avoid arguments, partly to comply with taxation requirements. Dykes and water-channels for irrigation were rebuilt. All this involved a huge amount of work, and to make sure it was done in time, large numbers of peasants attached to the pharaoh's estates, and effectively part of his property, were called up according to a kind of *corvée* system which existed from the earliest times. Similar

into the ground, rather than prepared the soil for them. The texture of the earth by now would be a rich, firm mud. Lumps would be broken up in advance of the sower and the plough by assistants with hoes. Spades and shovels were unknown. As well as emmer wheat and barley, flax was grown to provide the linen with which most Egyptians clothed themselves, though cotton was later introduced. Flax was also used for making rope and matting.

After planting, maintenance work, especially on irrigation, had to continue. Water was carried laboriously from lower to upper levels in pots attached to yokes, as the lifting device known as the *shaduf* was not invented until the New Kingdom. The *shaduf*, which survived well into modern times and could still be seen in the twentieth century AD, consisted of an upright support to which a cross-pole was fixed. At one end of this was a bucket, and at the other a counterweight. The water-wheel did not appear until Ptolemaic times.

As the seeds began to sprout, they had to be protected. The farmer's lot has been depicted by contemporary scribes as a hard one:

> He spends eight hours ploughing, and the worms are already waiting. He eats half his crop himself, the rest is taken by the hippopotamus. There are many mice in the fields, and locusts descend on them. Even cattle devour his harvest, and sparrows steal it. Alas for the farmer! The little that is left, thieves take from his barn. Then the scribe-officer arrives to count up the harvests; he has bailiffs with him who wield sticks, and black men with palm-stalks. 'Give us the grain,' they say. 'There is none!' So they hold him by the legs and beat him, then tie him up and throw him into the ditch. His wife is bound too, and his children, and their neighbours make haste to abandon them to save their own grain.

Pests were certainly a problem during the season of *Peret*, Coming-Forth, the Egyptian autumn; and although small boys were deployed to scare off the birds, anyone working in the fields had to watch out for snakes: the Egyptian cobra is two metres long; the horned viper – which forms a standard hieroglyph – was another reptile which had to be contended with; and the black-necked cobra, now rare in Egypt, is capable of spitting venom three metres into a victim's eyes, causing blindness.

Snakes were appeased by treating them as deities,

weeks later monsoon rains in Ethiopia had a similar effect on the Blue Nile and the Atbara tributary. The resultant floods reached Egypt in August, and during the latter part of that month and throughout September the river valley was flooded. If the floodwaters rose too high, whole communities could be at risk. Ancient Egyptians sited their towns and settlements on mounds or higher ground to save them from being swept away, but the mud-brick buildings were not expected to last forever and as decades and

levies on manpower were made at other times of the year, when less work was required in the fields, to undertake work on great monuments, such as the pyramids. It has been argued that this work had the secondary effect of keeping the people busy, so that they would not have time to reflect on their lot.

When the fields were ready, the time came, in October, for ploughing and sowing, which took place simultaneously – sometimes the seeds were strewn in front of the primitive plough, so that it turned them and cobra-headed Renenutet was the goddess of the harvest. The crops were reaped using sickles, and there followed the processes of threshing and storing the grain. The season of *Peret* came to an end in mid-February, and was followed by *Shemu*, the dry season, or spring, which lasted until the end of May or early June. This would have been the period when the peasants could find themselves co-opted for other tasks, from assisting with major building works to going to war.

LEFT: Sennejem and his wife are depicted on the wall of Sennejem's tomb. Egyptians viewed the after-life as an idyllic pastoral world, which is why agricultural scenes often adorn tombs.

BELOW: The young pharaoh wearing the uraeus or sacred serpent. The snake was a symbol of kingship in Egypt and was worn on the crown or headdress of royalty.

year. However, properly managed state granaries provided insurance against those possibilities and it was seldom that Egypt faced real material crisis.

The weather was predictable, the climate hot but not unbearably so, and the Great River – the Nile – provided the means of producing a virtually consistent supply of food. As for the landscape, that too was ordered, even monotonous. The location of the capital city was quickly established: at the junction of the Delta (from the Greek letter 'delta' on account of its shape) and the river. The northern part of the country was known as Lower Egypt, because, as the Nile flows north, its lower reaches are towards the Mediterranean. Upper Egypt, where the upper reaches lie, is the southern part. The country as a whole was called Kemet, 'The Black Land', after the fertile silt the Nile deposited annually during its flooding. The desert beyond went by the name of Deshret, 'The Red Land'.

In a country where the scenery and the weather hardly varied, and which was bounteous in its resources, Ancient Egyptian culture took shape. As the great French Egyptologist, Serge Sauneron, pointed out, 'Art, thought, lifestyle, manner of expression – everything in this land was marked by a static concept of things whose eternal rhythm did not change, but remained as they had originally been created.'

We live in a very different world, one of doubt and change. Adaptability, and the need to find new solutions all the time, dominate our thinking. For the Ancient Egyptians little changed, except towards the very end of their civilization. Their world was fixed: it worked, and, according to their experience, it had always worked. There was little need to question anything. What had been laid down to begin with was what mattered. Everything could be referred back to a common root of experience.

With such a plentiful water supply, the land was occupied long before pharaonic times. Although North Africa became hotter towards the end of the last Ice Age (about 12,000 years ago), there were long periods of rainfall, especially in the three millennia following 9000 BC, and again after 5000 BC and 4000 BC.

During the period *c.* 5500–2350 BC large areas of high desert uplands, and low-lying desert too, were inhabited

EARLY EGYPTIANS

Before 12000 BC: Lower and Middle Palaeolithic
Periods. Upper Palaeolithic (I). Nomadic
food-gatherers.

c. **12000:** Upper Palaeolithic (II). Camps of
fishing communities in Kom Ombo basin.

c. **8000:** Final Palaeolithic or Mesolithic Period.
First bows and arrows.

c. **4500:** Neolithic-Chalcolithic Period.
First identifiable periods of
pre-dynastic culture.

c. **3500:** Pre-dynastic cultures.

c. **3100:** Beginning of Dynastic Period.

by a very wide variety of animals and plants, and by peoples, at first hunter-gatherers and later pastoralists, who
profited from the fecundity of the land. The remains of
fishermen's camps dating from about 12000 BC have
been excavated near Kom Ombo, and other artefacts
from that period down to *c.* 8000 BC indicate that man
found it best to inhabit the flood-plain area in the neigh-
bourhood of the Nile, where he could hunt the aquatic
and woodland game as well as the creatures from the
drier steppe land beyond, which came to the river to
drink. Animal remains that have been found from those
times show the range of wildlife that lived in the region:
hartebeest, gazelle, wild ass, wild cattle as well as water
buffalo, but also hyena and ostrich, along with more
familiar denizens like hippo and crocodile. In the Eastern Desert there were elephant, rhino, giraffe, oryx, ibex,
barbary sheep, fallow deer and lion, among others. However, meteorological changes early on meant that some of
these species disappeared from the area. Rhino, elephant
and some species of gazelle had gone by the time of the
Fourth Dynasty, by when the kind of dry climate we
associate with modern Egypt had begun to set in.

It is possible that the period of transition from man as
hunter-gatherer to pastoralist took place over the period
9000–6000 BC, but that is a 'dark age' of which little certain knowledge exists. Perhaps it took place because the
reserves of wild animals had been over-hunted; certainly by
6000 BC there were agricultural communities dotted all
over the place. The earliest human farming societies arose
in modern Lebanon, Palestine and Jordan in the period
10000–8000 BC; the people who formed them were
slightly built, with long heads. Egypt may have been settled
in the north by some of these peoples, though settlers were
also arriving in the south, from further south and the west.

The modern period of aridity set in around 2500 BC,
but because of the Nile and the Delta, a limited area
along the river remained cultivable and habitable, as it
does to this day. Egypt, as Herodotus observed when he
travelled there in the fifth century BC, was 'the gift of the
river'. The Nile was not only a provider of the neccessities
of life, but also a means of fast and efficient transport
the length of this attenuated land. The wind blew
steadily from the north, so that ships heading upriver,
against the current, could raise their sails and benefit
from it. Ships travelling downriver stepped their masts
and let the current do most of the work. A picture of a
ship under sail was the hieroglyph for travelling south,
and one of a ship without sail or mast meant 'travelling
north'. The north wind was cooling, too, providing a
kind of massive beneficent air-conditioning for the
whole land. Houses were built with open windows facing
north to catch this wind.

The Delta comprises a fruitful wetland. This part of
the country was Lower Egypt, the country of the Red
Crown, protected by the cobra-goddess, Wadjet, whose
name means 'the green one' or, 'she of the papyrus'. Here
in the Delta the papyrus plant grew. Papyrus, emblematic of Lower Egypt, has now died out in its original
habitat except for artificial plantations and, still in the
wild, on the reaches of the White and Blue Niles, tribu-
taries far to the south. But in ancient times it flourished
in the Delta and not only provided paper but could also
be bound together to make boats, huts or, in the earliest
times, temples. It was even adaptable to the humbler
resources of rope, matting, baskets, raincoats (when
occasionally needed in the far south) and sandals.

A branch of the river Nile runs north from modern

El-Ashmunein to debouch in the fertile Faiyum Depression south-east of Memphis, and there are oases in the Western Desert, the most famous of which, not least for their wine-production in ancient times, were Dakhla and Kharga. In antiquity, when the land in Lower Egypt was much marshier and wetter, villages and farms in the Delta were founded on the desert borders and on sandy islands rising from the morass. In the Faiyum, Lake Moeris absorbed the floodwaters of the yearly inundation. The name Faiyum itself derives from *payom*, which simply means, 'the water'.

Southwards of the apex of the Delta near where Memphis was situated, lay the realm of Upper, or southern, Egypt. This part of the country was the domain of the vulture-goddess, Nekhbet, and its crown was the *hedjet*, or White Crown. The emblematic plant was the lotus, or water-lily. Three types grew, of which perhaps the fragrant blue lotus was the most enduring symbol.

In Upper Egypt, the river runs a straight course along its valley, finally passing out of Egypt and into Nubia. Its length, from the Mediterranean to the southern border, traditionally set at modern Aswan, is about 1250 kilometres.

The fertile countryside owed its existence to rich deposits of silt and mud that were thrown on to its banks by the Nile when it flooded at the start of the Egyptian year, in June. The process began about 10,000 years ago and only ended with the construction of the Aswan Dam, built by Soviet engineers between 1960 and 1970, which thereafter has controlled it.

There is a considerable difference between the cultivable land of Upper and Lower Egypt. In modern times, the maximum stretch on the Nile in Upper Egypt is about seven kilometres on either bank; whereas in Lower Egypt, the Delta, where so much of the water deposits its silt before debouching into the sea, commands an area of 15,000 square kilometres of arable land. A similar ratio would have existed in ancient times, and has some bearing on the relative importance of north and south in the country's history.

One of the largest of the Old Kingdom pyramids, Khufu's pyramid, named after the Fourth Dynasty king, is approximately four-and-a-half thousand years old.

PAPYRUS

The papyrus on which the Ancient Egyptians wrote is also the name of the plant from which it was made – the paper reed, *Cyperus papyrus*, which grew in huge amounts along the Nile and especially in the Delta. It has ceased to exist in the wild in Egypt, though some is grown in pools in front of the Egyptian Museum and the Agricultural Museum in Cairo.

The name means 'pertaining to the king' in Ancient Egyptian, and may indicate that the ruling house had a monopoly on papyrus – which was in fact the case in Ptolemaic Egypt. It is the root of our word 'paper', though of course paper today comes mainly from wood-pulp.

In antiquity, paper was made by slitting the stems of the papyrus reed and cutting them into thin strips, which were placed side by side and then covered with another layer at right angles to them. They were then sprinkled with water and beaten with stone hammers to release the starches within them, which then, with the water, served to bond the strips together. The sheets, anything between fifteen and fifty centimetres wide, were then laid out to dry. When ready, they were glued together and wound on to wooden rods. Some 'lengths' thus produced measured up to forty metres for a tract or literary work; but papyrus was used for letters and drawings on individual sheets as well. Scribes used red and black ink, made from

A Nineteenth Dynasty scene from the scribe Hunefer's *Book of the Dead*, which shows Osiris (seated on the throne) passing judgement on Hunefer's soul. The scribe is led by Horus while Thoth – the Ibis-headed figure on the left – takes notes.

water or saliva mixed with pigment, and used reed brushes, whose splayed ends were created by chewing. A scribe carried a special palette which held his ink and brushes. Scribes are often depicted with their pens stuck behind their ears.

Parchment, made of thinly stretched hide, was also used, though far less often. Ostraca (singular: ostracon) were shards of pottery or flakes of stone used to make rough notes or preliminary sketches.

NATURAL RESOURCES

The sun and the river were the fundamental elements in the lives of the Egyptians of antiquity. But the rich natural resources of the country would, as time progressed, play almost as big a role in its development, and contribute to making it, at the height of its power, the wealthiest land of the ancient world.

Egypt had access to plenty of gold, which was early recognized as a metal rare enough to command enormous buying power. Neighbouring rulers observed enviously that there was as much gold as sand in the Black Land, and although this is clearly an exaggeration, there was more than enough to ensure Egypt's supremacy once its civilization had established itself. Curiously, for a long period in the earlier dynastic times, silver, which was rare in Egypt and had to be imported from Western Asia and the Mediterranean, carried a higher value within the country than gold. But in Ancient Egyptian there was never a word that expressed 'silver'. 'White metal' was the closest formulation.

Lower Egypt yielded natron, the naturally occurring salt used in the hugely important process of mummification, as well as in rituals of purification. North of Memphis limestone and quartzite could be mined, and to the south-east of the town there was copper. Further south,

at Hatnub, and elsewhere in the Eastern Desert, there were alabaster quarries. In the Eastern Desert too, to the north-east of Thebes, were deposits of sandstone, porphyry and gold, as well as granite at Aswan and greywacke, an agglomeration of pebble and sandstone, in the Wadi Hammamat. Gold was to be found at many locations in the Eastern Desert, and in great volumes in the mines of Nubia, ancient Kush, which was controlled by Egypt for much of the Dynastic period. There, too, diorite, dolerite and gneiss were to be found, the old hard igneous rocks that lie beneath sandstone and limestone. Between Thebes and Kush, near Kom Ombo and Aswan and the sacred island of Elephantine, there was gold again, and granite and amethyst, as well as sandstone and red chalcedony. Near the Red Sea coast, approximately due east of Edfu, emeralds were to be found.

But all these were luxuries, the materials which contributed to art, architecture and religious observance. It cannot be denied that, second only to the country's enormous agricultural riches in the form of the alluvium deposited annually by a generous river, was its wealth in stone. The silt provided the means to live well; the stone provided the means to express that beneficence.

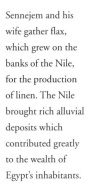

Sennejem and his wife gather flax, which grew on the banks of the Nile, for the production of linen. The Nile brought rich alluvial deposits which contributed greatly to the wealth of Egypt's inhabitants.

AGRICULTURE

In Ancient Egypt, everything grew, everything reached its peak, harvests were gathered; and daily the sun rose and fell, and annually the river flooded and receded.

Although few trees grew in Ancient Egypt, there were more then than there are now. Indigenous trees included the Egyptian willow, and the tamarisk, which is still plentiful, the acacia and, not native, but introduced very early, the sycamore fig. None of these was much good for building anything. As late as the Eighteenth Dynasty an attempt was made to cultivate olive trees, but that was not too successful, and it was only much later, in Ptolemaic times, that the olive tree took root. Two kinds of palm, the dom-palm and the date-palm, the former cultivated for drink, the latter for fruit, have been grown since the earliest times. The country was agricultural in its economic base, and along with domesticated animals, principally goats and cattle, barley and wheat were grown to provide the staple food, bread, though varieties of beans and lentils, as well as onions and garlic, lettuce and celery, were also cultivated. Herbs were used both in cooking and medicine. The rich could eat luxury fruits such as the persea, which tastes like a sweetish apple and is similar in size, though more oval in shape. Fish and pork were generally avoided by wealthy people.

There were at least fifteen different kinds of bread, and

During the harvest season, crops such as emmer wheat and barley were gathered (below) and winnowed (left).

it has been argued that barley-bread was eaten by the poor, and wheat-bread by the rich. The basic loaf was probably not unlike modern *pitta*. Bread was made from flour produced on a stone quern and particles of stone, sand and other impurities in the bread led to the erosion of the teeth which scientists have noticed in many preserved examples, though this is less marked in upper-class mummies, who in life would presumably have eaten finer bread. But even among them abscesses were common. The Egyptologist Eugen Strouhal has pointed out that 'if a tooth fell out, Egyptian dentists were able to fasten it to its sound neighbours with gold or silver wire'.

The peasant would eke out his bread with beans and

IMPORTS AND EXPORTS

For its basic needs, Egypt was very largely self-sufficient, but it was poor in timber, and as its society became more sophisticated, demand grew among the upper classes for luxury goods. Olive oil, for example, would be bought in from Crete. Lapis lazuli, barter system similar to that used domestically, and Egypt offered in exchange for the goods it needed either straightforward amounts of gold, or manufactured articles which relatively unsophisticated trading partners would find attractive. Sometimes the barter system would be light local trading vessels could be made of papyrus, any craft intended to carry heavy cargoes, such as obelisks from the granite quarries in the south, or timber from Byblos, needed to be built of wood. In return for the cedarwood, Byblos received gold, manufactured goods, and ebony

known to the Egyptians as *khesbed*, was prized in the decoration of the most opulent tombs, and used extensively in jewellery and in the making of amulets. It was always considered far superior to imitations in faience (a type of ceramic compound based on crushed quartz) or glass. Already known in the pre-dynastic periods, it had to be imported from as far away as Badakhshan, in north-eastern Afghanistan, though quantities must have come via the Middle and Near East through subsidiary trading. The remains of an Asiatic Bactrian camel have been unearthed from a ninth-century BC Egyptian site, and during the Twenty-second Dynasty King Takelot II sent King Shalamaneser III of Assyria a selection of exotic animals, including two such camels. The dromedaries one sees in modern Egypt did not appear until the time of the Persian Occupation, around 500 BC.

Foreign trade almost certainly operated on a

as basic as each side laying out for display what it had to offer, then withdrawing from or adding to its pile until agreement was reached.

Trade with the developed states of the Mediterranean was more refined, and conducted on a regular basis, as Egypt for long periods had a controlling or diplomatic presence in Palestine and Syria. The ancient east-Mediterranean port of Byblos, sited in modern Lebanon, was where the Egyptians sent their sea-going ships to collect the timber they lacked themselves. The famous 'cedars of Lebanon' grew in the hinterland in abundance until the Egyptians managed, even in antiquity, to over-exploit them. The Egyptians were not natural sailors, unlike the Greeks, and tended to follow coastal routes when venturing on to the Mediterranean and Red Seas; but water-travel was ingrained in them and journeying by boat on the Nile was an absolute necessity. Although skiffs and

ABOVE: Egypt had its own supply of gold, which held divine symbolism as it never tarnished. Lapis lazuli scarab bracelet, with gold, cornelian and green faience.

and ivory, the latter two commodities themselves first imported by Egypt from the land of Punt, which may have been in the region of modern Eritrea.

Punt was a supplier of gold, aromatic resins, various hardwoods including ebony, and exotic animals such as cheetahs and dog-headed baboons. Punt acquired a mythical status in the eyes of Ancient Egyptians, partly because of its remoteness, and partly through the extraordinary things that arrived from it. The best documented period of trade with Punt was during the reign of Queen Hatshepsut (1473–1458 BC), and details of it are recorded on the walls of her funerary temple at Deir el-Bahri.

onions and river-fish, as well as the occasional duck or other river-bird. To drink, he would have beer, which frequently made up at least part of his breakfast. Ancient Egyptian beer, made from barley or wheat, was opaque and thick, not very alcoholic, but highly nutritious. Dates and pomegranates were available and used as sweeteners, as well as honey.

For those who could afford it, the most popular meat was beef, though goat and mutton were also eaten, as well as the flesh of game animals such as antelope. There is a famous depiction of men force-feeding hyenas. It has been argued that this was part of an attempt to domesticate the beasts, perhaps for the purpose of hunting. It seems unlikely that the animals were being fattened for the pot, since it's hard to imagine that the taste of their flesh would be agreeable. Vines were cultivated even in pre-dynastic times and the rich drank wine with their meals. There were even vintage wines and some are mentioned in royal records from as early as the First Dynasty.

Barley is added to water – the first stage in making beer; fish formed part of the staple diet for the poor; a lamb butcher displays his wares.

MEDICINE

A medical profession existed in Ancient Egypt and it operated on a highly skilled level, though some thinking about how the body operated was primitive. The heart was regarded as the seat of the mind, and the brain was regarded as an unimportant organ chiefly useful for keeping the sinuses clear. However, a number of medical texts survive which show that the Ancient Egyptians did know a good deal about anatomy, and for the most part their medicine was based on science not magic, though the Egyptians didn't really distinguish clearly between the two. The doctors were good at treating injuries and could recognize the difference between simple and compound fractures. Fractures were set using palm ribs, strips of bark or wood bound with linen or plant fibre bandages. Linen bandages were also used for dressing wounds. A surgeon's tools included knives, forceps, and wooden and metal probes. Knives would be heated to lance a boil or abscess in order to cauterize the wound, and in heating the instrument the doctor would also unknowingly have sterilized it.

The Ancient Egyptians identified about 200 different types of illness, although it is not always easy to relate the descriptions to modern ailments, perhaps because the doctors simply didn't know what the functions of various organs actually were.

Illnesses abounded, and some of them are still to be found in Egypt today. The mud-brick houses in which most people lived tended to be damp, leading to various disorders, such as tuberculosis and bronchitis; poor ventilation and lack of chimneys led to other lung diseases, which were also caused by sand inhalation. The Nile and contaminated water (beer was drunk far more than water) generally led to diseases such as bilharzia, which gave rise to blood in the urine, and the lack of any great sense of hygiene (and its relation to better health) in the cities led to a large number of other complaints such as piles and cystitis. Bilharzia, an illness caused by a parasitic worm which uses water snails as an intermediary host, is still not uncommon in Egypt. The eggs laid by the parasite within the body enter the bloodstream, the bladder and the guts. As well as blood in the urine already mentioned, symptoms include enlargement of the genitalia and hair loss. The disease is an ancient one: a pre-dynastic body preserved at the British Museum in London carries the earliest known evidence of it.

In ancient times there were several similar maladies,

including infestations of thread-worms, tape-worms and liver-flukes. Smallpox and poliomyelitis, as well as, possibly, malaria were known, and a variety of diseases of the bone, such as spinal osteophytosis and arthritis. It was not uncommon for people to suffer from a failure in bone development that led to dwarfism, a condition which remained in the population on account of inbreeding. Dwarfs often feature in Egyptian art: they were frequently attached to the court but carried no stigma. Indeed, they married and led normal lives.

Added to the maladies, there was also always the risk of snakebite in the fields. There was also the risk of attack by crocodiles or hippos.

Whilst the wealthy in Ancient Egypt were obsessed with hygiene and cleanliness, the vast majority of the population lived in poor, unsanitary conditions.

MEASUREMENTS AND VALUES

The Egyptian bureaucracy was complex and the scribes who ran it needed to have access to a precise method of measuring the value of things. Tomb paintings of everyday life frequently portray scribes seated under trees with pen and paper to hand, counting cattle or assessing sacks of grain.

Counting was based on a unit of ten – there were ten days in the Egyptian week, followed by a day of rest, for example. There was no symbol for 'nought', and scribes therefore left a blank to indicate it between numbers. Symbols have been identified for 1, 10, 100, 1000, 10,000, 100,000 and 1 million, the last often carrying the sense of 'countless'. The frog and the tadpole have been identified as symbols for 10,000 and 100,000 – understandably as they existed in such huge numbers on the banks of the Nile and in the Delta.

The Egyptians did not develop mathematics in general to the sophisticated degree attained by the Greeks, but they did develop the science to a point which suited them for practical purposes, especially in the field of geometry, necessary for their ambitious building programmes.

A system of fixed weights was also introduced, and archaeologists have discovered a great many of them, made of stone, pottery and bronze. The earliest come from the dawn of the Egyptian civilization. Sometimes they are in the shape of bulls' heads, others are inscribed with their 'value'. The most common was called the *deben*, a unit of about 93.3 grams. Later on another unit, the *kite*, was introduced, weighing 9–10 grams, and the *deben* was standardized to weigh 10 *kite*. The *deben* was used to measure copper, silver and gold; the *kite* was used for silver and gold alone.

Capacity was commonly measured in a unit called the *hin,* just under half a litre, ten of which made up a *hekat*, sixteen of which equalled a *khar*.

Units of length were important in architecture, land-measurement, and in laying out large murals. The principal unit was the *royal cubit*, at 52.5 centimetres deemed to approximate the length of a man's forearm. This was made up of 28 'digits', or thumb-widths, or 7 palm-widths. A 'short-cubit' of about 45 centimetres was used by artists, and there were other variations during the foreign occupations towards the end of the Empire's existence. Area was measured by the *aroura*, 100 square cubits.

In a society without money, values of goods, crops and cattle had to be exactly measured for purposes of taxation and remuneration. This was resolved by a complex system in which a notional agreed value was ascribed to any given 'goods' of whatever type, which was their market value. This value could be expressed on paper or as tokens and therefore be much more easily exchanged: if a man were paid 100 loaves and 3.5 goats a week, for example, he could hardly receive, store or consume such things physically. Tokens or paper-valuations could be exchanged for the real thing as needed, or yielded up to the scribe tax-gatherers. The stone and copper weights already described could be used to express the value of an object. For example, a manufactured object such as a coffin might be valued at 25.5 *deben* of copper. This could be paid for either in the value in copper, or in a mixture of commodities whose values were predetermined. For instance, the coffin might be purchased, to follow an example given by J. J. Janssen, with 13.5 *deben* of copper, plus two goats (each valued according to size at three and two *deben*), two logs of wood at one *deben* each, and a hog at five *deben*.

Weights for use in scales were often cast in the shape of animal heads.

SOCIAL STRUCTURE

Society was strictly regimented: at the top was the pharaoh and his immediate family. Then came the aristocracy, whose importance varied in magnitude across the centuries. This upper, administrative class often overlapped with the religious class, since priests could also be secular administrators and their religious work was quite unrelated to the work of most of their modern counterparts. (Religion was a matter of state. Temples were not open to the public, nor were services held in which the common people took part.) The aristocracy also provided the military leaders. Within these elite classes there were of course many ranks, and from their number came the landowners and big farmers who formed what might very loosely be described as a middle-class. But by far the greatest portion of the population was made up of peasant-farmers and their families, whose working lives were as tied to the land as to the seasons.

Family life was close and informal. Much has been said about the incestuous brother-and-sister marriages of the

RIGHT: Egyptian aristocrats lived in large detached villas, often with an outside courtyard and elegant gardens.

FAR RIGHT:
A family makes an offering in the courtyard of their home. Religious rites took place in public and private. Note the 'lock of youth' on the otherwise shaven head of the boy.

DOMESTIC RELATIONS

The following maxim is taken from the 'Instructions of Ptahhotep', attributed to a Fifth Dynasty vizier:

If you are excellent, you shall establish your household
and love your wife according to her
standard:
fill her belly, clothe her back;
perfume is a prescription for her limbs.
Make her happy as long as you live!
She is a field, good for her lord.
You shall not pass judgement on her,
remove her from power, suppress her.
Her eye when she sees anything is her
stormwind.
This is how to make her endure in your
house:
you shall restrain her. A female
who is in her own hands is like rainwater:
she is sought, and she has flown away.

Egyptian Royal Houses, but these were not always the norm and were usually entered into to protect the dynastic line. Among ordinary people this was not the case, although marriage between cousins, and even uncles and nieces, took place to keep property within the family.

People often married in their early teens. There was no formal ceremony, though at times during the dynastic period the material interests of the husband and wife would be protected by a legal document in case of divorce. If the man instigated the divorce, the woman would get back her dowry and any marriage 'gift' or additional settlement brought with her on marriage, as well as a share of the marital property. If the woman started divorce proceedings (and she was perfectly free to do so) she would still have her dowry returned, as well as a share of the marital property. There was no shame or disgrace attendant on divorce, and both parties could

and often did marry again. Apart from the nobility, Egyptian society was generally monogamous. Marriage must frequently, indeed more often than not, have taken place by arrangement, in order to cement or extend property; but love as the emotion we recognize was known to the Ancient Egyptians and that is incontestably proven by the relatively large number of beautiful and erotic love poems that have come down to us from that distant time.

Attitudes to misbehaviour such as adultery varied in the course of the history of the country, but it was generally frowned upon and punishments for guilty women were harsher than those for guilty men. Homosexuality by and large seems to have been tolerated: there is even a short story concerning a pharaoh's affair with one of his generals.

Although women were by no means consistently treated as equals throughout the history of Ancient Egypt, they did enjoy a great degree of equality, and could own their own property, run a business of their own, be partners in a business, be signatories to legal documents and adopt children in their own right. Women could also inherit land and property. They were fully protected in law and their husbands had to take a responsible attitude to them. 'Books of Instruction', which form a major part of Ancient Egyptian literature, offer advice on correct social behaviour: 'Love your wife, feed her, clothe her and make her happy,' says Ptah-hotep. 'But don't let her gain the upper hand!' Another writer, Ani, counsels: 'Don't boss your wife about in her own house when you know she is efficient. Don't keep saying to her, "Where is it? Bring it to me!" – especially when you know it is in the place where it ought to be.'

What women did not get was a formal education. Schools, often attached to temples, were for boys, and only for the sons of the noble, administrative, priestly and military classes. They attended school from about the age of five to as old as fifteen.

A notary's office at Saqqara. The notary was an official responsible for maintaining judicial order. This included the issue of marriage, birth and death certificates, and the settlement of civil disputes and property transfers.

RACIAL ORIGINS

Egypt enjoyed a rich culture and civilization. But where did the original inhabitants come from? Over the centuries intermarriage with Libyans and Palestinians in the north, and Nubians in the south, would have tended to modify any 'pure' original race.

In the south, the indigenous people were small and fine-boned, with wavy hair, and long, narrow skulls. In the north, the inhabitants were bigger, and their skulls were larger. At first the two halves of the country developed independently, but the fortune conferred upon them all by the bounty of the river led quickly to a shared sense of superiority to 'outsiders'. Not only the generosity of the land, but its isolation, shut in as it was by deserts to the east and west, by the sea to the north and by the expanse of Africa to the south, combined with its own internal wealth, gave the Ancient Egyptians a feeling of natural greatness. They would have to deal with their neighbours, but always, it seemed, from a position of condescension and advantage. This was a double-edged sword, because they clung to what they knew and what was already known. In many ways they were unconcerned with intellectual development past a given point of certainty, but thereafter their own consistency of power carried with it an underlying weakness.

Although the peoples of Lower and Upper Egypt did not always trust each other, and were open to very different influences from their separate neighbouring lands, they were united in the belief that they were more fortunate than any other nation. A faint arrogance was combined with a certain defensiveness as well, for the Egyptians were not a complacent race. They worked hard, and although they were not naturally given to great military expansionism, they could and did organize armies to defend their territories and subdue vassal races, and under certain kings did indeed mount major military campaigns.

Egypt was a multicultural society.
Its rich resources brought traders
to Egypt's cities from the Mediterranean
north and the African heartlands to the south.

RIGHT: Nubian soldiers were recruited into the Egyptian army and valued for their skills as bowmen.

ECONOMICS

Organization in general was another matter – to put it crudely, Ancient Egyptians operated on the principle of 'if it isn't broken, don't mend it'. Although a sophisticated barter system operated, money as we know it wasn't introduced until very late on, in the Ptolemaic period, when the land was ruled by outsiders. There was no earlier Egyptian word or concept approximate to our sense of 'economics'.

If a system worked, there was no need to develop it. Similarly, although the central administration of what was effectively a long, narrow land (owned almost entirely by the pharaoh – i.e., the state) was complex, and involved intricate methods of calculating, for example, taxation, no fully developed mathematical system ever emerged. The scribes, who made up the class of elite administrators who ran the country and could best be described in modern terms, very broadly, as 'civil servants', used a system of counting in which, except for commonly used fractions such as two-thirds and three-quarters, which had their own signs, no other fraction had a greater numerator than one. Thus, two-fifths would be written out as 'one-third-plus-one-fifteenth',

Women played a major role in the Egyptian economy, often owning stalls or running them.

Mass production of beer produced a proliferation in the manufacture of pottery and pots such as these.

and more complicated fractions had to be expressed as whole series added up. Only one extant papyrus record, known after its discoverer as the Rhind Papyrus, presents a table of fractions in which the numerator is two.

The attitude to any form of mass-production was similarly unambitious. In temple bakeries, bread had to be produced in large quantities. We would immediately approach the problem of how to do this by creating a large oven in which many loaves could be baked by perhaps a handful of bakers. But the Egyptians simply took the ordinary domestic oven and replicated it over and over again. There was enough manpower, there was enough wealth, so there was no need to look for a more efficient solution.

Although these are examples of what might appear to be intellectual sluggishness, the great achievements of the Egyptians when their imagination was engaged should not be forgotten, the most obvious examples of which are in the realms of architecture and writing.

EARLIEST
TIMES

EARLIEST SETTLEMENTS

Roughly shaped flint axes have been discovered in sites south of Abydos which date to as long ago as 200,000 BC, and finds from later periods have shown that the not-always-welcoming region which became Egypt was settled and remained so from the very earliest times. There is more evidence of human activity from 100,000 BC and from 30,000 BC. We have already seen that the earliest communities of which we have concrete traces, near Kom Ombo, were centred on fishing, and excavations have unearthed a vast quantity of fish bones near Qena, dating from about 12,000 BC. The remote ancestors of the Ancient Egyptians probably ate their fish smoked, to judge by the carbon waste from fires that also marks the site.

The land was rendered uninhabitable by the floods in the earliest times, and man had to retreat to levels above the Nile flood plain to exist with any security. But the presence of water in such quantity was an irresistible lure.

The earliest settlements were on the low spurs of the desert, out of reach of the inundation and the swamps. It isn't known precisely when the earliest settlers began to cultivate fields on the floor of the valley, but it must have been hard work even to clear a plot sufficient for their needs. However, once this first step had been taken, the water of the river would repay the investment generously, as yearly it would offer up fresh supplies of rich soil. Each year the inundation would fertilize the earth and grain could be sown in the same place; so it wasn't long before early man, recognizing the beneficence of the land, settled down. The hunter-gatherers gradually became settled cultivators.

The first period of settlement that can be identified archaeologically over a measurable time is called the Badarian Period, dating from about 5500 to 4000 BC, although a site at Merimda on the edge of the Delta, about ninety kilometres north of the Faiyum, has been discovered which pre-dates Badarian culture by several centuries, and gives evidence of a separate, northern mini-civilization. Other Delta sites have also come to light. The Delta itself, as we know it today, was formed about 6500–5500 BC.

The name 'Badarian' derives from a district in which a pre-dynastic settlement, near the modern village of el-Hammamiya, containing significant artefacts was excavated. Several burial sites were discovered, mainly oval in shape (although there were more elaborate rectangular tombs), in which the body was contracted into an embryonic posture and laid out facing the west, contained either in a basket, or simply shrouded. Animals – dogs, jackals, sheep and cattle – were buried in the same cemeteries as people, and this is an indication of early animal-cults. The cow was revered as a mother-goddess, and the jackal was associated with a god of the dead.

Badarian people believed in life after death, and no burial was without the deceased's possessions, however modest. The tombs of the rich contained much finery. The art of the time was the basis for a tradition which changed little in fundamental style over the millennia: acute observation of nature coupled with an ability to reduce animals and plants to their essential qualities. Mummification was a later development: in the earliest burials, the bodies were placed directly into the sand, which acted as a natural preserver since it desiccated them. Only later, when tombs became more elaborate – reflections of the houses in which the dead had dwelt in life – and the corpse was not in direct contact with the sand, did artificial means have to be found to preserve the body for the afterlife. As early as the Second Dynasty the Ancient Egyptians had devised a means of preserving the body by placing linen pads soaked in solutions of resin between the individually wrapped limbs, the pads being shaped to follow the contours, so that if the flesh rotted, the pads would preserve the form. It was of crucial importance that the body was whole, but if a part of the actual corpse had decayed or was simply missing, for example, a finger, it could be replaced with a wooden substitute. The whole attitude to death seems obsessive, yet the Ancient Egyptians weren't so frightened of the mystique surrounding mortuary rites that they desisted, from the earliest times, from tomb robbery. No consistent embalming process was developed until much later, and the hope of a secure life in the hereafter was sustained through spells as much as chemical efficacy.

THE RIVER

The Nile was the bringer of life. It was referred to simply either as 'The River' or 'The Great River'. The inundation of the river was worshipped in the form of the god Hapy, an androgynous figure with a pot belly (a symbol of wealth), a beard, and pendulous breasts, wearing a headdress of river plants. The Nile was the source of the moisture by which crops could be cultivated regularly in a land where rainfall was more or less non-existent, and it was the thoroughfare by which ships could trade and carry tax-collectors and administrators throughout the land. It was secure, because beyond the margin of fertile soil on either side were vast stretches of desert, which an invading enemy could not hope to penetrate, and it ensured a food supply, which meant that Ancient Egyptians of all classes seldom suffered real want. This meant in turn that the workforce and potential army were reliably strong – another source (apart from the rich mineral and agricultural resources of the country) of confidence and superiority for the Black Land.

ABOVE: A fisherman guides his papyrus canoe through the shallows along the banks of the Nile.

LEFT: A funerary papyrus document from c.1100 BC shows the Nile as a formalized strip dividing the tiers of agricultural activity and worship. The looped sequences in the bottom left-hand corner represent irrigation canals.

The birth of architecture, best known to us through the tombs they built, took place about this time, and what remains from that distant period is already quite sophisticated. Most First Dynasty kings were buried at Abydos, and most Second Dynasty rulers found their last resting place at Saqqara, a name derived from Sokar, a Memphite god of the dead. Some Egyptologists have argued that Abydos contained largely the cenotaphs of kings, whose lasting presence and power in the south needed to be emphasized for the sake of political stability, and that the tombs themselves were chiefly centred at Saqqara from the first. However many experts disagree with this.

Mud-brick was the preferred medium, though stone was already in use, not only in building, but in sculpture, itself another form of artistic expression that developed early on. The reign of the last king of the Second Dynasty, Khasekhemwy, produced two magnificent statues of the ruler, one in schist and the other in limestone. Both show Khasekhemwy sitting on a low-backed throne, the whole form solidly cube-shaped. His right fist is clenched on his thigh, and his left hand rests on his right forearm. On his head is the White Crown. This confident, powerful manner of depicting the sovereign as the epitome of authority was to endure as an artistic convention for three thousand years.

Linen was already known to them, and the people wore beaded jewellery. Their pottery was of various types, from containers and vases with red or brown bodies and black tops, to others with polished bodies either entirely red or black. Their flint artefacts were, by contrast, rather basic. The beads they wore were mainly glazed, and appear to have been imported, as do the smaller number of copper beads and copper-finished articles. They also used shells for decoration, which came from the Red Sea or the Persian Gulf, and they wore amulets, which may originally have been hunting charms, since among the forms they took were such things as hippos, or a gazelle's head carved in bone. They had bracelets in ivory, bone or horn, sometimes artfully decorated. Utensils, such as spoons and ladles, were fashioned from horn or bone and often the handles were decorated with the carved heads of animals.

These early people also used cosmetics, much beloved by Ancient Egyptians of both sexes, which were sometimes kept in beautifully carved, minute ivory vases. Everyone had to grind his own cosmetics on palettes of slate or stone, and people of the Badarian culture used rectangular palettes. A favourite cosmetic was derived from ground green malachite, mixed with fat, resin or castor-oil. This was used as an eye-liner, and its purpose was not just decorative: the fatty medium in which the malachite was compounded caught grains of sand; and the malachite itself deflected the sun's rays and deterred flies.

The Badarian culture people were hunters and fisherfolk, but they were also cultivators, growing wheat and barley, and these, along with their domestic animals, sheep and goats, were of Asiatic origin and must have originally been acquired through some contact with Asia. Even at this still relatively early stage, the people were of mixed racial origin, since some had fine skulls and others thick, heavy ones. No evidence of houses remains, suggesting that their way of life may have been locally semi-nomadic, and that they lived in tents.

Mummy of a ram, one of the animals associated with Amun, the tutelary deity of Thebes; now in the Egyptian Museum, Cairo.

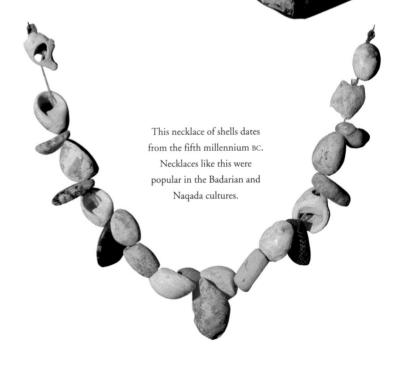

This necklace of shells dates from the fifth millennium BC. Necklaces like this were popular in the Badarian and Naqada cultures.

NAQADA PERIOD

The next culture also takes its name from a place, Naqada, north of Thebes, and is divided into two or (latterly) three phases, though the last, Naqada III, was only two hundred years in duration, and is sometimes known as the proto-dynastic period, a time of transition between the earliest times and the more-or-less traceable dynasties.

Naqada I lasted from 4000 to 3500 BC. It was characterized by circular mud-huts which may have been dwellings or warehouses, and earthenware decorated with white criss-crossed lines. The only houses that have been identified with any certainty are at el-Hammamiya, where the remains of nine circular buildings have been found, between one and two metres across. Simple agriculture, supplemented by hunting and fishing, was the basic means of living – very similar to those of the people of the Badarian culture.

The graves of Naqada I were similar to Badarian ones, and though little has been recovered from them – even less than from the previous period – a pair of miniature sandals in ivory has been found, indicating that there was a tradition of burying representative belongings (or models of the real thing) as grave-goods with the deceased. An innovation of this period seems to have been ivory pins, and some weaponry has survived in the form of a disc-shaped mace-head and some long flint knives, though all may have been for ceremonial purposes, and the knives seem far too delicate for use in battle. Copper goods were still rare, and gold scarcely appears at all.

Very little is known in detail about the political or social organization of these people, but they were town-dwellers who lived in fortified settlements. Some of their grander tombs contained artefacts which were clearly of magical or ritualistic use, which indicates that shamans were important members of society. Among these finds are vases and figurines in the shape of a fertility goddess, often reduced to essentials of belly, breasts and vulva. The people of the Naqada I period used more elaborate make-up palettes than their immediate ancestors, carving them in the shape of turtles, birds, fish and hippos.

The Naqada II period spans the years 3500 to 3100 BC and ushers in a new and vital influence on the people of Upper Egypt. The cause of this was the immigration of a new people. It's likely that they first arrived not as invaders but as traders and, finding the Nile Valley a hospitable and fertile place, gradually settled down there, merging with the existing older population. One clue about where they came from may be drawn from the ship-pictures which decorated the pottery of the period. One place other than the Nile Valley proper in which the same style of decoration can be found is the Wadi Hammamat, which links the Nile in southern Egypt with the Red Sea. The famous Egyptologist William Matthew Flinders Petrie (1853–1942) deduced that the newcomers entered Egypt by this route, and the hypothesis is borne out by the fact that the earliest artefacts associated with them were found at Koptos, Naqada itself and Diospolis Parva, all near the Nile end of Wadi Hammamat. Egyptian tradition has also always maintained that the country was unified and civilized by the first king, Narmer or Menes, from the south. Narmer's monuments have been found throughout

Some Naqada pottery is among the finest Egypt has ever produced. Dating from around 4000 BC these pots, now in the British Museum, show the fine craftsmanship that the period is known for.

southern Egypt and he also traded with settlements in the Delta and even Palestine.

The newcomers brought with them a great creative and expansionist instinct. Their presence turned a gifted prehistoric race into one with the capability of forming a great nation.

Practically speaking, they brought a more systematic approach to agriculture and possibly also conducted the earliest experiments with irrigation and the digging of canals for that purpose. It has been argued that the infrastructure needed to regulate irrigation was itself one of the fundamental factors in unifying the country, for such a project could not be undertaken by one settlement or even one district alone.

We have, however, no idea precisely how agriculture was organized, or who owned and/or controlled what land. Sowing and harvesting had to be organized on a large, collective scale, and by the early dynastic period, from about 3100 BC onwards, the king certainly 'owned' vast estates. Early on, therefore, land which originally might have been administered by the local or district headman on behalf of the community had passed to royal control. Ancient Egypt was divided into (traditionally) forty-two administrative districts, each called a *sepat* but more commonly known now by their Greek name of *nome*. These districts were probably based on large, at least semi-autonomous, estates of very early date. How the transition took place is still unclear, but what is certain is that by the end of the Naqada II period a king who had consolidated power in Upper Egypt began to annex Lower Egypt.

The reason for this expansion northwards isn't hard to find. The fertile Faiyum and the Delta offered enormous possibilities to an ambitious people.

The cemeteries of the period indicate a much more complex and class-divided society than before, although the dead were still buried in a foetal position, wrapped in linen or mats, and surrounded by personal effects for use in the afterlife.

Polished earthenware of red, black and black-top was still current, as well as unpolished patterned vessels. Their forms took on a greater variety, and the decora-

tions now predominantly featured ships: the Nile was from the very earliest times the thoroughfare of the country. Travel was fast and efficient. It has been calculated that it took three to four weeks to sail from the First Cataract to the Mediterranean. The appearance in society of specialists – craftsmen, sailors and even administrators – can be dated to this period. The cylindrical seal appeared, a product of Mesopotamia, where it had been known much earlier. With it came the beginnings of a written record.

Alongside the pottery appeared exquisitely worked stoneware – bowls and vases in the shapes of animals and birds made from alabaster, basalt, porphyry, schist, serpentine and, above all, the plentiful and easily worked limestone. The availability of copper and limestone in the area around Memphis and its position at the apex of the Delta, led to an early rise in the district's importance.

More sophisticated flint tools had appeared too, and there was an increase in the amount of jewellery in all forms, especially beads and amulets, while gold, obsidian and lapis lazuli were being used as materials. Make-up palettes became even more ornate and some knitted fabric has been discovered. Silver began to make an appearance: a silver ceremonial adze, and a model of a hawk, one of the earliest divine symbols (as the hawk flew close to the sun), have been discovered. Copper-work became more diverse too: harpoons, daggers, maces, knives, needles, finger-rings and pins, as well as axes and adzes. Craftsmen also worked with electrum (white gold).

During the last phase of pre-dynastic history, known as Naqada III, some of the settlements which had been the cradles of the preceding cultures, notably Naqada itself, and Nekhen (Hierakonpolis) to the south of it, and Thinis to the north, began to develop into powerful mini-states. The Confederacies of Thinis and Naqada had access to the Eastern Desert with its gold and other mineral resources. Naqada too lay near the Nile end of the Wadi Hammamat – the main route into the Eastern Desert and to the Red Sea. Nekhen controlled the route south to Nubia, and it is probable that King Scorpion, who may have been the last great king of the pre-dynastic

OPPOSITE:
A pre-dynastic sand-burial, resulting in natural mummification. This example, nicknamed 'Ginger' because of the colour of the man's hair, is preserved in the British Museum, London.

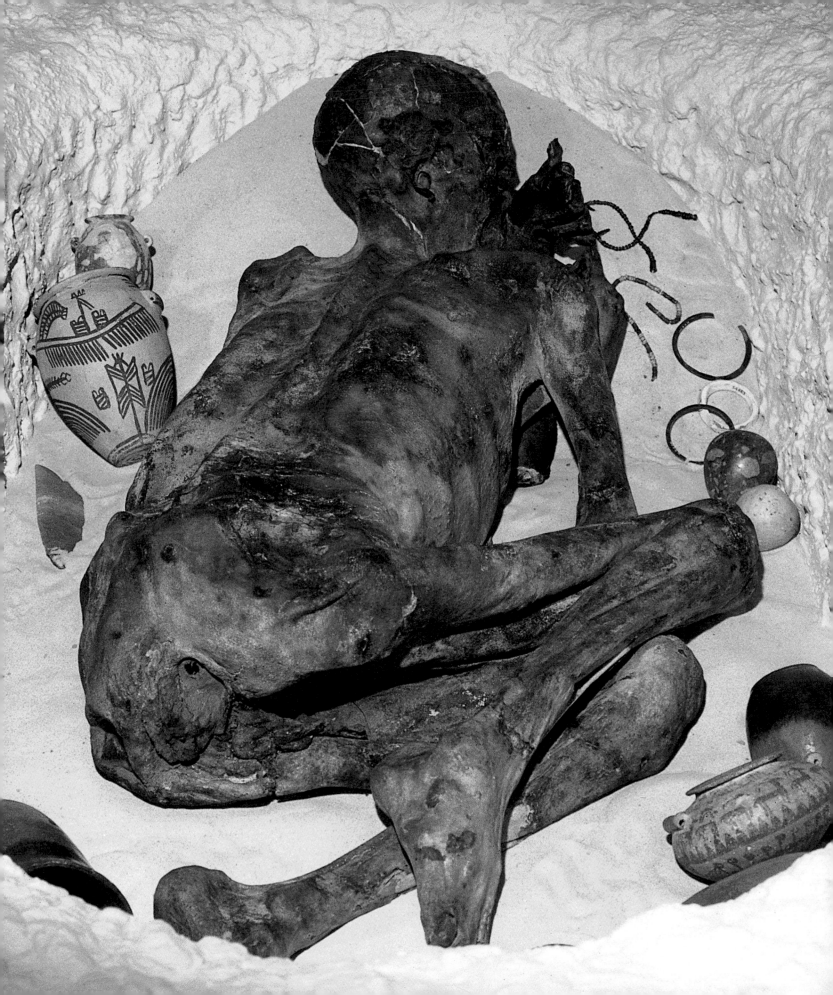

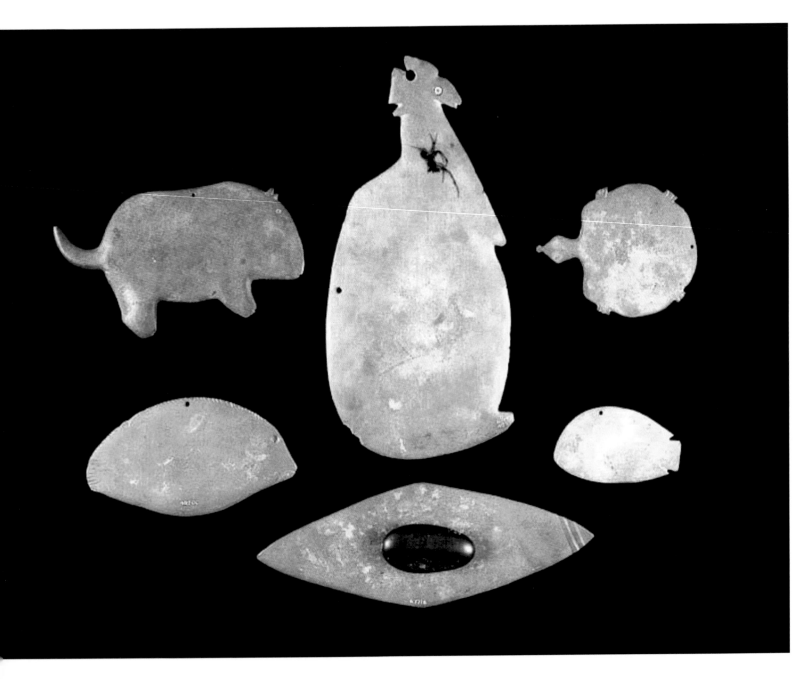

period, ruled from here. It was from the Confederacy of Thinis, however, that the unifying kings of the First Dynasty emerged.

Early royal tombs comprised a burial chamber and a number of other rooms, below ground but marked at ground level by rectangular mud-brick structures which could be quite large, up to sixty metres long and twenty metres wide. Grave-goods were stored in them. They had

walls which sloped gently inwards from the ground up, and they are known by the Arab word for a kind of bench they resemble: *mastaba*. That of King Den at Saqqara is a notable example. When it was excavated in AD 1936, it was found to hold in its storerooms, among other things, 60 wooden tools, 305 flint tools, 493 arrows and 362 jars of alabaster, crystal and schist.

Meanwhile, the towns that formed the cores of the

Animal-shaped palettes of slate used to grind cosmetics, dating from around 3300 BC.

confederations were no longer collections of tents or mud-huts, but properly planned and laid-out cities of mud-brick, fortified and solid, with temples and monumental buildings. Members of the highest caste were buried in massive brick tombs, and kings began to associate themselves with the local deities, just as later the pharaohs would be associated closely with the chief gods.

These finely carved flint knives are over five thousand years old.

There was also a new theme in art: warfare; though this may have conveyed a sense of ability to defend rather than a desire to attack. Rulers were depicted as bulls, hawks or lions, slaughtering hapless enemies. Everywhere themes were emerging which were to endure throughout Ancient Egyptian culture, such as the image of the king holding a crouching victim by the hair with one hand, about to smite him with a mace held in the other.

The confederations of Thinis, Naqada and Nekhen merged into one kingdom before embarking on campaigns of military expansion to both north and south. These would result in the foundation of the land of

Ancient Egypt as it became established in dynastic times, and it was from this proto-kingdom that the new rulers of the whole land would emerge; but to the south lay several autonomous confederations, including an important one at Elephantine, and to the north were many more, especially at Memphis and in the Delta. The period of transition is unclear, and overshadowed by the legendary king Menes, who may have been the historical king Narmer, though this is not at all certain. As the Egyptologist Bill Manley has succinctly put it, 'Traditionally, the state of Egypt was created when the legendary king Menes led the armies of Upper Egypt to defeat the kingdom of Lower Egypt, and then founded his new capital at Memphis. The story of Menes, however, belongs to mythology, as do the twin kingdoms, and it seems certain that Egypt became a unified cultural and economic domain long before her first king ascended the throne.' Political unification probably also proceeded gradually, perhaps over a period of a century, as local districts established trading networks, and the ability of their governments to organize agriculture and labour on a large scale increased. Horus, the local god at Nekhen but already widely known and worshipped, became a national god, if not *the* national god, after unification; Set, tutelary deity of Naqada, and Ptah, the god of Memphis, both also enjoyed early national status.

This mixture of developing interdependence, through trade and perhaps through the need to cooperate on such projects as irrigation, for the Nile was common to all and vital to all, set the stage for the takeover by force of the weaker confederations by the stronger, who also saw that control of the Nile was ultimately necessary for their security. Arguably unification was a by-product of this necessity, and a central administration became the only efficient means of controlling the country. From early on, administration became a skill that was handed on through families, and as time passed, it became harder for an outsider to break into these domestic cartels, though the court was always open to real talent if it had the luck or the political ability to manifest itself. The means of recording and communicating matters of state in writing was the cornerstone of Egyptian power.

THE EARLY DYNASTIES

The First Dynasty dates from the year its founder, Narmer, ascended what was to become the Golden Throne in about 3100 BC. The shadowy figure of Menes, recorded by Manetho as the first king and founder of the First Dynasty, may be a conflation of Narmer and Scorpion. We are aware that Scorpion really existed because his name is mentioned on fragments of an ancient ceremonial mace-head, where a picture shows him wearing the White Crown of Upper Egypt. Menes has his supporters among early historians: Herodotus and Manetho claim that he founded Memphis; Manetho further tells us that he was killed by a hippo after a reign of sixty-four years, while the Sicilian historian Diodorus Siculus, who lived about 40 BC, assures us that the king was attacked by his own dogs, but rescued by a crocodile which carried him across a lake to safety, as a result of which he built the city of Crocodilopolis on the shore, decreeing that from thenceforward crocodiles should be allowed to live and breed unmolested in the lake.

However, Menes remains a kind of Egyptian King Arthur, and the likeliest scenario for the transition between pre-dynastic and dynastic times is that Scorpion subjugated the south, while Narmer took the conquest northwards. Knowledge of these early years comes from two sources: the Palermo Stone and the Narmer Palette.

The Palermo Stone comprises broken fragments of a basalt stela from the Fifth Dynasty. Both sides are inscribed with important historical data concerning the rulers up to then and from before the dynastic era. The main piece is in Palermo, in the Sicilian Archaeological Museum, but there are other pieces in Cairo and London. Unfortunately important sections are missing, so that there is no clue to the Stone's provenance. However, the annals of the kings it records go well back beyond history into mythology. The Stone also records festivals, military campaigns and the passing of laws, as well as trade with countries as far away as Syria, and the record of mining expeditions to Sinai.

The Narmer Palette (in the Cairo Museum) is made of mudstone (a coarse-grained, gritty shale, readily reduced to mud by the action of frost, of which there was little fear in Egypt). The Palette gives us our primary proof of

Narmer's existence, though there is also a limestone votive mace-head, now in the Ashmolean Museum, Oxford, which also 'mentions' him. Both were discovered in Hierakonpolis and both date to around 3100 BC. Whether the scenes depicted on the mace-head and the Palette show actual historical events, or symbolical summaries, remains the subject of lively debate among experts.

Only fragments of the mace-head survive, but the Palette has miraculously remained not only intact but in almost perfect condition. Both sides show a relief carving of Narmer, identified by his written name inscribed in early hieroglyphs. Interestingly enough, on one side Narmer is shown wearing the White Crown of Upper Egypt, like Scorpion before him. He is standing over an enemy in the pose we have already established as emblematic: in his left hand he holds the kneeling foe's hair. In his right, arm upraised, is a cudgel with which he is about to brain him. Above and in front of him to his left is a hawk or falcon, symbol of Horus, lording it over another, but now an emblematic rather than realistic, enemy. Two things are striking: the early appearance of the hawk or falcon as a god associated with the king, and the artistic convention whereby the action and the characters in it are flattened out. That this durable convention of Ancient Egyptian art should have been established so early must give us pause.

The obverse of the Palette shows Narmer again, somewhat smaller, and this time, highly significantly, wearing the Red Crown traditionally and (later) historically associated with Lower Egypt. Now the battle is over –

CREATION MYTHS

Isis, the sister-wife of Osiris,
is one of the oldest and most
important goddesses in the
Ancient Egyptian pantheon.

J ust as there are many gods who overlap with
each other, perform the same function, and
are more or less important in different areas of
the country, so, in a civilization that lasted so long
and reflected such a wide diversity, there are
several main creation myths.

The first concerns nine primal gods: Atum,
Shu, Tefnut, Geb, Nut, Osiris, Isis, Nephthys and
Set. It tells how Atum (later identified with the
sun-god Ra) came out of the pre-existing sea,
Nun, after he had created himself or had been
born of Nun. He created an island in the sea, the
primal mound which is celebrated throughout the
Egyptian religion and which the architecture of
temples reflects. Ra-Atum then divided day and
night, and, taking the form of the bird called
Benu, alighted on the *benben* pillar. The bird,
whose name means 'to rise', would later evolve
into the Phoenix of the Greeks, and may
originally have been either a yellow wagtail or a
heron. Either way, the *benben* stone or mound on
which it sat symbolized the primal mound and
had its origin at Heliopolis. This stone – a pillar
originally capped by a small dome, was probably
the origin of the obelisk with its pyramidion top.
The derivation of its name also comes from 'to

rise'. Life's regenerative force was associated from
the very beginning with the sunrise.

Ra-Atum, alone, then created Shu and Tefnut,
the god of air and the goddess of moisture. Shu
and Tefnut, brother and sister, then slept together
and produced Geb, god of the earth, and Nut,
goddess of the sky. Geb lay beneath Nut, and her
body, arched over him, formed the sky. Their
children were the sisters Isis and Nephthys, and
their husbands, Osiris and Set, who were to
develop the complicated pantheon that succeeded
them.

But this creation myth originated at Heliopolis.
Other local priesthoods and centres of power also
laid claim to a *de facto* primal myth, in order to
attest their political superiority. At Hermopolis,
for example, a rival cosmogony was evolved which
postulated Nun again as the primal sea, but
associated him with Kek (darkness), Amun
(air/'the hidden force'), Heh (infinity) and their
consorts, in all forming a cosmogony of eight gods
and goddesses. However, the strongest 'rival' to
the Heliopolitan tenet was that of Memphis. Here
the creator-god was Ptah.

Ptah belonged to a triad. His consort was the
lioness-goddess (reminiscent in many ways of the
later Hindu Kali), who was a creator-destroyer:
Sekhmet, and the less important Nefertem,
represented by the blue lotus, and perhaps the son
of Sekhmet. Ptah, associated from early on with
craftsmen, probably drew the bulk of his power
from the place of his cult. It is odd, however, that
he is presented, as Osiris frequently is, as a
mummiform god and it is equally interesting that
his heart – in Ancient Egyptian thinking the
centre of all intellect and emotion – is supposed to
have brought the world into being through
thought and the spoken word.

THE SUN

It is no wonder that the Ancient Egyptians associated their fundamental conceptions of deities with moisture and light. The river and the sun were recognized from the first as the sources of life, and venerated in many forms accordingly.

The sun was the most fundamental god, in common with all religions. As Aten, it was represented in the form of the sun's disc, and this god's cult was especially revered during the short but iconoclastic reign of the Eighteenth Dynasty pharaoh Akhenaten, who banned all other deities in favour of this one, whose power was then further refined into a sense of the life-giving force of the sun's rays. Akhenaten's adoption of the Aten in favour of all other gods has been viewed as the birth of the concept of monotheism.

The sun is also associated with Atum, the creator-god and sun-god of Heliopolis, and the originator of the primal nine gods of that city. He was associated with the bull, the lion and the scarab beetle – the last because it was active when the sun was at its height, at noon, when most other beings were sheltering from the sun's power. The scarab also rolled a ball of dung before it: the ball symbolic of the sun. In the ball were its eggs, which when ready gave birth, as it were, to its

young, who emerged from the ball, symbolizing for the Ancient Egyptians who observed this, a spontaneous life-force, though this view has been challenged. At times Atum was represented as a snake – a primal and often threatening form to which he was expected to revert when the universe collapsed and all things returned to their original state.

The third major god connected with the sun was Ra – first encountered by association with the second king of the Second Dynasty, Raneb. Often depicted as a hawk-headed human with a sun-disc on his head, he became the dominant sun-god as other sun-deities became fused with him. His centre was at Heliopolis, and the important strategic position of this city may have led to Ra's domination over other sun-gods.

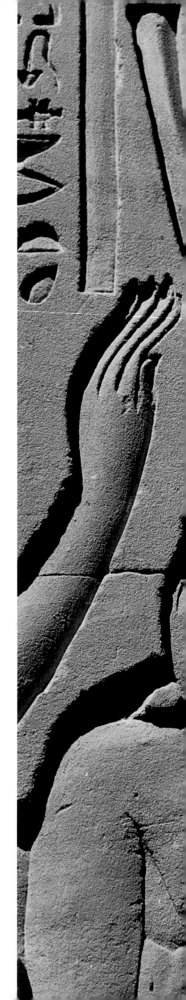

The sun – Ra – was a fundamental Egyptian deity. Here it is represented (above) as a disc supported by a scarab beetle on a gold bracelet, and (left) between the horns of a mummified Apis Bull.

standards are borne before him, as he reviews an array of decapitated corpses of the defeated enemy.

Other than these two valuable sources of information, there is little evidence of what actually happened during the first two dynasties. Narmer's queen was Neithhotep, and his successor was Aha, as far as we know; but Aha may have been a king who reigned concurrently and took over the reins of power when Narmer died. It is also possible that Aha wrote a treatise on anatomy, but this is yet to be proved. Aha was followed by Djer. Seventeen of the fifty-odd years of his reign are recorded on the Palermo Stone, but what is written has to do more with religious ritual than historical events, though it is possible that he fought in the north, against the Libyans, and also in Sinai.

Djer's successor was Djet, but here there is confusion. Somewhere in the line, unusually for these early times, there may have been a Queen Merneith. It has been argued that she was the daughter of Djer, the wife of Djet and the mother of his successor, Den. However, the fact that there were few actual female pharaohs does not mean that women, in the royal house as in society, did not have an important social and political role. The Queen Mother, the king's Chief Wife and the king's Chief Daughter were all key figures in the hierarchy, and the complex rules of succession dictated that the next king should be the son of the Principal God (i.e., the pharaoh) and the Principal Wife. The next Principal Wife in line would be the Principal Daughter, so the next ruler needed to marry her to substantiate his claim to the throne. As the next ruler was usually the son of the king and queen, it followed that he would marry a woman who was either his sister or his half-sister.

Den was the first king to wear the double-crown: a combination of the Red Crown of Lower Egypt and the White Crown of Upper Egypt – thus proclaiming himself king of the two lands, and though this had probably been established earlier, the convention of the combined

The double crown was first worn by King Narmer. The crown represented the kingdoms of Upper Egypt and Lower Egypt united under one ruler. Here it is shown on Ptolemy IX Soter II, Temple of Horus, Edfu.

crowns found its expression now. He was the first king to have been known by the title 'He Who Belongs To The Sedge And The Bee' – references to other signal attributes of Lower (bee) and Upper (sedge) Egypt. But following this dramatic moment, the First Dynasty seems to have petered out after a couple of minor kings, and no-one knows exactly why it came to an end.

The first five kings of the Second Dynasty are similarly shrouded in mystery, and the division between the two royal houses can so far only be based on conjecture. It is known that the sixth king, Peribsen, introduced the cult of the god Set into Heliopolis, and that his successor Khasekhemwy conducted numerous campaigns in Nubia.

Early palaces, which were also the administrative centres (revenue, tax inspectorate, armoury, granaries and public works), were built of mud-brick, the staple building material in early times, and one which has continued to the present. Because of the friability of the material, very little evidence of the earliest examples has survived.

Socially, a system began that was to serve as a matrix for succeeding generations of administrators: the king became established as god on earth and head of state. The chief executive was a kind of vizier, but under him were chancellors of the Red and White Houses – executives for, respectively, Lower and Upper Egypt. There would also be relationships with foreign powers, mainly mercantile and diplomatic, for the Ancient Egyptians were not naturally bellicose, despite some intense military activity involved in unification. We know that Djer is the possible author of a treatise on anatomy, and we also know that he founded the first royal palace at Memphis and there encouraged the arts and architecture.

Specialized craftsmen were employed at Memphis for the making of luxury goods both for use in life and in the hereafter. They had their own district to live in, and their very existence was a testimony to the material well-being of society. Earthenware was now utilitarian, but vessels of alabaster, basalt, breccia, diorite and other rocks showed the art of the stone carver and polisher at its height. Limestone-cutting reached a new level of sophistication in the walls of tombs, and this

and by comparison we may reflect that communism as a controlling doctrine lasted less than a century, and that the USA's control of world power will probably end within a similar period.

From early on a sophisticated and centralized system of taxation was developed. Because the Ancient Egyptians had no concept of money *per se*, taxes were paid in kind, largely in the form of storable commodities like grain, which were placed in the royal granaries partly as a kind of early gold standard and partly for distribution amongst the people in the event of a poor inundation and consequent bad harvest. Much later, the Seven Plagues of Egypt recorded in the colourful and magnificently vengeful texts of the Old Testament, recall the kind of misfortunes that could befall the Ancient Egyptians.

The inundation dictated levels of taxation, and in years of surplus, supplies of food were used in trade with neighbours for other commodities which in lean years would have been in short supply, such as wood from Lebanon and Syria or olive oil from Palestine and Cyprus.

All the early kings must have been able military campaigners, but if they left records of their achievements, these are yet to be found. Den certainly campaigned in Sinai; we also know the name, from this period, of one of the first administrators – Den's vizier, Hemaka; and during his reign occurred the first recorded *Sed* festival – a celebration which traditionally (though not strictly) marked the first thirty years of a king's reign, after which it could be held more frequently.

Den was succeeded by Anedjib, and two more kings followed him before the First Dynasty came to an end in circumstances which have not yet been fully explored. The Second Dynasty consisted of seven kings, whose reigns, like those of the First Dynasty, covered a period of about 200 years. Little enough is known of it, but what is important is that by the time it ended, in about 2690 BC, in the words of Egyptologist Barbara Watterson, 'a unified state with a strong centralized government had emerged, and Memphis was firmly established as the capital city of Egypt. These two factors, and important cultural advances, brought Egypt to the brink of its first golden age, the Old Kingdom.'

ABOVE: Silos such as these were used to store grain levied as tax by the state.

LEFT:
The development of more sophisticated tools went hand-in-hand with the development of a class of artisans and craftsmen.

achievement went hand-in-hand with the development of copper tools. Carpentry, as better types of wood in larger pieces arrived from the north, became more ambitious in tandem with the availability of better tools: inlay and complex joints were introduced. Jewellery-making and metalwork developed similarly, and gold began to be used to a prodigious extent, especially in the tombs of the rich.

Djer's successor, Djet, was another patron of the arts, and under the next king, Den, Egypt began to enjoy the economic supremacy that was to ensure its position as the leading nation of the world for nearly three millennia. There is nothing in history to match this hegemony,

THE PYRAMID BUILDERS

THE OLD KINGDOM

Egyptologists date the beginning of the Old Kingdom from the start of the Third Dynasty. This dynasty didn't last long – only about seventy years, and it left little historical record behind it. In fact the administrators of the Old Kingdom, which embraced the Third to Sixth Dynasties, seem to have been either disinclined or uninterested in marking contemporary events in stone, and little remains, from that great distance of time, of the papyrus records of day-to-day happenings. We have little to go on other than statements of family relationships, the names and titles of officials, and those of members of the royal family, though these do become more discursive as the Old Kingdom progresses.

The Third Dynasty, short though it was, was nevertheless a period of great development. As the cult of the afterlife grew and became more formalized, so it may have become a means of maintaining the status quo, as well as of advertising the king's authority. The first and greatest expression of this was the pyramid, the massive tomb structure everyone immediately calls to mind on hearing the words, 'Ancient Egypt'. The pyramid formed part of a temple complex, with attendant buildings and a causeway running either to the river or to a man-made rectangular sacred lake, but its own massive form was an unequivocal statement of might.

The Third Dynasty comprised five kings, of whom the second, Djoser, was by far the most important. Djoser may well have been a commoner who managed to rise to the top through sheer ability. He is best remembered now for his monument, the Step-Pyramid at Saqqara, the area to the west of Memphis, which was to become a great necropolis and temple-centre. Saqqara's name derives from that of Sokar, the Memphite god of the dead. The necropolis at Saqqara at its greatest extent was large, measuring eight kilometres in length and between 500 and 1500 metres wide.

The Step-Pyramid was the invention of Djoser's principal minister and architect, Imhotep, a man subsequently so revered in Ancient Egyptian culture that he was deified after his death. Imhotep not only invented the pyramid as a form, but conceived the formal idea of the funerary complex, and initiated the first large-scale building in stone in the Empire's history. Imhotep also grasped the psychological value of the pyramid: it took enormous effort, time and resources to build. It was thus a powerful symbol of the king's ability to organize the people he ruled, and even, lying as it did near to his seat of power, acted as a marker of the city in which he reigned and which was the home of his centralized administration. The city was also something new.

Imhotep refined the shape of the tomb, building up the original *mastaba* into a series decreasing in size, ascending to heaven. The pyramid drew its form from the primal mound of earth, the 'High-Sand', and from the *benben* stone from which it took its formalized shape. For the next thousand years, pyramid-building became a fundamental factor in Ancient Egyptian society, though the sheer size of the earliest pyramids would not be matched in later times as the emphasis placed on a royal burial lessened.

There are few more impressive things in the Egypt of today than the Step-Pyramid of Djoser, over one hundred years older than the Great Pyramid of Khufu. When it was new, in about 2650 BC, it must have struck even sophisticated people with an awe approaching fear, with its sides cased in white stone, towering above the enclosure wall of limestone, complete with massive, but false, gates. And as a visitor passed through the narrow, colonnaded entrance to the complex, he must have been struck by the imitation in stone of building materials he was already familiar with – wood, reeds and matting, all in great detail, from the fences, the 'log' roofs, and the 'tree-trunk' columns to the 'wooden' doors carved in stone as if they had been swung open on their hinges.

In the private underground galleries the dark corridors were covered with faience tiles in imitation of mats and screens, framing panels of exquisite low-relief carving. Columns would be decorated with papyrus or lotus capitals, and it would take a mass of them to hold up a roof. They needed to be solidly made, too, because gateways were constructed by the simple means of columns supporting a lintel of stone placed on top of them: the Ancient Egyptians never invented the arch.

The Step Pyramid of Djoser as it is today, 5000 years since its construction.

The last king of the Third Dynasty was Huni, who may have been the father of the first king of the Fourth, Sneferu, remembered in later literature as agreeable and benevolent. Already, it appears, the united kingdom had been able to lay aside its warlike guise and, enjoying prosperity, devote itself to a development of the humanities. By the Third Dynasty too, the art of mummification had made significant advances.

That Sneferu's reign might have been one of heightened sophistication is indicated by a much later (Middle Kingdom) story that describes the king, bored, wandering aimlessly through his palace until the magician Djadjaemankh suggests that he should seek diversion on the lake in the grounds. This he does in a boat crewed by girls from the harem, on the king's command dressed in nothing but fishing-nets. One of them loses her hair ornament, and before the party can continue, Djadjae-

mankh is ordered to roll back the waters so that the ornament, a malachite fish, can be found, and so it is, lying on a potsherd at the bottom. Beautiful silver bracelets from this period have also survived from the otherwise looted tomb of Sneferu's Chief Wife and half-sister, Hetepheres, the mother of Khufu. That tomb-robbers were already operating in remote antiquity is attested by the fact that Hetepheres' grave was plundered only fifteen years into Khufu's reign (he succeeded Sneferu in 2589 BC). When Khufu found out about the robbery he ordered that his mother's coffin and her surviving grave-goods should be transferred to another location, but it is possible that no-one realized that the coffin itself had been opened and resealed after his mother's body had been removed to strip it of its jewellery and amulets, which would have meant unwrapping the mummy. The corpse was irretrievably lost, but this early desecration,

BURIAL

The Egyptologist Donald B. Redford has pointed out:

> Cemeteries were separated from the living and placed, usually, but by no means always, on the western desert edge; consequently death involved a journey from the home of the living to the house of the dead in the desert. The Realm of the Dead was in fact projected over the trackless desert wastes, and out here only the instincts of a canine – jackal, dog or wolf – would prevail. Such a quadruped could always be seen prowling among the tombs or over the desert, seeming to find his way where no path existed. And thus it is no surprise that, in Middle Egypt especially, where the low sandy desert emerges at a gentle gradient from the valley floor, the canine should have become the essential town deity, protecting the dead and leading them to the west.

and the relatively frequent incidence of grave-pillaging from early on, indicates that there was always a section of society that believed none of the mythology of the afterlife, or was desperate enough to ignore it.

Three pyramids were built during the reign of Sneferu, one at Meidum and two at Dahshur, all of them moving away from the step-construction and representing the first experiments with smooth-sided pyramids. For the first time, the tomb chamber was inside the pyramid, not beneath it, which led to the development of the corbel roof to support the weight of the pyramid above the tomb chamber. The one at Meidum may have been started by Huni, and began life as a type of step-pyramid, but the two at Dahshur seem from the first to have been conceived as smooth-sided. The southern one is 'bent' –

Royal mummies were buried in gilded coffins and elaborately decorated sarcophagi.

The great pyramids
of Giza which lie
on the Giza Plateau,
today part of
Greater Cairo.

the upper half is at a different angle from the lower – but the northern, 'Red' pyramid was true. The latter is second only to the Great Pyramid in base area, and may have been Sneferu's actual last resting-place.

Of course there has been a great deal of theorizing about what pyramids were, and even whether they were tombs at all; but the high period of pyramid building lasted a relatively short time, and did not significantly outlast the Fourth Dynasty.

This period of building experimentation could only have been indulged in during a period of security. There was no external military threat during this period, and only an occasional raid by the small standing army was needed to keep the tribes that lived along the country's frontiers in line. Thus it was that throughout the Fourth Dynasty the great period of pyramid-building continued. It was during this dynasty too that the art of sculp-

ture reached an early peak, as extant statues of its rulers demonstrate. Relief sculpture rapidly became popular and is to be seen on surviving buildings everywhere. There were two types – true relief, in which the figures stand out from the stone, and sunken relief, in which they are carved into it. The latter, being quicker to execute, is more common, but the artistic standard of both is always consistently high.

The most famous pyramid of all, the Great Pyramid, was constructed at Giza during the reign of Sneferu's successor, Khufu, as his monument. Already recognized in the Ancient World as one of its seven wonders, it would when new have been an extraordinary sight, gleaming white on the desert plain and visible for kilometres around. Herodotus, visiting Egypt around 450 BC, relates a story that Khufu put his daughter out to prostitution in order to pay for the stone. The biggest of the three famous pyramids at Giza, its construction is impressive: there is an error of only about twenty centimetres at the bases, though the average length of each base is about 250 metres. The right angles at the corners are virtually exact, as is the angle of slope of each face; but statistically the most impressive factor is the volume of the building. Like the other pyramids, the Great Pyramid of Khufu is a solid structure apart from the small

ARTS AND CRAFTS

There are many depictions of craftsmen at work in the tomb-paintings, and through them, and the wooden and clay models made during the Middle Kingdom, as well as actual tools which have survived, we can get a detailed impression of the way these people went about their work. Design changed as fashions altered and new technologies developed, enabling us to date various artefacts with a degree of accuracy; but the way workshops seem to have been organized remained pretty much unchanged down the centuries.

By the end of the Old Kingdom production by individuals had given way to specialized factories where a number of craftsmen of differing specialist skills worked together to manufacture any given object. These men worked, not necessarily for themselves or as a cooperative, but for the crown, or a temple. If, as was the case of the tomb-workmen in the Valley of the Kings during Ramesside times, they were effectively state employees, even their tools would not be their own, but the property of the state, and they would be handed out to them in the morning and collected again at night. Tools, especially ones with metal components, were expensive, and the scribe-administrators responsible for them were strict in their surveillance.

The first specialists were the tool-makers themselves, but even in dynastic times when bronze and copper were freely available, there was still a place for makers of flint tools, which were used in rituals and in the art of embalming. Metalworking and smelting were skills acquired early, though the art of smelting was imported from Asia Minor. Bellows, however, were not invented until the New Kingdom.

Next come the craftsmen in stone and wood. Stone vases of extraordinary delicacy and superb finish have been discovered from the very earliest times, polished and bored using sand and water, abrasive stones, and drills furnished with hard stone bits.

Stonemasons cut everything from the easily workable limestone to the much harder granite using saws, sand and water, and trimmed blocks with an astonishing degree of accuracy. Sculptors would have their stone cut by masons, mark out their designs with a piece of ochre, then carve out their statues.

Carpenters were especially prized because wood was such a valuable and rare commodity; at the top of the pecking order would have been the shipwrights, but furniture-makers for the elite in society would not have been far behind them. The range of tools the carpenters and cabinet-makers used was relatively narrow: they had the axe, the saw, the adze (a very widely used tool), the mallet, the drill and the chisel. The most common article of furniture was the stool, which came in a variety of heights and levels of sophistication in design.

Pottery and ceramic vessels of every conceivable kind, and to fulfil every possible purpose, were produced from early on, some with complex and delicate decoration. Pottery-factories are one of the most obvious examples of mass-production, with rows and rows of storage jars (for example) laid out in the sun to dry outside the workshop, before being fired in ovens in which temperatures of up to 800°C could be achieved.

Akin to the potter was the maker of mud-bricks. Glass-workers may have enjoyed slightly higher status, for glass tended to be a luxury item.

The making of glass was a royal monopoly, and the depiction of glass-making is absent from the tombs of the nobility and the bourgeoisie; kings' tombs of the New Kingdom seldom showed domestic scenes, so they provide no clue. Fortunately many glass artefacts have survived.

Jewellers used a good deal of faience in their work, but they were used to working with gold, silver, electrum, and many precious and semi-precious stones, of which turquoise was one of the most common. In Ancient Egypt, the jeweller's craft early on became highly sophisticated, and examples of work of unbelievable delicacy have survived. Everyone wore jewellery of one kind or another, even if only in the form of amulets to ward off evil; but the greatest examples were designed and made for the royal house.

Other skills which everyone profited by were tanning and leather work, weaving and spinning.

The glass fish vessel (centre), dating to c.1350 BC and now in the British Museum, would have been used as a cosmetics container, while the glass bottle (far left) was for perfume or medicinal use.

BELOW: Craftsmen made sandals out of papyrus, which priests wore for reasons of purity and cleanliness. Other people wore leather sandals.

The famous monumental Sphinx at Giza whose features may be those of the pharaoh Khafra.

inner chambers and access corridors. It has been estimated that it consists of 2,300,000 limestone blocks weighing an average 2.6 tonnes. The size of the task of erecting the monument, which also provides an indication of the relatively large population of Egypt at that date, can be judged by the fact that it has been calculated that the construction would have taken 100,000 men slightly fewer than twenty years to complete.

Khufu was succeeded by Djedefra, whose reign was short and perhaps curtailed by a coup. His successor was Khafra, another pyramid-builder at Giza, whose name is most famously associated with that other iconographic symbol of Ancient Egypt, the Great Sphinx, which lies next to the causeway to his pyramid. The ancient Greek *sphinx* means 'strangler', though the origin of the name is more probably derived from the Ancient Egyptian *shesep ankh* – 'living image'. Usually, as is the case of the Great Sphinx, the image is of a creature with a lion's body – an obvious symbol of power – and the head of a man, most frequently the king, and commonly wearing the royal *nemes* headcloth. The Great Sphinx was carved out of a natural outcrop of rock, whose original shape may have suggested the form it was to take, and its face is almost certainly a portrait of Khafra.

Khafra's successor was Menkaura, who built the last of the three large pyramids at Giza. It is much smaller than the other two but he was having it cased in expensive granite from Aswan when he died. His successor, Shepseskaf, had the job finished in mud-brick.

The transition from the Fourth to the Fifth Dynasty is

unclear. A successful raid on Libya by the second king of this dynasty, Sahura, is recorded, and in the funerary chapels of the period, for by now nobles and prominent commoners were having themselves buried in state, small details of people's private lives begin to appear. Smaller and more exquisite pieces of statuary appear in a variety of forms and materials: people, animals and plants were represented in copper, limestone, basalt, alabaster, gold and granite.

The most important Fifth Dynasty tomb, however, at Saqqara, was that of the dynasty's last king, Unas, who died about 2345 BC. The rooms and corridors inside his pyramid are for the first time, as far as we know, covered with long columns of incised inscriptions inlaid with blue pigment, intended to help Unas into the afterlife, and to triumph over any obstructions and enemies encountered there.

These writings are now known as the Pyramid Texts, and they were to become a regular feature of the tombs of the kings of the next dynasty, as well as a matrix for succeeding Books of the Dead, as they are now commonly known. The Pyramid Texts are a forerunner of the Egyptian 'Books-of-what-is-in-the-Hereafter'; collections of magic spells which make success in the afterlife possible. They combine ideas from the Osirian myth of the Underworld with the Heliopolitan notion of a heavenly paradise. The Pyramid Texts are the most ancient mythological and religious works of literature known in Ancient Egypt.

As time went on, inscriptions became more descriptive and slightly less formal. There was more incidental and personal detail, and murals appeared depicting scenes from everyday life: children playing with animals, the business of bird-trapping, trading, markets, tending stock, harvesting and so on. And within the coffins themselves, painted on the inside so that the dead could read them, 'Coffin Texts' began to appear, as the original Pyramid Texts became available not just to the king, but, in modified form, to the aristocracy and, ultimately, to the bourgeoisie.

Details of the handover between the Fifth and Sixth Dynasties are again obscure. During the latter dynasty

trading expeditions, by river and by donkey, beyond the southern frontier had become established, and brought back luxuries such as ebony and other hardwoods, incense, ivory, various oils and animal skins. One of the principal explorer-pioneers of the new trade routes was the governor of Aswan, Harkhuf, and a letter from the child-king Pepy II survives, expressing delight that Harkhuf is bringing him back from the far south a 'dancing dwarf'.

Pepy II is reputed to have come to the throne aged six and to have reigned for ninety-four years – the longest in history. Although his extraordinarily long reign was a period of relative stability, the last twenty-five years or so may have seen Ancient Egypt in decline and some argue that Pepy himself seems to have gained a reputation in old age as a homosexual voluptuary – neither attribute attracting great regard in Ancient Egypt, though other ancient texts indicate that Pepy was highly respected.

The Old Kingdom came to an end with the death of Pepy's successor, Queen Nitiqret, in about 2181 BC, and its collapse is mirrored in a gloomy and pessimistic literature (in sharp contrast with the optimism and material practicality of earlier times), and best represented in the 'Admonitions of Ipuwer'. These were probably composed at a later date, but closer to the events than other similar works which belong to the Middle Kingdom, which began slightly more than two hundred years later. The Admonitions may be no more than an artistic exercise. However, their drama cannot be denied, and so immediate is their tone that it is hard to imagine their not having been inspired by some actual catastrophic event, whether experienced by Ipuwer himself (though this is highly unlikely) or handed down to him as an oral or folk memory. Ipuwer laments the collapse of order and describes a society turned on its head, tombs robbed, the rich in rags, the official abused, and the peasant tilling his field carrying a shield to defend himself against an undefined marauder, though there are hints that foreigners have invaded the Delta. The Admonitions are conservative in tone, and bewail the fact that in this 'bad time' servants and slaves have taken possession of valuables they don't understand.

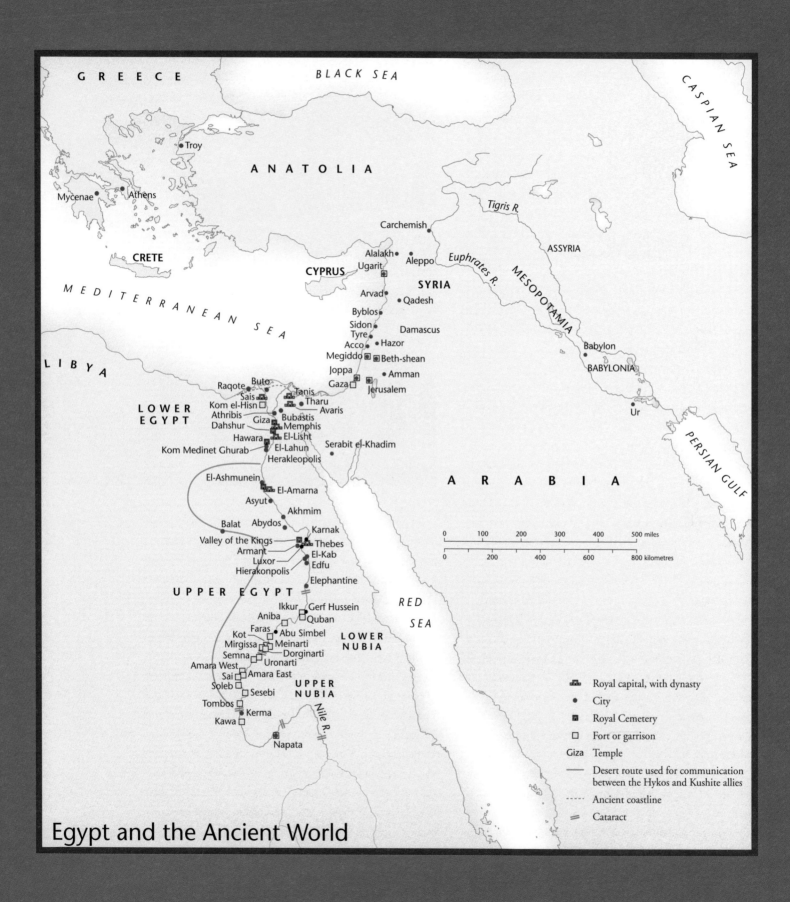

GREECE

BLACK SEA

CASPIAN SEA

• Troy

ANATOLIA

Mycenae •   • Athens

CRETE

Carchemish •

Tigris R.

Alalakh •   • Aleppo   ASSYRIA
Ugarit ⊡

CYPRUS   SYRIA

Euphrates R.

MESOPOTAMIA

M E D I T E R R A N E A N   S E A

Arvad •   • Qadesh
Byblos •
Sidon •
Tyre •   Damascus •
Acco •   • Hazor   Babylon •
Megiddo □ ⊡ Beth-shean   BABYLONIA
Joppa •
Gaza ⊡   • Amman
Jerusalem •   Ur •

LIBYA

Raqote • • Buto
Sais ⊞   • Tanis
Kom el-Hisn □   Avaris
Athribis • Bubastis

LOWER
EGYPT

PERSIAN GULF

Dahshur • Giza Memphis •
Hawara •   El-Lisht •
Kom Medinet Ghurab • El-Lahun •
Herakleopolis •

Serabit el-Khadim •

A R A B I A

El-Ashmunein •
• El-Amarna
Asyut •
Akhmim •
Balat •   Abydos •
Karnak •
Valley of the Kings — ⊡ Thebes
Armant • El-Kab •
Luxor •   Edfu •
Hierakonpolis •
Elephantine •

UPPER EGYPT

0   100   200   300   400   500 miles
0   200   400   600   800 kilometres

RED
SEA

Ikkur • • Gerf Hussein
Aniba •   □ Quban
Kot   Faras • • Abu Simbel   LOWER
Mirgissa □ □ Meinarti   NUBIA
Semna □   • Dorginarti
Amara West □   Uronarti
Sai □   Amara East
Soleb □
Tombos □   Sesebi
        • Kerma
Kawa □

UPPER
NUBIA

Nile R.

• Napata

⊞ Royal capital, with dynasty

• City

⊡ Royal Cemetery

□ Fort or garrison

Giza Temple

── Desert route used for communication
     between the Hykos and Kushite allies

- - - Ancient coastline

≈ Cataract

Egypt and the Ancient World

THE MIDDLE KINGDOM

The shadowy First Intermediate Period continued from the beginning of the Seventh until the middle of the Eleventh Dynasties, and during this period the Two Lands were fragmented once more. The kings of the Seventh and Eighth Dynasties seem to have controlled Memphis. Manetho, the third-century BC priest and historian based in Heliopolis or Mendes, speaks of seventy kings ruling for seventy days. The Eighth Dynasty may have been more substantial. One of their kings, possibly Ibi, was buried near Pepy II at Saqqara, indicating a continuing power base at Memphis.

The governor of the twentieth *Nome* (district), Meryibra, seized power, established a base at Herakleopolis and founded the Ninth and Tenth Dynasties, which both reigned from there. The first kings of the Eleventh Dynasty ruled in Thebes alone. These five dynasties overlapped and their history is obscure – what is known of it is complex.

Thebes, far to the south of Memphis, was a relatively new provincial power, but during the Tenth Dynasty a local official called Mentuhotep became governor and lost no time in placing members of his family into positions of power. From this start Thebes began to assert its independence and indeed dominance of neighbouring cities, and as its power and confidence grew, so it became more aggressively expansionist. Mentuhotep was succeeded by Intef I, II and III. By the time of Intef III in about 2060, Thebes was the chief city of Upper Egypt. Intef declared himself king and granted his immediate predecessors the same honour. Mentuhotep thus posthumously became the founder of the Eleventh Dynasty.

With the accession to the Golden Throne of Mentuhotep II, fifth king of the Eleventh Dynasty, in about 2055 BC, the country was reunited and the era of the Middle Kingdom began. Mentuhotep II was one of the most important kings of Ancient Egypt, a second Narmer, pulling the country out of chaos and back into unity. His power base remained Thebes.

The first decades of Mentuhotep's long (fifty-year) reign were spent in war, consolidating his power over the Two Lands and wiping out pockets of resistance from the Herakleopolitans and others, 'clubbing the eastern lands, striking down the hill-countries, trampling the deserts,

enslaving the Nubians ... Medjay and Wawet (Lower Nubia), the Libyans and the Asiatics ...' as one contemporary inscription at Dendera has it. Once order had been re-established, state building work resumed on a monumental scale. Literature began to flourish too, and the period of the Middle Kingdom produced perhaps the greatest writing of the whole empire. With the reunification of the country, trade resumed, from the Mediterranean coast to Nubia, and from Aswan to the Red Sea across the Eastern Desert via the Wadi Hammamat. The land of Punt had perhaps not been visited since the Sixth Dynasty. Now an expedition of 3000 men was funded, led by Chief Steward Henenu. Each member of the expedition was supplied with a staff and a leather water-bottle, and the donkeys of the pack-train carried among other supplies sacks of spare sandals to replace those worn out on the march across the hot sand. They also carried enough to supply each man with two jars of water and twenty biscuits a day, as well as

This famous wooden model from Assyot is of an army on the march. It dates from the Tenth Dynasty.

TOWNS AND CITIES

Having mastered the arts of mathematics and particularly geometry early on, having learned to measure and, above all, possessing plentiful building materials in the form of mud-brick (easy and cheap to make), and abundant supplies of workable limestone, it is no wonder that the Ancient Egyptians involved themselves in the construction of sizeable towns, palaces, temples and monuments from almost the beginning of their civilization.

Because the country was rich and fertile, the population grew fast, and towns along the river were quickly settled. For the most part, ordinary dwellings were built of mud-brick, stone being reserved for the most important palaces and temples, and, of course, for mighty tombs, such as the pyramids.

Towns were built on an approximate grid-system, sometimes divided into quarters by two principal thoroughfares intersecting at right angles. Houses were constructed in terraces and would not look unusual to the modern eye. However, though town planning existed, it was not well developed. Haphazard shanty-towns grew up on the settlements'

fringes, and there was little or no organized sanitation: rubbish of all kinds quickly piled up.

The most important locations were the royal cities, such as Thebes and Memphis, as well as Pi-Ramesse and Tanis, chosen by pharaohs as their chief seats, and the centres of the nation's government. After them came the regional capitals and centres of religious importance, such as Saqqara and Abydos.

One of the best examples we have of urban architecture is the village that was inhabited by prosperous specialist craftsmen who worked on the tombs in the Valley of the Kings. Their village at Deir el-Medina is still remarkably intact and gives us important information about how ordinary Ancient Egyptians lived. Houses here were about five metres wide by fifteen deep. Typically, the entrance room was used as a household chapel, presided over by the god who was revered as the protector of the hearth, the lion-dwarf Bes. Beyond it was the main room, its high ceiling supported by columns, with a dais along one wall which probably served as a table by day and a sleeping platform by night. Below the dais was a cellar. Leading off from

this room would be one or two smaller chambers, used for sleeping or as storerooms, and at the very back a final room, unroofed, served as the kitchen. At another workmen's village there is evidence that the houses had bathrooms and privies. The flat roofs were also used for living and sleeping.

The houses of the better-off stood in their own walled grounds, with trees and a rectangular pond. Walls would be whitewashed to reflect the heat, and windows often faced north to catch the cooling, prevailing north wind. Larger houses had more than one storey and sometimes stood on their own platforms to help prevent damp from rising into the mud-brick walls. The house of a major official or businessman would contain workshops and storerooms on the ground floor. The first floor would comprise rooms for receiving guests, and offices. The second floor would contain the private apartments. A stairway linked all floors with the flat roof, with further storage and living spaces.

The large burial ground at Deir el-Medina.

PUBLIC BUILDINGS

Public buildings were often massive. The great temple of Amun at Karnak covered thirty-one hectares, and was almost certainly the largest religious building ever constructed by any culture. Ancient systems of standing stones have recently been discovered in the desert west of Abu Simbel, dating from about 6000 BC; but early temple buildings would have been constructed out of wood, matting, and reeds, whose forms are echoed in the the great stone pillars with their lotus and papyrus capitals of the hypostyle halls at Karnak, for example. The best-known and most obviously impressive examples of temple-building are the Old Kingdom pyramid mortuary temples. Temple architecture was strictly dictated by tradition and religious tenets: the temple, as you progressed through it, grew lower, more intimate, and darker. Its *sanctum sanctorum* was the shrine where the image of the god was kept, and the temple itself was viewed as the god's house, though elements of its architectural schema also reflected the primal mound rising from the water of Nun. Temples were not public places of worship,

TOP LEFT: The closed buds of the papyrus plant feature on the tops of the columns supporting part of a temple built by Tuthmosis III. The temple was home to species of plants brought back from countries defeated by the pharaoh and his army.

LEFT: The festival hall of Tuthmosis III.

ABOVE: The gate of Ptolemy III Euergetes I
at the Karnak temple precinct.

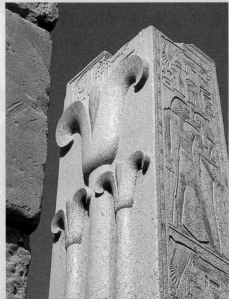

LEFT: The lotus flower features
on column carvings at Karnak.

but private shrines where the priests enacted daily
the rituals surrounding the god.

Some of the greatest surviving examples of
temple architecture are at Karnak, and the best
preserved of all is the stone-built temple of Horus
at Edfu, built as late as the Ptolemaic Period,
around 230 BC. The plan of construction is an
entrance-way via a towering processional gateway
flanked by pylons. This gave into a courtyard,
beyond which lay the hypostyle hall with its forest
of columns, and beyond that still, the shrine.

THE HYPOSTYLE HALL

trade-goods for Punt, and supplies of timber. Shipwrights also accompanied the expedition.

Henenu's orders were to re-establish trade with the fabulously rich land of Punt. Armed groups of scouts went ahead of the main force to get rid of any hostile troops of desert nomads, and fifteen wells were sunk along the route, with guardposts, to ensure a water supply for future trade expeditions. When he reached the coast, Henenu had a fleet of ships built and despatched them to Punt with the goods for trade. His mariners returned in due course safe and sound and laden with exotica from Punt, which Henenu, after establishing a port and garrison, loaded on to the donkeys before setting off for home, pausing on the way to carve an inscription celebrating his exploits.

Egypt entered the prolonged period of peace and prosperity which defined the Middle Kingdom. The last king of the Eleventh Dynasty, Mentuhotep IV, was probably usurped by his vizier, who proclaimed himself

The great temple complex at Karnak was dedicated to Amun, the tutelary deity of the city and by extension the chief god of the land. The complex was vast, covering about 120 hectares of the East Bank at Thebes. It was not only the most sacred religious site in Egypt, it was also a centre of administration and the law: an economic powerhouse whose vast estates across Egypt may have employed as much as fifteen per cent of the country's population. Its magnificent hypostyle hall was forested with towering columns twenty-six metres high, painted and carved to look like papyrus. The great hall was dark, illuminated only by shafts of sunlight filtering through slatted stone windows set high in the walls. All Egyptian temples were built to represent the primal mound of creation, where, according to one of the creation myths, the god Horus, in the form of a falcon, first alighted to bring order to the earth. The hypostyle hall reflected the notion of the papyrus reedbank that grew from the primal-swamp to hold back the waters of chaos. It was seen as a sanctuary of truth, order and justice.

RIGHT: The magnificent columns, which are still standing today, of the biggest of the halls at Karnak – the Hypostyle Hall, and (far right), a reconstruction that reflects the scale of this impressive site dedicated to truth, order and justice.

LEFT: The god Amun represented in a statue at Karnak. He was a Theban tutelary deity, elevated to the principal national god at the beginning of the Twelfth Dynasty. A creator-god, more generally he was worshipped as a force behind all things, believed to be the divine father of all pharaohs. Guises he was worshipped in included the goose, the snake and the sun.

LITERATURE

Apart from the vast amount of day-to-day and administrative writings that have come down to us there is also a large body of literature, all essentially anonymous, though some of the books of 'Instruction' or 'Admonitions' have been ascribed to various dignitaries and high officials. There are stories, mythical, moral and purely entertaining, some of which eerily adumbrate familiar Greek myths. There is a large amount of poetry, of which the love-poetry is especially delicate. Curiously, no dramatic work has yet come to light, and it is possible that drama played no part in Ancient Egyptian society. Most of the excerpts that follow are from the 'golden age' of the Middle Kingdom.

FROM 'THE TALE OF SINUHE'

This is the story of a courtier, exiled from Egypt, who longs to return to his native land:

> A night is assigned to you with oils,
>   and wrappings from the hands of tayet.
> A procession shall be made for you on the day
>   of burial,
> with a mummy case of gold,
> a mask of lapis lazuli, a sky over you,
> and you on a hearse,
> with oxen dragging you,
> and chantresses before you.
> The dance of the dead shall be performed at the
>   mouth of your tomb,
> and the funeral invocation recited for you;
> sacrifice shall be made at the mouth of your
>   tomb-chamber,
> with your pillars, built of white stone,
> in the midst of the royal children's.

FROM 'THE TALE OF THE ELOQUENT PEASANT'

This story deals with a peasant who has been robbed by a landowner. The peasant takes his case to the High Steward, who, impressed by his eloquence, lets him go on pleading his case through nine petitions just for the pleasure of listening to him speak on the nature of truth and justice, before finally granting his suit.

> Do Truth for the Lord of Truth ...
> may you avoid doing evil! The goodness of the
>   good man is alone good before him.
> Yet truth itself is for eternity,
> To the necropolis in its doer's hand it descends;
> he is entombed, earth joined with him.
> But his name is not effaced on earth;
> he is remembered for goodness.
> It is the standard of god's word.

FROM 'DIALOGUE BETWEEN A MAN WEARY OF LIFE AND HIS SOUL'

> Death is to me today
> like a sick man's recovery,
> like going outside after confinement.
> Death is to me today
> like the scent of myrrh,

The John Rylands Demotic Papyrus. Sixth century BC.

> like sitting under a sail on a windy day.
> Death is to me today
> like the scent of lotuses,
> like sitting on the shore of Drunkenness.
> Death is to me today
> like a well-trodden path,
> like a man's coming home from an expedition.
> Death is to me today
> like the opening of the sky,
> like a man's grasping what he did not know.
> Death is to me today
> like a man's longing to see home,
> having spent many years abroad.

Amenemhat I and founded the Twelfth Dynasty in about 1985 BC. He had to reassert his power over all of Egypt, and did so; and it was he who first elevated the Theban tutelary deity, Amun, to principal national god. Amenemhat also moved his capital from Thebes to Itjtawy, probably located beside El-lisht just south of Memphis, from where it was easier to control the whole land. The name Itjtawy means 'Seizer-of-the-Two-Lands'. As regnal years during this dynasty often overlapped, it may be that Amenemhat also introduced the system, which became common among Egyptian rulers when the throne passed from father to son, for the son to act as co-regent with his father for a handover period, which had the dual benefit of teaching the successor the manner of ruling, while reinforcing the succession at the same time.

Amenemhat died in 1955 BC and his heir, Senusret I, took over the reins of power. His reign saw the further enrichment and expansion of the Black Land: Lower Nubia was conquered, with its valuable gold mines, and the temple of Ra-Atum at Heliopolis (On) was rebuilt. By the time of his immediate successors, Amenemhat II and Senusret II (who died in *c.* 1874 BC), Egypt was playing an increasingly important role in the culture, commerce and politics of Western Asia. These were kings who became the legends of later ages: Senusret III (1874–1855) was a great though autocratic reformer who cut the power of the nobility and centralized power (like an early Louis XIV), and reshaped and rationalized the national administration into three principal districts, Upper, Middle and Lower Egypt.

Senusret III built and refurbished a system of eleven mud-brick forts in Lower Nubia, and also had a channel dug to render the rapids at the Second Cataract of the Nile navigable by warships and merchant ships. He pushed the southern boundaries further south than any king before him, establishing a lonely garrison fort at Semna, only sixty kilometres north of Wadi Halfa. A stela set up there by him amply indicates the Egyptian's contempt for his enemies:

> The Nubian hears only to fall at a word ...
>
> If one is aggressive towards him, it is his back that he shows ...
>
> They are not people of much account ...

His principal purpose was probably to protect the trade route south and maintain Egypt's monopoly on gold, ivory and animal skins.

Such was Senusret III's energy and ability that by the time his son, Amenemhat III, came to power, Egypt was indisputably the greatest nation on earth. The turquoise and copper mines of Sinai were being worked more heavily than ever, the arts and crafts flourished, and Egyptian influence was felt from Syria in the north to Upper Nubia in the south.

Amenemhat III ruled until 1808 BC, and was succeeded by Amenemhat IV. Amenemhat IV was already a relatively old man by then but he managed to maintain the status quo within the Empire during an eight- or nine-year reign. He was succeeded by Queen Sobekneferu, probably a daughter of Amenemhat III and a sister or half-sister of Amenemhat IV. Her reign was short and unspectacular – it lasted only from about 1799 to 1795 BC.

The last two dynasties of the Middle Kingdom saw a new period of decline. The Thirteenth and Fourteenth Dynasties were once more minor ones, the former lasting from 1795 to 1650, the Fourteenth from 1750 to 1650 – it will be seen that there was considerable overlap. According to Manetho, the Thirteenth Dynasty consisted of sixty or seventy kings. They ruled from Thebes, and none of them seems to have lasted long – the average reign being about two-and-a-half years, the succession being determined not by bloodline but by usurpation or possibly election, with the exception of a mini-dynasty of three brothers who succeeded one another.

The weakening of Egypt, whatever the reasons for it were, attracted immediate outside attention. The people of Syria-Palestine, whose harvests were unpredictable and who lived under a constant threat of starvation, looked enviously at the fecundity of the Black Land. Egypt was far too rich a prize to ignore, and it was not long before the country faced invasion. It would have started in the form of border skirmishes and infiltration, before the last two dynasties of the Middle Kingdom had breathed their last.

EMBRACING GREATNESS

THE NEW KINGDOM

The precise time and nature of the invasion of the foreigners from the north is uncertain, and the first incursions, towards the end of the Thirteenth and Fourteenth Dynasties, were a matter of infiltration rather than invasion. The Fourteenth Dynasty may have hung on in the Western Delta for some time after the northern rulers had established themselves in Egypt. The term of their rule is known as the Second Intermediate Period, during which three dynasties ruled in different regions concurrently.

The northerners, who came from ancient Retenu (modern Palestine), and countries to its north and east, are commonly known today as the Hyksos, described by Manetho as 'shepherd kings', but more realistically represented as 'Asiatics' (the translation of the word the Egyptians themselves used for the interlopers, *Aamu*). But this still doesn't give us much of a clue about their precise identity. By this time Egypt was a multicultural society, but the word 'Asiatic' covered a multitude of races: the Egyptian word for mankind, *remet*, applied only to Egyptians, and despite their tolerance of other peoples in their midst, foreigners remained in their eyes not so much second-class citizens but beings whose very existence was on a lower level. Things, however, were about to change.

The Hyksos were very well organized militarily, and even if there had been a national standing army to defend Egypt at the time, it would have been hard to repel them. As things were, some local attempts were made, leading to isolated battles, skirmishes and the sacking by the Hyksos of individual towns, but there was no all-out war. Once in power, the Hyksos readily adopted the culture of their host country: they built temples, worshipped the gods, copied the literature and slipped into the mores of the Egyptians. Interestingly, they elevated Set as their principal deity. The god was especially revered in Avaris (Hutwaret), the region where they first established themselves; and it is possible that they identified Set with one of their own gods. They also honoured Ra, and were entirely tolerant of the existing cultural and religious status quo.

But they brought something with them too. Through

their occupation of the country the Hyksos supplied a huge transfusion (literally) of new blood, and with it, an influx of new ideas – religious, artistic and practical. In the last, it was in the art of war (in which the Hyksos excelled) that their influence had a special impact. Bronze swords and daggers, the composite bow and, above all, the horse-drawn war-chariot, led to a revolution in military strategy and tactics. This stimulus paved the way for the great Eighteenth Dynasty, and the achievements of two famous military pharaohs, Tuthmosis III and Rameses II.

The rule of the Hyksos began about 1650 BC. They reigned successfully through the century that was covered by the Fifteenth and Sixteenth Dynasties, which ran concurrently from different power centres, the Fifteenth

New Kingdom Egypt was the first period in which Egypt had a professional army.

being dominant. Towards the end of the reign of Apepi, around 1560, the Egyptians began to reassert themselves. The Hyksos never penetrated far south, and native kings retained power at Thebes as the Seventeenth Dynasty, which also ruled at the same time as the Fifteenth and Sixteenth. The Seventeenth Dynasty was isolated and poor, but fiercely independent. The mummy of one of its kings, Seqenenra Taa II, who ruled *c.* 1560, has been recovered. The terrible wounds on his head have suggested to Egyptologists that he may have died in battle against the Hyksos (though this is not certain). He was known as 'The Brave', however; and his successor, Kamose, who ruled from about 1555 to 1550 BC, launched the offensive that was eventually to lead to the expulsion of the Hyksos and usher in the Eighteenth

Dynasty, which some consider the greatest in the history of Ancient Egypt, and with it the period known as the New Kingdom, which covered the Eighteenth, Nineteenth and Twentieth Dynasties.

The first king of the Eighteenth Dynasty was Ahmose, perhaps a younger brother of Kamose. Ahmose reigned for twenty-five years from 1550, and he it was who finally expelled the Hyksos, but probably only after a long and hard fight. The Jewish historian and soldier Flavius Josephus, who lived in the first century AD, quotes Manetho as saying that 240,000 Hyksos left Egypt peaceably as the result of a treaty signed after Ahmose had repeatedly tried and failed to take Avaris. Ahmose's campaigns were praised to the skies (as were those of all pharaohs) by contemporary Egyptian historian-propagandists. Ahmose also campaigned in Nubia, pushing the southern frontier as far south as Buhen and appointing a viceroy to govern the annexed country. His military activity to the north, however, was restricted to a brief expedition into Phoenicia.

Ahmose was succeeded by two more warlike pharaohs, Amenhotep I and Tuthmosis I, the latter a middle-aged career soldier when he succeeded his brother-in-law Amenhotep. These two kings consolidated the victories of the dynasty's founder and secured the country's borders.

A standing army was reinstated after the expulsion of the Hyksos, who had taught the Egyptians the dangers of complacency, as well as how to arm themselves efficiently. Soldiers were equipped with the composite bow, the battle-axe, swords and spears. Military standards were introduced to rally companies, and discipline was reformed and enforced. Soldiers were recruited from the ranks of freeborn Egyptians. Conscription was modest in normal times but nevertheless force was usually necessary to separate the unwilling recruits from their pleading families, and the pressgangs were almost always backed up by police. Doubtless sons were concealed and bribes changed hands to avoid the draft.

The navy existed as a transport and communications system for the army, since there was, as yet, no concept of naval warfare, though some examples of river piracy have been discovered. River ships were lightweight and of shallow draught, their superstructure consisting of tall cabins from which lookouts could scan the banks of the Nile. Sea-going ships were sturdier and fully decked, and had deeper keels, but otherwise their design was simple. They were built for speed, with long, clean hulls; they were not designed to carry large supplies of food and fresh water.

Tuthmosis I's successor, Tuthmosis II, was his third son, two older boys having predeceased him. Tuthmosis II married his half-sister, Hatshepsut, daughter of the king and his Chief Wife Ahmose, who may have considered herself superior to him by birth. He, too, was a vigorous soldier and conducted important military campaigns, definitively and brutally crushing a further Nubian rebellion, as well as contributing to the temple-building at Karnak, the temple-complex at Thebes, which remained an important power-base of the kings of the Eighteenth Dynasty, though Memphis, with its cooler climate and better geographical location, retained its position as capital. Reference is, however, sometimes made to the 'Northern' and 'Southern' Capitals.

Tuthmosis II had a weak physical constitution and died young, probably only in his early thirties. He perhaps

LEFT: As is the case with many of the military innovations in the New Kingdom period, the chariot was actually copied and adapted from Egypt's Syrian enemies.

Like many pharaohs of the New Kingdom, Tuthmosis III prided himself on his personal military prowess.

knew that Hatshepsut had strong personal ambitions, and accordingly made arrangements to have his only son, another Tuthmosis, born to him by a concubine called Isis, appointed his successor.

At the time of his father's death, Tuthmosis III was still a child. Hatshepsut ruled on his behalf as regent for the first few years following her husband's death, but in that time she may have collected a powerful clique around her. The head of this was her chief aide and administrator, Senen-mut, who may also in time have become her lover, but there were other influential members in the clique, including Hapuseneb, the High Priest of Amun, Nehesi, the Viceroy of Nubia, and the Treasurer, Thuty. It was not long before Hatshepsut had herself proclaimed pharaoh, claiming descent through the sun-god, whom, she

claimed, in a story strikingly reminiscent of Amphitryon, took the form of her father to impregnate her mother. Although a woman, her images do not distinguish her from other pharaohs, and she wears the ceremonial (false) beard.

Tuthmosis III was permitted to continue as co-regent, but this was a nominal honour, and he had no power. It would take twenty years before he was strong enough to assert himself. He was married to his half-sister, Neferure, the daughter of his father and Hatshepsut, and spent most of his time in military training, for which he had a keen affinity, though it was noted that he was short in stature.

Hatshepsut's fall, after a peaceful and successful reign mainly notable for a major trading expedition to Punt and a remarkable mortuary temple, which has survived

SPORT AND GAMES

The Greeks were puzzled that the Egyptians didn't exercise their bodies regularly and indulge in sports in the way that they themselves did, but for many Egyptians the building-up of the body by daily exercises such as wrestling and gymnastics was regarded as something to be avoided; they believed that such a course might impart a dangerous and excessive energy to it. To the Ancient Egyptians, the body was home to eight elements crucial to immortality, which had nothing to do with physicality. These were the *khet, ba, khou, ren, ka, ib, khaibit* and *sahu* – body, soul, intelligence, name, double, heart, shadow and husk. In addition, the Egyptians believed that a muscular body denoted that its owner belonged to a class obliged to do physical labour. A certain plumpness was an indication of wealth, and scribes would have been horrified to have well-developed arms. Inky fingers and soft limbs denoted status for them. But this is a general rule, and it is clear that among the Eighteenth Dynasty pharaohs some set store by their physical prowess, especially those whose talents lay in the art of war. Likewise, charioteers would have needed to be strong, and after the introduction of the horse, upper-class young men aspiring to belong to the chariot corps would certainly have taken exercise.

Connected to military training were archery, chariot racing, which became very popular, ship-handling and big-game hunting. Amenhotep II's horsemanship when he was still crown prince is celebrated in a stela inscription:

Now when he was still a lad he loved horses and rejoiced in them. It was strengthening of the heart to work them, to learn their natures, to be skilled in training them, to enter into their ways. When it was heard in the palace by his father ... the heart of his majesty was glad ... 'Let there be given to him the very best horses in my majesty's stable which is in Memphis, and tell him: Take care of them, instil fear into them, make them gallop ...' Now after it had been entrusted to the king's son to take care of the horses ... he trained horses without their equal.

The introduction of the chariot and the composite bow made big-game hunting much more exhilarating too, and this and similar sports were perceived as having the practical advantage of sharpening the senses for war.

Less elevated people with a taste for blood sports went out in boats to harpoon hippos and crocodiles in the Nile, netted or speared fish, and brought down birds with throwsticks, a kind of boomerang-shaped weapon.

Young men, especially from the time of the New Kingdom onwards, also took part in sporting activities such as running, wrestling, boxing and fencing as part of their military training – activities which in time spilled over into civilian life and became leisure activities. Running became part of the celebrations during the *sed* festival. The king himself would do a long-distance solo run to prove that he was still physically fit. By the Twenty-fifth Dynasty, long-distance races were organized, and athletic events such as long-jump and high-jump were introduced, as well as weightlifting. Swimming was a popular activity, and one of the few, apart from dancing and acrobatics, in which girls participated.

Less active pastimes involved board-games, of which several different examples survive, though unfortunately no-one yet has been able to deduce how they were played. One perhaps had a similarity to draughts; all appear to have been position games for two players. One game for up to six players was *mehen*, the snake game. It was played on a large board laid out on a floor and used pieces in the shape of balls, lions and dogs.

Charioteering became a sport for the elite and a new breed of young heroes called 'maryannu' competed in chariot races and became the celebrities of their day.

RIGHT: Egyptian sport was as much about training for war and physical combat as it was recreation. Winning archers became the best bowmen on the battlefield.

LEFT: Board games like this one, called *senet* and invented by the Egyptians, are still played in parts of Africa and the Middle East today. Clay, wood, stone or ivory pieces in the shape of animal or human heads are moved around the board along 'houses' that represented good or bad fortune. To determine how the pieces can be moved each player uses throwsticks or knuckle bones.

at Deir el-Bahri in the Valley of the Kings, came in about 1458 BC. A record of her trade with Punt remains on two obelisks at Karnak which have survived, and at her mortuary temple. The Egyptians exchanged weaponry and jewellery for Punt's highly desirable exotic goods. During her reign, Amun was consolidated in his role as chief god, and his cult (and attendant priesthood) gained great power. A strong pharaoh could always control the priesthood as well as his army and his household, but the possibility exists that things may have been running out of control in Hatshepsut's reign, especially towards the end. The priests and temples dedicated to Amun absorbed vast amounts of property, land, personnel and resources, which was detrimental to Egypt's general well-being. A great deal, too, was syphoned off by corrupt officials. Senenmut took full advantage of his position to feather his own nest: he managed the estates of the god, and held many lucrative and advantageous offices, amongst which were Chief Steward of Amun, Steward of the Barque Amen-Userhet, Overseer of the Granaries of Amun, Overseer of the Fields of Amun, of the Cattle, of the Gardens, of the Weavers, and of the Works of Amun.

Whether Hatshepsut died naturally, or was ousted from office, or even assassinated, is unclear. The premature death of her daughter, Tuthmosis' Chief Wife, eleven years into her reign, would have weakened her position, and the fall of Senenmut from power in the nineteenth year probably dealt it a crushing blow. It is unlikely that her body was buried in the tomb she had built to receive it. As soon as she was gone, Tuthmosis, in a gesture which recurs in the course of Ancient Egyptian history, had her name erased from all monuments and stelae, her statues were destroyed and her obelisks tumbled. Her name is blotted out – she is removed from the historical record. Fortunately for archaeologists, this business was not carried out nearly as efficiently as the new pharaoh would have wished. Her two prominent obelisks remained at Karnak, for example, and clearly it was out of the question to raze a building of the scale of Hatshepsut's mortuary temple, modest as it was by comparison with what was to come later.

Once in power, Tuthmosis immediately established his authority, and went on to become one of the greatest of all pharaohs; some would argue the greatest of all. He gained personal respect by his own acts of bravery and prowess and is reputed to have been a formidable athlete, archer and charioteer; but he was also a strong and able administrator.

As well as conducting a regime that was notable for its military achievements and campaigns – the story of 'The Battle of Megiddo' fought against Mitanni is told in Chapter Six of this book – he carried out a great range of

ABOVE: Hatshepsut's image can be seen defaced in this pylon in Karnak. All references to Hatshepsut were obliterated by her successor Tuthmosis III.

OPPOSITE: The funerary temple of Queen Hatshepsut at Deir-el Bahri.

political and civil reforms. Nubia and the Sudan were brought definitively under control, and the new stability ushered in a period of economic boom that facilitated a reform of the administration, a vast building programme, and generous sponsorship of culture and the arts. He adopted a policy of taking hostage the sons of the rulers of the neighbouring countries he conquered, and bringing them up as Egyptians. This not only ensured their fathers' compliance, but when they were ready to take over their own thrones, they were sent home as fully indoctrinated 'honorary' Egyptians.

In general, immigrants were tolerated but were not always assimilated. Asiatic prisoners-of-war in Egypt were mainly assigned menial work, but skilled craftsmen could advance themselves. As Egypt was a far richer and more sophisticated country than their homeland, life in the Black Land could be advantageous. Weavers, copper-smiths, shipwrights, goldsmiths and members of similar trades often stayed, married, and became Egyptianized. The Egyptians were always ready to promote talent, which worked to their advantage, and at least as far as language was concerned, there was assimilation: hundreds of foreign words were adopted, of which at least a quarter had a military application.

Tuthmosis was succeeded by his son, Amenhotep II, who carried on his father's tradition, boasted of his personal athletic and military skills, including ship-handling, and reigned for about twenty-seven years. By this time some foreign gods had developed cults in Egypt, and Amenhotep's chariot team was protected by a Syrian goddess, Astarte, and an Amorite god, Reshef, both war deities.

Amenhotep's successor was Tuthmosis IV, who reigned for a decade. Aware of the threat posed by the growing power of the Hittites to the far north, he made an alliance with Egypt's old enemy, Mitanni. The balance of power this effected resulted in forty years of peace in the Near East.

Pharaoh Tuthmosis III appeared before his people to address them and to receive tributes from defeated enemies. The balcony structure from which a pharaoh would do this was called the Window of Appearances.

THE AGE OF ATEN

By the time the next king, Amenhotep III, ascended the throne in about 1390 BC, Egypt had reached the apogee of its fame and power. Diplomacy and trade by now had largely replaced warfare, and the country enjoyed peace, security and enormous prosperity, fuelled by the secure Nubian gold trade. This was a time when the humanities flourished, and in religious matters new philosophical ideas were beginning to be aired: it was a long and gradual process, but even during the reign of Tuthmosis III some intellectuals had begun to question the monopolistic power of the priesthood, and wonder if there might not one day be a reform of the vast pantheon of gods. Interest was stirring in the idea of the Aten, a god represented by the sun's disc. By the time of Amenhotep II, this god, whose physical form was less concrete than those of his fellow deities, began to be represented as having rays which culminated in hands, representing care and protection. His cult began to gain popularity.

Meanwhile, as the arts flourished and developed, Amenhotep III, who was to enjoy a long reign of some forty years, devoted himself to worldly pleasures and embarked on what the *Cambridge Ancient History* describes as 'a programme of self-glorification more elaborate and on a far grander scale than any previously undertaken'. He had the central colonnade of the temple at Luxor constructed, and the famous 'Colossi of Memnon' are all that remain of his lost mortuary temple, the dimensions of which were indeed colossal. In addition, his palace, the 'House of Rejoicing', encompassed about one hundred hectares. But he also had the sense to make a marriage outside his own immediate family and took as his Chief Wife Tiy, the daughter of Yuya and Tjuyu, neither of them close members of the royal family. Tiy's father, Yuya, held the important military posts of Master of the Horse and Lieutenant of Chariotry, and may have been related to Amenhotep's mother, Mutemwiya. Amenhotep III's marriage to Tiy was announced to the world by means of a large stone scarab on whose flat underside Tiy's titles were incised. Tiy was an unusual queen in several ways: she appeared regularly on public monuments by the king's side, and her name was linked with his in official pronouncements. She was also involved in foreign affairs, conducting correspondence with the King of Mitanni after her husband's death.

By marrying outside the immediate royal house, Amenhotep had broken with tradition. He sought to secure the inheritance by marrying one of his own daughters by Tiy, Sitamun, and fathering her children. He also had himself proclaimed a god in his own lifetime: normally, a pharaoh would be recognized as the son of Ra-Amun during his life, and deified on his death. As the power of the Hittites and the Assyrians

Named by the Greeks, the Colossi of Memnon stood at the entrance to the funerary temple of Amenhotep III on the West Bank of Thebes. These two colossal structures are all that remain of what was once a mighty mortuary complex.

grew, he made other diplomatic marriages: to Gilukhepa, daughter of King Shuttarna II of Mitanni, to another Mitannian princess, Tadukhepa, and to a princess of Babylon. However, the threat posed by the Hittites and Assyria did not go away, and to make matters worse the princelings in Syria-Palestine were restive, perhaps sensing the softer reign of Amenhotep III, whose military instincts were not strong.

At home, Amenhotep took steps to curb the growing influence of the priests of Amun, whose wealth and arrogance threatened to upset the balance of power, and it may be that his promotion of the cult of the Aten was as much inspired by political as by philosophical considerations. He died, if we can judge by a realistic image of him that has been preserved, old and debauched in about 1352 BC, and was succeeded by the son of his Chief Wife Tiy. Also

This famous unfinished maquette is a portrait of Queen Nefertiti, Chief Wife of the iconoclastic pharaoh, Akhenaten. The bust is now in the Egyptian Museum at Charlottenburg, Berlin.

named Amenhotep (the name means: 'Pleasing-to-Amun'), this king promoted the cult of the Aten to such an extent that he changed his name to Akhenaten ('Glorious-Spirit-of-the-Aten'), declared all other gods to be of no importance, stripped the priesthood of its power, closed the temples and cut off their revenue; and moved his capital to an entirely new, purpose-built city some 300 kilometres to the north of Thebes, a place now called el-Armana.

Akhenaten married Nefertiti as his Chief Wife, the daughter (probably) of Ay, a high official at the court, possibly Master of Horse. Ay was also the brother of Akhenaten's mother, Tiy, and we can perhaps see Tiy's influence in arranging the marriage to consolidate the position of her family.

Nefertiti is, after Kleopatra VII, probably the most famous Egyptian queen, owing to the portrait bust of her that has survived, now in the Egyptian Museum in Berlin-Charlottenburg. She bore Akhenaten six daughters, who figure prominently in representations of the royal family, but no son is ever mentioned. During this reign, artistic expression took a new turn towards greater realism, and the king and his consort are portrayed much as they may have looked in life, and in informal poses, rather than as idealized and remote. Akhenaten himself is shown with a soft body, having a large belly and pendulous breasts, as well as an elongated head and skull, perhaps the result of some inherited disease. His physical defects have been the subject of much speculation.

During his short reign (about 1352 to 1336 BC), Akhenaten concentrated on promoting the Aten to the exclusion of most other affairs, and neglected the territories gained by his forefathers in Syria-Palestine. This, coupled with the king's intolerance of any gods but Aten, who remained exclusive and remote, led to a sharp decline in the popularity of the royal family. Apparently oblivious to this, Akhenaten ruled from his new city, Akhetaten ('City-of-the-Horizon-of-Aten'), the centre of a cultivated but rarefied court, where the arts flourished.

Meanwhile, the Asiatic part of the empire began to crumble. Cities freed themselves of Egyptian rule, and the king disregarded requests for help from those which remained loyal to him. The governor of Byblos,

Ribaddi, sent more than fifty letters to Akhenaten, which were ignored.

This state of affairs was not pleasing to leading Egyptians outside the charmed circle of the court at Akhetaten. Akhenaten died in *c.* 1336 BC, aged about thirty, and to speculation that he was assassinated. He was one of the most intriguing of all the pharaohs, and much has been written about him. In *Moses and Monotheism*, Sigmund Freud speculates that Moses (an Egyptian name) may have taken the root ideas of Atenism and left Egypt after the fall of the king to make his way north and found a new religion. Other writers have gone so far as to identify Moses with the king himself! Many scholars have commented on the similarity between a hymn to the Aten attributed to Akhenaten and Psalm 104.

The king's successor was not a son/brother, but a noble called Smenkhkara, who may have been a son of Amenhotep III, or a son of Akhenaten by another wife, Kiya. Smenkhkara ruled for only a year at most. His successor, who came to the throne while still a boy, was

BELOW: The golden mask that covered the head and shoulders of the mummy of the youthful pharaoh Tutenkhamun, which is now in the Egyptian Museum, Cairo.

HYMN TO ATEN

Akhenaten himself may have been the author of this beautiful hymn in praise of Aten. It bears an uncanny resemblance to Psalm 104.

O thou great living Aten ... Lord of heaven and
  earth ... thou risest beautiful on the horizon of
  heaven ... shining on the eastern horizon,
  having filled every land with thy beauty!
Thou hast made the heaven afar off in order to
  shine in it.
Thou hast made the seasons in order to nurture
  all that thou hast made.
Thou settest on the western horizon and the
  land is in darkness in the manner of death.
Every lion comes forth from his den and all the
  serpents bite.
Dawn comes only when thou risest on the
  horizon.
The whole world, people do their jobs.
The fish in the river leap before thee; thy rays are
  within the sea.
Ships sail both north and south.
Thou settest each one in his place, thou
  providest their needs – each one with his
  food.
How manifold is what thou hast done.

Tutankhaten. Famous for his nearly intact tomb, discovered by Howard Carter in 1922, this pharaoh soon changed his name to Tutankhamun, and his consort, Ankhsenpaaten, also changed her name to expel the 'Aten' part and replace it with 'Amun'. This signalled a return to the state of religious affairs which had existed before the cultural revolution of Akhenaten. Tutankhamun returned to Thebes, and the new city was abandoned. Soon it would be empty, and left to be covered by the eternal sands of the desert. As for Akhenaten himself, his name was excised from all monuments, and all his works were laid waste.

The boy-king Tutankhamun must have spent all his life governed by advisers, of whom the middle-aged Ay and the commander-in-chief of the army, Horemheb, would have been prominent. It is clear that during his short reign the priesthood of Amun was reinstated, the status quo restored, and the beginnings of an attempt made to contain the damage done to the northern part of the empire. However, the young king died (again, possibly killed) in about 1327 BC, not yet out of his teens and after a reign of only nine years. His death appears to have been followed by a brief but potentially disastrous power-vacuum, when his widow sent a message to the powerful king of the Hittites, Suppiluliumas, to send one of his sons to marry her and reign as King of Egypt. Suppiluliumas duly sent his son Zananza, but the prince was intercepted and assassinated, possibly on the orders of Horemheb, who may have been working in concert with Ay, who now took the crown and married Ankhsenpaamun himself. Ay reigned for no more than four years and was succeeded by Horemheb, who staked his claim by performing the Opening of the Mouth ceremony on his predecessor, and by marrying Mutnodjmet, Ay's daughter and Nefertiti's sister. The ultimate fate of the rest of Akhenaten's family is unknown.

Horemheb was already old by Egyptian standards when he came to power, but he reigned for nearly thirty years, dying in about 1295 BC. He was the last pharaoh of the Eighteenth Dynasty, and during his rule he managed to restore to Egypt much of its former greatness. Having no direct heir, he left the empire to his vizier, a former army colleague called Rameses, who already had a son, Sety.

After the brief transitional reign of Rameses I, which lasted little more than a year, Sety I continued the work begun by Horemheb of repairing the damage done to the empire by Akhenaten's neglect of it. He also attacked the Hittites, who had moved down into the northern part of Syria-Palestine, and for a time succeeded in driving them back.

Sety was followed by Rameses II, another of the great pharaohs, whose long reign of sixty-six years (c. 1279 to 1213) dominated the dynasty. When he died, he was over ninety years old and had fathered at least fifty sons and thirty-eight daughters. He was a great military ruler, and one of the most prolific builders: his 'Great Temple' at Abu Simbel, 250 kilometres south-east of Aswan, and the 'Small Temple' dedicated to the goddess Hathor and to his deified Chief Wife, Nefertari, remain as a testimony to the mighty scale of his building work, as does his mortuary temple, the Ramesseum, at Thebes. Additionally, this triumphalist pharaoh usurped many monuments of his predecessors, inserting his name in place of theirs. An early archaeological description of the remains of one of his statues inspired Shelley's famous sonnet, *Ozymandias*.

The inconclusive Battle of Qadesh, in about 1274 BC, ultimately led several years later to a peace treaty with the Hittites, who had hitherto remained hostile. In his late sixties, Rameses married a Hittite princess to cement the diplomatic bond between the two countries, which offset the threat posed by the rise of Assyria. Peace was maintained between the two powers for the remaining lifetime of the Hittite Empire and both nations enjoyed eighty years of stability and prosperity.

Rameses II's successor was his thirteenth son, Merenptah, already in his early fifties when he came to the throne, and faced with the need to restore and rebuild the army, and mend fences with his neighbours. By the fifth year of his ten-year reign he had to fight off a vast coalition of Libu (Libyans), Meshwesh and Kehak peoples with the 'Peoples of the Sea' – Sherden (Sardinians), Sheklesh (Sicilians), Lukha (Lycians), Tursha (Etruscans) and Akawasha (Achaeans) – all led by the Libu prince Mauroy, which advanced on the Western Delta with the intention of colonizing it.

The Egyptians met the coalition in battle, and after a fight which lasted six hours they routed them. A granite stela in Merenptah's mortuary temple at Thebes celebrates the victory: 'Great joy has come to Egypt, rejoicing comes forth from the towns of the Black Land ... Sit down happily and talk ... The soldiers can lie sleeping ... The herds in the fields can be left without herdsmen ... There is no shout of alarm in the night ... He who plants his crop can be sure of eating it.'

But after Merenptah, the Nineteenth Dynasty died out over the next two decades in a series of short reigns riddled with palace intrigue. And the threat from Libya, always tempted by the fecundity of Egypt, did not go away. In any case a stream of Libyan immigrants entered Egypt and settled during the next several years.

The Twentieth Dynasty saw the beginning of a gradual but irreversible decline. Its first significant king was Rameses III, and after him every king of the dynasty shared the same name. It ended with the death of Rameses XI in 1069 BC.

Rameses III came to the throne in 1184 and ruled for about thirty years. Initially he was involved with continuing skirmishes with Libya and various coalitions of small neighbouring states, but by the eleventh year of his reign a period of peace meant that prosperity was restored. Rameses embarked on a building programme, though not as ambitious as those of his forebears; there was a major expedition to Punt, and the king led a final period of territorial expansion. But the end of the reign was marred by serious palace intrigue and an attempted coup. The end of Rameses III's rule also marked the end of Egypt's undisputed role as an imperial power.

After his death the country entered a new period of

Isis embraces the pharaoh Rameses I. This painting from 1180 BC is at the tomb of Amon-Hir-Khopshef, who was the son of Rameses III.

POPULATION

Ancient Egypt knew three different kinds of community: the village, the port and the city. Villages were agricultural communities; ports, trading places, and cities centres of administration and culture. The largest of these were the capitals of the districts, or *nomes*, into which Egypt was divided. There were forty-two *nomes* at the time of the New Kingdom. Cities were densely populated and surrounded by villages. Large tracts of the country were virtually uninhabited.

Before the New Kingdom the population of the country has been estimated at about one-and-a-half million. During the Eighteenth and Nineteenth Dynasties this increased hugely, reaching perhaps five million by the twelfth century BC, the population swelled by large numbers of immigrants. The greatest centres were at Memphis and Heliopolis, where up to half the population may have lived, and Memphis was probably the first city in the world to have a population of one million. Other large cities were Thebes, Saïs, Pi-Ramesse and Herakleopolis.

The government remained centralized, and wealth stayed in the hands of the elite, though the administration of the country responded to the needs and concerns of the farmers who formed its economic base. Immigrant communities lived peacefully within an essentially stable society, as indicated by the fact that there were relatively few military garrisons in Egypt itself.

Whilst the vast majority of the population of Egypt were farmers, many people lived in the towns or cities, seen as the greatest in the ancient world.

ANIMALS

Animals played a major part in Ancient Egyptian culture. Many of them were revered as gods and most were associated with some form of ritual or magic. Farmers lived in the same buildings as their stock, and from early on animals of many kinds were mummified for eternity in the same way as humans.

As early as the Naqada II period some animals were being ritually buried: cattle, crocodiles, hippos, elephants, gazelles, dogs, baboons, lions and geese have all been found. In later periods, cats and the sacred ibis (a species now vanished from Egypt) were mummified and interred in their millions.

Although animal cults increased during the New Kingdom, they reached their zenith in the Late Period, from about 750 BC. During this time millions of animals and birds were killed and mummified as offerings to the gods they represented or were affiliated with. Not only cats and ibis, but falcons, rams, dogs, baboons, shrews, mongooses, snakes, fish, scarab and jewel beetles, gazelles, cattle and possibly even lions were subjected to this treatment.

It is not however paradoxical to note that animals were loved and cherished. Domestic animals were valuable and it would have been an act of madness

Animal worship was of long duration. The Apis Bull cult lasted until at least the middle of the fourth century AD; and the Early Church father Clement of Alexandria, who lived from *c.* AD 150–215, observed scathingly that 'the god of the Egyptians appears on a purple couch as a wallowing animal'; Herodotus made the mistake of thinking that all animals were sacred to the Egyptians.

to maltreat them. Cattle, sheep, goats and pigs were among the earliest to be domesticated. Camels were at first known only in the wild, and were probably not fully introduced until the time of the Persian invasion of about 525 BC. Oxen were used as draft animals, and to draw the plough. From the earliest times, donkeys were the only beast of burden. Later on, after the introduction of the horse, mules and hinnies were also bred. The donkey was never used for riding, except by the peasants. The horse, by contrast, was regarded as a noble animal.

The Egyptians were experts in domestication and they kept a diversity of pets, including dogs and cats, but also vervet monkeys, baboons (sometimes used as 'guard-dogs'), dorcas gazelles, pintail ducks, hoopoes and geese. Lions

TOP: Donkeys and mules were important as beasts of burden and were ridden by peasants and farmers, in contrast to the upper classes, who would ride horses.

ABOVE: Amulets of sacred animals. From left to right: bronze cow representing Hathor, lion, jackal, ram, ibis and the Apis Bull. The green and blue colours are turquoise and faience, both mined from the Late Pre-dynastic period onwards.

LEFT: Faience statue of a hippopotamus, from the Twelfth to Thirteenth Dynasty.

were kept as royal pets, though these may have been declawed and had their teeth removed. Berenike II, the wife of king Ptolemy III Euergetes I, is said to have loved to walk in the palace gardens accompanied by her tame lioness. Cheetahs and, occasionally, leopards were also kept domestically.

decline. Despite the fact that Rameses III had left the country in good economic health, the hitherto efficient tax-collection system began to falter, and this affected the country badly. A smallpox epidemic and poor harvests in ensuing reigns added to the deterioration of the Black Land. By the time of Rameses IX (*c.* 1126 to 1108), economic depression was affecting everyone. There was a marked increase in the incidence of tomb robberies, and it is from this period that 'Tomb Robbers', the story recounted in Chapter Seven, comes. Meanwhile, there were continued incursions from Libya, either in the form of skirmishes and raids, or of what would now be called

The Ramesseum – the funerary temple of one of the greatest of the pharaohs, Rameses II.

illegal immigrants, attracted by what was still, despite everything, a country with magnificent natural resources.

Rameses XI, who reigned from 1099 to 1069 BC, was the last of the Twentieth Dynasty. But by then the pharaoh was king in name only: by the nineteenth year of his rule, a new high priest in Thebes, Herihor, possibly married to a sister of the king, assumed power in the south, taking the titles of Commander-in-Chief and Viceroy of Nubia. In the north, power was wielded not by Rameses but by an administrator called Smendes, who may have been a son of Herihor. Rameses remained

titular pharaoh of the whole land, but on his death Smendes ascended the throne, founding the Twenty-first Dynasty and ruling the north as Smendes I. The south continued to be governed from Thebes by the ruling priest-administrators there.

Smendes established his capital at Tanis. His relations with Thebes remained good, perhaps because of the family relationship that existed between the two sets of rulers. Smendes ruled from 1069 to 1043; the High Priest of Amun in Thebes, Pinudjem, was in power from 1070 to 1032. He had married a daughter of Rameses XI, and one of his sons, Psusennes, became the third king of the Twenty-first Dynasty at Tanis. This dynasty, the first of the four which make up what is known as the Third Intermediate Period, also had good trading relations with Syria-Palestine. Meanwhile, Libyan settlers continued to arrive, and some of the immigrants rose to positions of power and status. One such, Sheshonq, established a power-base at Per-Bastet, known to the Greeks as Bubastis (modern Zagazig), in the Eastern Delta, the centre of the cult of the cat-goddess, Bastet. Sheshonq married into the royal family, and when his father-in-law, the last king of the Twenty-first Dynasty, Psusennes II, died in 945 BC, Sheshonq succeeded him, founding the Libyan-Bubastite Twenty-second Dynasty. He moved quickly to instal one of his sons as High Priest of Amun at Thebes and sugared the pill by undertaking building work on the city's Temple of Amun at Karnak, which had last received attention in the Nineteenth Dynasty. This attempt to reunify the country if only partially met with some success, but tensions remained between north and south and in 836 BC, during the reign of Takelot II, civil war broke out. The war lasted ten years, but its end did not bring a return to stability. Takelot was succeeded by his brother, who ruled as Sheshonq III from 825, and seven years into his reign found himself faced with a rival, Pedubast, who set himself up as pharaoh at Leontopolis, and founded the Twenty-third Dynasty. To confuse the picture further, the Libyan princelings of Herakleopolis and Hermopolis also declared their autonomy, so that for the next century Egypt was ruled, at least nominally, from four centres.

THE
LONG
EVENING

FOREIGN RULE

In an effort to curb the power of the high priests of Amun at Thebes, Rameses XI had appointed a man called Panhesy as Viceroy of Nubia. He seems to have held sway in Nubia until his death, but after his demise Nubia regained its independence, largely owing to the squabbles in the north and the lack of a coherent leadership of the whole of what had once been a united Black Land.

A power vacuum followed Panhesy's death, but Nubia, left unmolested, became a unified country with its own natural resources and in about 747 BC a Nubian, Piankhy, established himself as ruler, based at Napata, his home town, a city far to the south and closer to the Fourth Cataract of the Nile than the Third. Piankhy adopted the full traditional trappings of a pharaoh, and resolved to take advantage of the chaos in the north by embarking on a campaign of conquest, in which he enjoyed the advantage of controlling all the southern trade routes. A faithful devotee of Amun, he was determined to celebrate as pharaoh the ancient festival of Opet in Thebes, and to that end despatched an army northwards in 728 BC.

Piankhy's army moved swiftly northwards, taking Thebes and, after a siege, Hermopolis, continuing into Lower Egypt to take the new town of Oxyrhynchus, and Herakleopolis, meeting and defeating King Tefnakhte of Saïs south of the Faiyum.

Having repulsed Tefnakhte, the only really powerful rival he had, and established himself in that part of Egypt which he had conquered, Piankhy withdrew, leaving trusted administrators and an army of occupation. He duly celebrated the Opet festival and installed his sister, Amenirdis, as the next God's Wife of Amun, a position which had eclipsed that of Chief Priest thirty years earlier and which had successively been occupied by daughters of the royal house since then, wielding power at Thebes on behalf of their royal fathers. (This useful arrangement had been instituted by King Osorkon III of the Twenty-third Dynasty in order to break the power of the high priests. As the God's Wife was supposed to remain celibate, she adopted a daughter, the Divine Adoratrice, as her successor: each Divine Adoratrice was a daughter of the pharaoh then reigning, and thus the succession and the power were kept under the control of the king.)

Piankhy's brother, Shabaqo, succeeded him and defeated and killed Bakenrenef (some sources say that he was burned alive), the son of Tefnakhte, who may have been ruling from as far south as Memphis. Shabaqo's armies took over the whole country and Shabaqo took up residence in Egypt itself, ruling from 716 to 702 BC. The Twenty-fifth Dynasty was thus established.

In the meantime, abroad, Assyria's star was rising. In 712 BC, Sargon II attacked and conquered Asdod, whose king fled for sanctuary to Egypt, but Shabaqo returned him to Sargon, pursuing a policy of appeasement to the great Near Eastern power. Shabaqo's successor, his nephew Shabitqo, reversed his uncle's policy and when Sennacherib of Assyria invaded Palestine in 701 BC, Shabitqo swiftly sent an army to King Hezekiah's aid. His soldiers were defeated, but the Assyrians failed to take Jerusalem, and although Sennacherib laid waste a large part of the country, he finally withdrew – events celebrated unhistorically in the Bible, 2 Kings 19, and also in Lord Byron's famous poem, *The Destruction of Sennacherib*.

The next king of Egypt was Taharqo, during whose twenty-six-year reign (he died in 664 BC) a substantial building programme was implemented. Egypt remained prosperous, but not as secure as it had been; the Assyrians continued to pose a threat, and in 674 BC an invasion, which got as far as the Nile, had to be repulsed. However, two years later the Assyrians were back. They established themselves in the Delta, and set up a puppet pharaoh, Nekau, a descendant of Bakenrenef, at Saïs, where he ruled from 672 to 664 BC.

The last king of the Twenty-fifth Dynasty was Tanutamani, who succeeded in defeating and killing Nekau; the Assyrians retaliated immediately, and pushed Tanutamani all the way down to Thebes, which they took and sacked. His forces broken, Tanutamani retreated to Nubia, where he died in 656 BC. The Assyrians placed Nekau's son Psamtek on the throne as the founder of the Twenty-sixth Dynasty, and withdrew. (Based as it was in Saïs, this dynasty is known as the Saïte.)

Despite its vicissitudes, this was a period that saw a revival of Egyptian building and sculpture along traditional lines. Some Saïte work reproduces the style of the Old Kingdom so faithfully that it is difficult to distinguish it. No doubt this deliberate archaism was partly inspired by nostalgia for a lost golden age, partly by nationalism, and partly by political propaganda. Saïte work is not just slavish imitation, however, and could tentatively be compared to the work of sculptors of the Renaissance in 'copying' the statues of antiquity. In the meantime, writing was becoming ever more cursive and phonetic, and hieratic was giving way to demotic for ordinary day-to-day business letters. Towards the end of the dynasty, the more informal demotic prevailed throughout the country.

The Saïte period also saw an increased interest in the navy, and a post, Master of the King's Ships, appears, occupied by various named officials during the reigns of successive pharaohs.

Psamtek accepted Assyrian overlordship, as did the princes of Lower and Middle Egypt, though Thebes remained loyal to the Nubians, who had done so much for the city. In 656 BC, however, Psamtek started to woo Thebes, with some success (perhaps Thebes was bowing to the inevitable since Nubian power had been subdued), sending his daughter Nitocris to be God's Wife of Amun. It was during this period that the family tragedy of the 'Murder In The Temple' unfolded, the story of which is told in Chapter Eight. Psamtek may have been encouraged to make his move not only by news of the death of Tanutamani, but by the fact that Assyria's power was waning. In 612 BC it was overrun by Medes and Babylonians; by 608 its empire had vanished.

Psamtek died in 610 and was succeeded by Nekau II, during whose reign Egypt and the new ascendant power in the east, Babylon, tussled over control of Syria, though Nekau also found time and the resources to begin cutting a canal to link the Nile with the Red Sea. Under him the navy developed its forces in the Mediterranean, with the introduction of triremes.

Nekau II was succeeded by Psamtek II (595 BC), who maintained a neutral position vis-à-vis the Babylonians, occupying himself with suppressing the Nubians who had continued to use pharaonic titles at Napata, and who took advantage of the desertion of the garrison established by Psamtek I on the southern frontier at Elephantine. The garrison, composed of 240,000 foreign mercenaries, had mutinied after three years' unrelieved duty and marched south. Psamtek II took the war to the Nubians and struck hard, so that they left Napata and moved even further south to establish their capital at Meroe.

Psamtek II's successor, Apries, took an army into Palestine to attack the army of King Nebuchadrezar. Apries failed to prevent the fall of Jerusalem, which led to the Jewish captivity in Babylon, though many Jews found refuge in Egypt and established a colony on the island of Elephantine. Apries also attacked Tyre by sea, an action which Herodotus recounts. If true, it is the first well-documented Egyptian naval strike. Naval development wouldn't have been unusual in a dynasty based so near

This plate dating from 1580 AD is in the British Museum. It shows Nebuchadrezar, seated on the throne, and his prisoner Zedekiah.

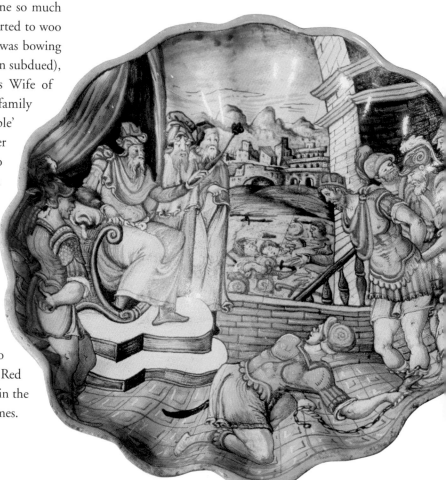

WIT AND HUMOUR

Much of Ancient Egyptian wit was visual, and satires like the erotic Turin papyrus (in which animals are depicted performing human activities, cats nursemaiding mice, and a battle between cats and mice) demonstrate this amply; but in various written tracts, such as the 'Satire on Trades', also called the 'Instructions of Khety', humour plays a strong role. It is humour we can readily recognize, as, just as in our society, the Ancient Egyptians had their fair share of ironists, satirists, mockers and wits as well as slapstick humourists and club bores. The 'Instructions of Khety', used as a copying book for generations, contains many good examples:

> I have seen the metalworker at his labour at the mouth of his furnace, with his fingers like a crocodile's, stinking more than fish roe ... The reed-cutter goes north to the Delta, to carry off arrows for himself; he has done more than his arms can do, the mosquitoes have killed him and the sandflies have butchered him, so that he is cut to pieces ... And the maker of pots is under the earth, though standing up with the living. He grubs in the meadows more than pigs do, to fire his pottery, and his clothes are stiff with mud, and his loincloth is in rags ... The sandalmaker is very badly off ... He's well, as well as a corpse, chewing on hides! ... and the washerman washes on the riverbank, and he is near the crocodile ... his food is mixed with shit, and no part of him is clean ...

There is much visual humour in tomb-paintings of scenes from everyday life: there are cavorting monkeys, animals doing humans' work, and hieroglyphs performing the same function as bubbles in strip cartoons. Thus we have people squabbling and cat-calling, swearing and abusing, sometimes in a good-natured way, and sometimes not. The actors in theses scenes are always rustics and realistically depicted, with paunches, thinning hair, stubble, and so on. Foreigners are almost always shown either in abject defeat or otherwise unflatteringly. Ostraca found in the workers' village at Deir el-Medina show sketches and cartoons evidently done for fun.

The cat deity Bastet cuts off the head of the serpent-demon Apophis (above), while (left) a cartoon shows a lion and an antelope playing senet. Unluckily for the antelope, it looks as if the lion is about to win.

Other written works satirize politics and religion: a Ramesside text portrays the royal family as cowardly, while some religious satires, such as one which mocks the important ceremony of weighing the heart (to assess whether the deceased is worthy to enter paradise) border on blasphemy. Sex, of course, plays a huge role in humour: 'Do not rejoice in your wife's beauty, her mind is set on a lover'; 'Man is more eager to copulate than a donkey; his purse is what restrains him'.

the sea, but generally the Saïte kings were more conservative than innovative.

Apries was evidently a warlike king, though not a victorious one. In 570 BC, the last year of his reign, he joined forces with the Libyans against the Greeks, who were beginning to unify and establish themselves as a power. The Greeks defeated the Egyptians amid much bloodshed, which led to a coup d'état against Apries by one of his generals, possibly backed by Nebuchadrezar.

drunkard, nevertheless managed during a long reign (570–526 BC) to soothe national pride and harmonize relations between native Egyptians and the large numbers of foreigners now living in the country. He developed the port of Naucratis, founded under Psamtek I in the Western Delta, and restricted Greek traders to it. Naucratis exported corn, papyrus, linen and other goods to Greece, receiving in return wine (which was better than Egyptian wine), olive oil and silver.

In the time of the last great Egyptian pharaoh Ahmose II, Egypt enjoyed a period of peace and prosperity. The country's diverse cultures flourished and relationships were cemented with Greece, Libya and the Mediterranean.

The usurper took the the throne as Ahmose II in the same year. Ironically Greek mercenaries, who formed a large part of the Egyptian army, remained loyal to Apries, but he was killed in a battle with Ahmose three years later. Ahmose shrewdly had the dead pharaoh buried with full honours, thereby legitimizing his own claim to the throne.

Ahmose II, often depicted as a boorish oaf and a

In the meantime, Cyrus the Great of Persia embarked on his own plan of empire-building. He annexed Babylon to the Persian Empire, and went on to take Syria and Palestine. When he died in 529 BC he controlled territories that stretched from the Aegean and the Mediterranean in the west, to the Persian Gulf in the south and the Black, Caspian and Aral Seas in the north, and to the frontiers of India in the east.

He was succeeded by his son Cambyses, who inherited his father's territorial ambitions. In 525 BC Cambyses invaded Egypt, overrunning the army of Ahmose II's son and successor, Psamtek III, who ruled for no more than a year, and bringing the Twenty-sixth Dynasty and the period of Saïte rule to an end. This Psamtek was initially imprisoned with his family, and only later executed because he was discovered plotting against Cambyses.

Cambyses took his armies as far as Nubia; an expeditionary force sent into the Western Desert towards Siwa vanished without trace, but apart from this setback he secured the kingdom and became pharaoh, founding the Twenty-seventh Dynasty, the first of the two Persian dynasties. The region of Saïs seems to have escaped relatively lightly, thanks to the collaboration with the Persians of one Udjahorresne, a former Egyptian naval officer who so found favour with the emperor that he was appointed priest of the temple of Neith at Saïs, which he had reconsecrated after its desecration by the Persians.

Cambyses did not stay in Egypt, and died in 522 BC after a coup. He was succeeded after a short period of uncertainty by Darius, called 'the Great', who successfully put down rebellions within the empire, extended it eastwards, consolidated it and codified its laws.

In his turn Darius also became pharaoh of the Black Land. A Zoroastrian by belief (under him Zoroastrianism became the state religion), he was tolerant of the mores of the nations under him and employed local officials as administrators. Egypt, together with the Western Desert and part of Libya, became a *satrapy* (province) under a governor and was brought to heel, though towards the end of his reign, Darius' defeat by the Greeks at the Battle of Marathon in 490 BC may have triggered a revolt that took place in the Delta. The revolt failed, and Darius' successor, Xerxes (486–465 BC), though still an absentee pharaoh, was far less *laissez-aller* than his predecessor, sacking all Egyptian officials except loyal army officers and imposing a firm rule on the land. He also reinforced the Persian secret police whom Cambyses had introduced with the first governor. This was not sufficient to quash the Egyptian spirit, however, and during the reign of the next Persian pharaoh, Artaxerxes,

there was another rebellion, led by a Libyan chieftain, which was eventually crushed in 456 BC.

This led to even firmer control by Persia of its province, and for a time, during the rest of Artaxerxes' reign and that of his successor, Darius II, the country was quiet. The flame of rebellion had not been put out, however, and in 404 BC, Prince Amyrtaios of Saïs raised a new revolt, successfully taking control of Memphis and Upper Egypt, and founding the Twenty-eighth Dynasty. The Persians were prevented from dealing with this by

The Persian king Darius, 'the Great', from a relief at Persepolis.

trouble elsewhere in their ponderous empire, but Amyrtaios died in 399, and with him died his dynasty, the shortest in the history of Ancient Egypt.

He had however re-established Egypt as an independent power, and the founder of the Twenty-ninth Dynasty, Nepherites, in his brief reign of six years, laid firm foundations for the kings who followed him, Hakor and Nepherites II. The army was reformed under the command of the Greek general Chabryas, who deployed his troops in the Delta so effectively that they withstood and held off the Persians despite a fierce three-year campaign.

In 379 Nectanebo took the throne as the first king of the Thirtieth Dynasty, helped by the Nile flood to repel a Persian expeditionary force which came through the Delta. Eager to re-establish an Egyptian identity, he inaugurated an ambitious programme of building in the Delta, though little of his works remain. His son, Teos, was the first to introduce an Egyptian coin, and continued the useful policy of alliances with the Greek states. By now Egypt was again so prosperous that Teos decided to take the offensive to the Persians, assembled a huge army, and invaded Syria-Palestine with great success. Unfortunately, however, at home his throne was usurped by his nephew and Teos ironically was forced to throw himself on the mercy of the Persian court. The nephew, Nectanebo II, ruled from 360 to 343 BC over a country that was prosperous and self-confident. Nectanebo encouraged another large programme of building and sculpture in the traditional Egyptian style, harking back to the days of true greatness. In reality, however, Persia remained a threat, and Nectanebo was to be the last native Egyptian pharaoh.

Artaxerxes III longed to restore Persian rule to the wealthy land of Egypt, and once again to control its trade with Africa. One attempt to reconquer, in 351 BC, had met with defeat at the hands of the Egyptian army under its able Spartan commander, Agesilaos. For his second attempt Artaxerxes gathered a mighty force of 300,000 men, together with a fleet of 300 galleys and beat the Egyptians back to Memphis, where Artaxerxes installed a *satrap* (govenor). Nectanebo established himself in Upper Egypt for a while, but by 341 Persia once again controlled the whole country. Nectanebo's fate is

ABOVE: Head of Alexander the Great, from a contemporary coin. BELOW: This incense burner is the only surviving example of a depiction of the Pharos lighthouse at Alexandria.

unknown. Artaxerxes ruled as pharaoh *in absentia* from 343 to 338, when he died, poisoned by Bagoas, his favourite eunuch. His victory established the Thirty-first Dynasty of Ancient Egypt, and he was succeeded by two more Persian kings, Arses and Darius III.

With Darius' defeat at the hands of Alexander the Great in 332, the end came not only for Persian rule in Egypt, which the Egyptians regarded as a great liberation, but for the Persian empire as a whole. For their part, the Egyptians had to get used to new overlords. Under Greek rule, native Egyptians would find themselves second-class citizens, denied the right to bear arms or to meet freely in groups to discuss grievances.

Alexander the Great, the first 'pharaoh' of the Macedonian Dynasty, spent little time in Egypt. Arriving in 332 BC, he founded the Mediterranean coastal city of Alexandria in 331, and then left to pursue his career of conquest, though he had taken pains to win the Egyptians round by showing respect to their religious beliefs, sacrificing to their gods, including the Apis Bull.

Alexandria was conceived as a large city – massive by contemporary standards, and clearly built with the precise purpose of rivalling and even surpassing Memphis. It was twenty-five kilometres in circumference and its grid-system streets radiated from two main boulevards. The entire population, both freemen and slaves, possibly numbered about 600,000. The harbour was dominated by the great Pharos lighthouse, a wonder of the ancient world, and in time large public buildings came to dominate a quarter of the city. There was the Great Library, the Academy of Muses or Museum, a university founded by the first Ptolemy, public baths, theatres, a hippodrome, and several gymnasia (the original Gymnasium was a club for intellectual and physical activities), and temples.

Alexander the Great died in Babylon in 323 BC, leaving his empire to be divided up among his principal generals, though they did not enjoy full control until after the deaths of Alexander's immediate heirs, his half-brother Philip Arrhidaeus and his son, whom he did not live to see, also Alexander. These two, with Alexander the Great, formed the whole of the Macedonian Dynasty, which lasted from 332 to 305 BC.

THE PTOLEMAIC PERIOD

The general to whose share Egypt fell was called Ptolemy. Having spent many years as governor of the country, he finally felt able to declare himself King of Egypt in 305 BC, at the age of sixty-three. The Ptolemaic Dynasty he thus founded with his wife Berenike lasted 275 years. This was the last dynasty, for at the end of it Queen Kleopatra VII Arsinoe ceded power to Rome. It was a complex and often bloody period.

The Ptolemies presented themselves completely traditionally as Egyptians: no untrained eye would guess that the temples at Edfu, Kom Ombo and Philae, for example, had not been built under a native regime. Allowing the locals to keep their religion, and giving them money to build temples, was, however, merely a political safety measure. Otherwise the Ptolemies, with few exceptions, never identified with their native subjects, and only Kleopatra VII, the last and one of the greatest of a morally and ethically threadbare dynasty, learnt Egyptian. If they were tolerant of the Egyptian religion, it was largely because they did not care about it; and the Greeks never had the destructive proselytizing zeal of the later Christians. For their part, the Egyptians came to hate and despise their Greek overlords as only members of an ancient, but flagging and superseded, culture can hate and despise those of a new and cocksure one.

Ptolemy I, who styled himself Soter, or 'Saviour', was a capable man whose first concern was to secure his frontiers and build up defences against the neighbouring Mediterranean states. He accomplished these aims and also gained control of Cyprus, parts of Libya, and Palestine. At home, his task as a foreign king was possibly made easier by the fact that the Egyptians were accustomed to the Greek language and people, and were in any case weary after two centuries of occupation and/or fighting. Abandoning the throne at eighty, he ceded it to his son Ptolemy II Philadelphus, who celebrated his accession with a great pageant in Alexandria, always a Greek city with virtual autonomy from the rest of the country, in which both Greek and Egyptian gods were honoured. Philadelphus enjoyed a long reign, from 285 to 246 BC, but it was not untroubled.

He had married Arsinoe I, a daughter of Lysimachus of Thrace, possibly a political alliance. When Lysimachus died in 281, his widow, Arsinoe II, Philadelphus' sister, came to Egypt to live with her brother and sister-in-law. It wasn't long, however, before this ambitious and ruthless woman had intrigued against her sister-in-law successfully enough to have convinced her brother that Arsinoe was guilty of treason. Arsinoe was banished to Cyprus where she died five years later. The surviving Arsinoe then married her brother, an alliance countenanced under Egyptian law but not by the Greeks, who regarded incest as illegal. The marriage was childless but it may have been one of convenience, since Arsinoe II brought with her most of Lysimachus' territory in the Aegean. She died in 269 BC, a couple of years after Philadelphus had made his first diplomatic contact with Rome, which by then had

LEFT: Basalt statue of Ptolemy I Soter, 305–283 BC. This statue is said to have been found in the lining of a well in the Delta area.

RIGHT: Calcite bust of Ptolemy II, 286–246 BC. Both pharaohs wear the *uraeus* and *nemes* (headcloth).

gained dominion over the whole of Lower Italy, and with which Philadelphus from then on maintained friendly relations.

Philadelphus died aged sixty-three, bloated, debauched and so gouty that he couldn't walk. He was succeeded by the son of his first wife, Ptolemy III Euergetes. Euergetes came to the throne in 246 BC, and his first task was to defuse a possible palace coup and smooth the ruffled feathers of the Egyptian populace, whom Philadelphus had neglected.

Euergetes reigned for twenty-five years. His wife, Berenike, a princess of Cyrenaica (north-eastern Libya), whom he had married in 247 BC, was a spirited woman. Originally betrothed to Euergetes in childhood, after her father's death her mother, Apame, had arranged for her to marry the son of the King of Macedonia, Demetrios. He duly arrived in Cyrenaica and the marriage took place, but not long afterwards he started an affair with Apame. Berenike became aware of this, and, ambushing them in bed, ordered the guards to spear her husband to death, which they did, and in their enthusiasm they killed Apame too, despite Berenike's efforts to save her mother. Berenike was much admired both in Cyrenaica and in Alexandria for this exploit.

While Euergetes was away campaigning in 240 BC, Berenike ruled in his name, but she was not effective at alleviating a bad famine which took hold at the time, leading to general unrest. On his return, Euergetes had a large temple built to Osiris at Canopis near Alexandria, but that did not placate the Egyptians. Their resentment grew, and was not mollified by the fact that Euergetes organized efficient famine relief, contributed to the upkeep of the Apis Bull at Memphis, and began construction, in 236, of the magnificent temple to Horus at Edfu in the antique style, which still remains to be admired today, and contributed to work at Philae, Aswan and Esna.

The result of the Egyptian resentment, ingratitude and discontent was that Euergetes turned from enlightened ruler to oppressor, and a dark mood prevailed over the last decade of his reign. Euergetes' quarter-century, however, was to be the best the Egyptians enjoyed under the Ptolemies. Soter, Philadelphus and Euergetes had made more than a promising start, but from now on a degeneracy would set in from which neither the ruling house nor the country would recover, characterized by palace intrigue, intermarriage and murder.

Euergetes' son, Ptolemy IV Philopator was in his mid-twenties when he came to the throne in 221 BC. Weak and vain, violent and libidinous, he fell under the influence of a Greek courtier, Sosibios, who isolated him by privily murdering several major members of the royal family under one pretext or another of disloyalty. Sosibios introduced him to a woman called Agathoclia, who became Philopator's mistress, indulging his sexual tastes. When he was fully in her power, she persuaded him to remove his mother, the dowager Queen Berenike, who continued as co-ruler, because, according to Agathoclia, she was planning to depose Philopator in favour of his younger brother Magas. Philopator had his mother and brother killed.

In 217 Philopator notched up his one real achieve-

This huge and impressive bust of Ptolemy IV, dating from the time of his reign, is now in the Alexandria Graeco-Roman Museum.

OPPOSITE: The Rosetta Stone, looted from Egypt by the French, and subsequently from them by the British. Now in the British Museum, London. This 'document' enabled the young Egyptologist Jean-François Champollion to decipher hieroglyphs.

ment, marching into battle with his sister, Arsinoe III, against Antiochus III of Syria who had invaded Palestine. He routed the Syrian, and after the battle Philopator celebrated by marrying his sister.

He was a poor ruler and did not care about the welfare of his people. When famine threatened again he did nothing, advised by Agathoclia and her brother, Agathocles. There was renewed unrest and Nubians invaded from the south and took back Thebes during the last three years of his reign, holding the territory well into the reign of his successor. For the next century rebellion and brooding discontent became the order of the day.

Philopator continued his life of excess, so disgusting his sister-wife that she retired from the court in 209 BC, only to be murdered five years later. Philopator predeceased her in 205. Their son was Ptolemy V Epiphanes, a child of four at his father's death. For a moment there was chaos, as Sosibios made a bid for the regency and failed. The mob in Alexandria rioted, and Agathoclia, her brother and their mother were dragged from their houses and torn to pieces. Epiphanes was fourteen years old when he had two coronations, one according to Macedonian custom and another, at Memphis, according to Egyptian rites. In 196 BC a stela was set up commemorating the event in two Egyptian scripts, hieroglyphic and demotic, as well as Greek. A fragment has survived and is now known as the Rosetta Stone. It was discovered by the French during the Napoleonic wars but was taken from them by the British and is now in the British Museum in London. It was by studying the Rosetta Stone that the young French linguist and Egyptologist Jean-François Champollion deciphered hieroglyphs at the beginning of the nineteenth century.

In 193 Epiphanes married Kleopatra, the first of seven queens of Egypt by that name. She was a daughter of Antiochus III of Syria, whom Epiphanes'

PARTIES AND FESTIVALS

Dance was an important part of Ancient Egyptian cultural life at all levels of society, both as a social pastime and entertainment, and in a religious context. Dance was accompanied by music – either simple clapping, chanting, or percussion instruments, or a combination of all three; and later by the lyre as well. Dance had many forms, from the formal, slow and lyrical, to energetic types which were close to acrobatics and gymnastics.

Music too had many forms, and dates back to the earliest times. Old Kingdom paintings show musicians as predominantly men; by the New Kingdom, they were predominantly women. One theme which occurs throughout the empire is that of the blind harp-player, who is usually male. The idea that the blind person has a more acute aural sense is one of ancient perception. The Egyptians

seem to have had no musical notation, at least none has yet come to light, and we have no idea what their music sounded like, though from the instruments they used we may glean inklings. Many instruments have survived as grave-goods.

Instruments included the tambourine and the drum for secular use. In religious ritual, the clappers, cymbals, bells and *sistra* were the principal instruments. The *sistrum* was a kind of rattle, used ritualistically, usually played by women. Egyptian stringed instruments included the harp, the lyre and a kind of lute, still known in a developed form as the *udd*. The design of these instruments varies little from their modern counterparts. The bow-harp was known from the Sixth Dynasty; the angular harp was an Asian import, perhaps via Mitanni, in the New Kingdom. The lute and the lyre came from

the Near East during the New Kingdom. They also had a type of trumpet, but this was more of a bugle, used for religious and military fanfares.

There were wind instruments, including a transverse flute, and a double-oboe, one pipe playing the drone, the other, the melody. There was also a kind of clarinet, the reeds being deployed more or less as in the modern fashion.

Throughout Ancient Egyptian history, musicians were engaged to entertain at banquets, parties and dinner-parties, the last being a favourite pastime of the Ancient Egyptian middle and upper classes. Garlanded guests wearing scent-cones on their heads would sit singly or in pairs at small tables where servants would serve them. Such scenes are found depicted frequently, perhaps most graciously during the Amarna period, where guests

OPPOSITE: *Muu* dancers lead the Apis Bull in its funeral procession. There are tomb paintings which depict dancers wearing these unusual basket type headdresses which is how we know exactly what they looked like.

LEFT: Found in the tomb of the wealthy Inkerhau, Thebes, this painting shows a harp player entertaining Inkerhau and his wife.

are shown being entertained not only by musicians, but by dancers and acrobats. In one such scene, a woman instructs a servant to 'Give me eighteen cups of wine, because I want to really get drunk. I'm as dry as a bale of straw!' In others, men and women are shown vomiting into bowls held by servants while their friends comfort them and the party goes on around them.

Holy days (holidays) and festivals were also marked by music. While the Greeks only had one annual festival per god, the Egyptians held many, and as the number of deities increased, so did the holidays; in the case of one village in the Faiyum it has been calculated that 150 days a year were

dedicated to gods' feasts. However, a large number of such festivals were observed only by the priests within the temples; otherwise no work would have been done. But there were still plenty of festivals, some lasting several days, in which everyone took part. There were also celebrations in which images of a god were paraded through a town or even launched on to the river in a ceremonial boat and taken for a tour.

Many festivals were associated with the idea of renewal and rebirth. Flowers, a potent symbol of rebirth and regeneration for the Ancient Egyptians, were presented in vast numbers as offerings to the gods: over three years at Karnak it

has been calculated that just over 4,750,000 bouquets were presented to the Great Temple of Amun.

One important festival, having much to do with regeneration, was the *Sed*-festival, or royal jubilee, celebrated by a pharaoh after completing thirty years of rule, and thereafter celebrated at three-year intervals, during which the king demonstrated his physical well-being in ceremonies which had their origins in pre-dynastic times. Other festivals and celebrations which occurred irregularly were centred on the death and funeral rites of kings, and of cult animals such as the Apis Bull at Memphis.

father had defeated, and her valuable dowry was the revenues of several of his territories. Epiphanes died young in 180 BC, leaving his widow with two sons, Ptolemy Philometor and Ptolemy Euergetes II, and a daughter, also called Kleopatra. Kleopatra I now became regent and ruled wisely and well, encouraging provincial Greeks to intermarry with Egyptians and so foster a greater cohesion and understanding. She also maintained peace for as long as her father was alive, but when he died in 176 BC and her brother, Antiochus IV, seized the throne in Syria, the Alexandrians called for war, arguing that the succession should go to Kleopatra's sons. In failing health herself, to protect her older son, she had Philometor crowned according to Macedonian and Egyptian tradition, and had him marry his sister. Kleopatra I died in the same year as her father.

The new young king followed foolish advice and made preparations for war with Antiochus IV. Both sides had appealed to Rome, now a major power, to arbitrate, each accusing the other of duplicity, but battle was joined before Rome could react and Antiochus was victorious, capturing Philometor and marching on Memphis. Meanwhile, the Alexandrians promptly proclaimed Euergetes II king. Antiochus at first moved against Alexandria, but then, cautious of Rome, withdrew to Syria, leaving Philometor behind in Memphis and Egypt in stalemate. Euergetes ruled Lower Egypt from Alexandria, and Philometor ruled Upper Egypt from Memphis. Trade between the two halves of the country ceased, and the economy, which had been reviving, slumped again.

The problem was solved, at least temporarily, by Kleopatra II, an ambitious woman, who proposed that all three of them rule the country together. Her brothers adopted her suggestion, and the triumvirate reigned from 170 to 164 BC, held together as much as anything by outside threats, not least from Antiochus IV, their uncle, who occupied Cyprus. Rome approved the arrangement, but it was never a happy one, and much political jostling and perfidy ensued. In 164 BC, Philometor went to Rome for help in resolving the problem, and Rome responded by awarding Cyrenaica

to Euergetes II and Egypt to Philometor. Meanwhile, the Alexandrians had turned against Euergetes II, who was much given to executing anyone who opposed him and whom they blamed for the country's economic slump. They called him 'Kakergetes' (the Evil-Doer) rather than Euergetes (the 'Doer of Good'). It was at this difficult time that the tragic events of 'The Twins', described in Chapter Nine, took place.

Hardly had Euergetes II taken over Cyrenaica than the country rebelled, which at least kept him busy for a few years, leaving Philometor and Kleopatra II in peace to run Egypt, which they did well. Philometor died in 145 BC after a troubled thirty-five years in power, and his son, Ptolemy VII Neos Philopator, succeeded him.

Unfortunately Euergetes II still had his eye on Egypt and returned to claim the throne for himself. Alexandria, switching allegiance once more, now welcomed him with open arms, but too late to prevent his sister from fleeing to Memphis with her son and most of the contents of the treasury. Kleopatra II's aim was to maintain control of the country, leaving her brother isolated in Alexandria. However, having failed to do a deal with Rome, Euergetes II countered by proposing marriage and Kleopatra accepted. Perhaps she thought

The image of Ptolemy Euergetes II from a coin dating around 116 BC.

it would give greater security to her hold on power; perhaps she thought it was better to share power than have to fight for it and risk losing all. Either way, she made a mistake. No sooner was he sure that he had made her pregnant with his own child than Euergetes II had Neos Philopator murdered. How Kleopatra II reacted to this is not known. For his part, Euergetes soon lost interest in Kleopatra II, if indeed he had ever had much. He sought neither her advice nor her company, and it is difficult to assess how much power she actually enjoyed. He began to take an interest in his niece, Kleopatra III, the daughter of Philometor and Kleopatra II. Despite the age difference and their complicated family relationship, in 140 BC, he married Kleopatra III. She was as ambitious and power-hungry as her mother, and the two women became furious rivals; but this was no marriage of convenience: she bore her uncle-husband five children in the course of time. Kleopatra II was still married to Euergetes as well, and for the next few years the mother-and-daughter-wives and the uncle-brother-husband ruled together.

This was not an arrangement destined to last, though Euergetes II hung on to power until his death in 116 BC. Thirty years earlier, Scipio Africanus the Younger, on an embassy from Rome, paid Euergetes an official visit and was repelled by the obese, debauched pharaoh. Scipio found the libraries and other cultural centres for which Alexandria had been famous, neglected – the scholars having fled in the face of the king's intolerance. The Alexandrians themselves had turned against Euergetes again: they were sickened at his marriage to his niece and appalled at the murder of his nephew. As long as the mainly mercenary army remained loyal, however, the unhappy population could do nothing. Nevertheless, by 132 BC a number of cities rose up in revolt. Euergetes reacted with violence, suppressing Thebes and massacring the inhabitants of Hermonthis and many other towns. He then rounded up a large number of students and young men in Alexandria and had them taken to the gymnasium, where he locked them in before setting fire to it. This action created so much rage against him that he was forced to flee to

Cyprus with Kleopatra III and their five children, as well as Ptolemy Memphites, his son by Kleopatra II, now a youth of about fourteen.

Kleopatra II was thus left in control of Egypt, but the Greek section of the population, far from accepting her as a welcome relief, were reluctant to accept a woman as sole ruler. She took the throne anyway, in 130 BC, at which Euergetes had their son Memphites killed and dismembered, sending the mutilated corpse to Kleopatra II in a box on the eve of her birthday. Despite this further act of savagery, Euergetes returned to Egypt in 129, capturing Alexandria. Kleopatra II withdrew to Syria for a few years, but by 124 she was back in Egypt, and for the next decade, hard as it is to contemplate, the incestuous triumvirate was reinstated. On his death in 116, Euergetes left the throne to Kleopatra III to pass on to her sons.

The successor, the army's choice, was the older son, Ptolemy IX Soter II. Soter II was already married to his sister, Kleopatra IV, another ambitious woman, and Kleopatra III, aware of this, persuaded her son to exile her to Cyprus.

By 107 BC, Soter II had remarried – another sister called Kleopatra V. Kleopatra II was still alive and clearly still active in the political life of the country, since she now managed to force the pharaoh to share power with his younger brother Ptolemy X Alexander, whom she had always favoured. Alexander's joining the ruling clique was facilitated by the death of Kleopatra III and his own marriage to Kleopatra Berenike, one of his brother's daughters. The two brothers maintained an uneasy power-sharing relationship until 88 BC, when Alexander died at sea, leaving Soter II to reign for the last eight years of his life with his daughter Kleopatra-Berenike.

On Soter II's death, a Roman protégé, Ptolemy XI Alexander II, was briefly king, but he was killed by an Alexandrian mob as the army stood by. His will bequeathed Egypt to Rome, but the actual inheritor was an illegitimate son of Soter II, who at least had the advantage of bringing some outside blood back into the line. He reigned from 80 to 51 BC, earning first the nickname 'Bastard', and later, Auletes ('Piper'), since he was a devotee of the flute. He married a half-sister, Kleopatra VI Tryphaena. His reign was undistinguished, and indeed he made Egypt a virtual vassal of Rome, cravenly bribing the greater power out of the public exchequer and allowing Rome to annex Cyprus. He ruled shakily in his last years, retreating to Rome between 58 and 55 BC, and leaving his wife in charge. Kleopatra VI was soon sidelined by her daughter Berenike and her husband, Archelaus, who started a programme of social and military reform; but when Rome restored Auletes in 55, he had them both murdered.

Auletes himself died in 51 BC, and the throne was taken by his eighteen-year-old daughter, Kleopatra VII Arsinoe. She was a woman of great character and charm, as well as considerable political and diplomatic ability, but she arrived too late to save Egypt from its inevitable fate. She made a dynastic marriage with the older of her two younger brothers, both called Ptolemy, but his faction immediately forced her from power and installed him as Ptolemy XIII, with the support of the people, whose favourite he was. Kleopatra withdrew to Syria. Meanwhile, Gnaeus Pompey, having lost his war for control of Rome to Julius Caesar, had fled to Egypt, where the new pharaoh had him killed. Far from being gratified, Caesar, in Egypt later himself, was appalled and obliged Ptolemy XIII to take back his unpopular sister and share power with her. Not long afterwards Ptolemy XIII was involved in a revolt with another of his sisters against Caesar, and drowned in the Nile during a mêlée with Roman troops. In 47 BC Kleopatra married the surviving younger brother, who ruled with her as Ptolemy XIV from 47 to 44.

Kleopatra was by now Caesar's mistress. The story goes that she seduced him in one night. At the time she was in her early twenties; he was thirty years older. She had a son by him, so when he returned to Rome she went too, and remained there, leaving Ptolemy XIV to rule alone. After Caesar's death in 44 BC she went back to Egypt and soon afterwards Ptolemy XIV died; some sources believe that he was poisoned by his sister, and he may have been disinclined to relinquish half his power to her. Kleopatra installed her son by Caesar,

Ptolemy XV Caesarion, to rule with her in his stead. She was not popular, but Caesar had left a Roman garrison in Alexandria to protect her.

After the break-up of the triumvirate of Octavian (Caesar's great-nephew and appointed heir), Mark

OPPOSITE: Kleopatra VII, whose fame has outlived Ancient Egyptian civilization itself. This enormous image is on the south wall of the Temple of Hathor at Dendera.

Antony and Lepidus, which had shared power in Rome following Caesar's assassination, Octavian controlled the western empire and Antony the east. The eastern empire included Egypt, and Antony wanted Kleopatra on his side, seeing Egypt as a means of outflanking Octavian. Kleopatra, fourteen years his junior, out-manoeuvred Antony diplomatically and also seduced him. They seem genuinely to have loved each other. In about 40 BC she bore him twins, Antony Helios and Kleopatra Selene, and five years later a son, Ptolemy Philadelphus. Antony and Kleopatra married in 40 BC and, nurturing their territorial ambitions, plotted to take over the whole empire. Octavian had been keeping a close eye on developments in Egypt ever since the alliance between Antony and Kleopatra became close, and tensions built until war broke out and battle was joined at sea off the Greek coast near Actium. Antony was a great land soldier, but not a naval strategist, and his forces and those of Egypt were defeated conclusively. Antony and Kleopatra fled back to Alexandria, where Antony committed suicide. Caesarion was sent out of the city loaded with treasure, hoping his escorts would manage to get him to India.

Octavian entered Alexandria on 1 August 30 BC. He allowed Kleopatra to bury Antony with full honours, and permitted her to continue to live unmolested in the palace; but she knew he intended to take her to Rome to take part, as a captive, in his triumph there, and vowed to starve herself to death. Octavian warned her that if she did, he would take reprisals on her children, but she outwitted him and committed suicide by means of a bite from a venomous snake on 12 August 30 BC. She was thirty-eight years old. Octavian had Caesarion pursued and killed in case he became the focus for a revolt, but he spared the other children, bringing them up with his own.

Octavian, who would become the Roman emperor Augustus, took on the titles and appurtenances of King of Egypt in 30 BC, and thenceforward rule of the Black Land for more than three centuries was through Rome. Native Egyptians would not enjoy power in their own country for more than 2000 years; their great civilization, and their great religion, were over forever.

LEFT: Julius Caesar, Roman statesman, general and lover of Kleopatra VII. He established his own ruling dynasty through his great-nephew Octavian, who eventually became the Emperor Augustus.

RIGHT: Mark Antony, Caesar's rival and successor as lover of Kleopatra. Antony and Kleopatra's forces were defeated at the sea battle of Actium in 30 BC, resulting in the triumph of Octavian and Rome over Egypt.

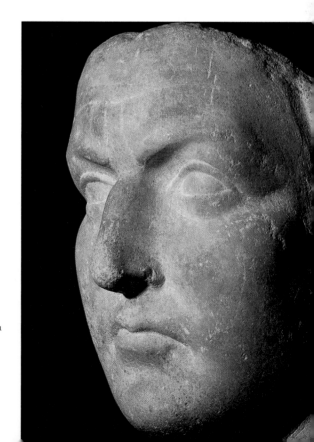

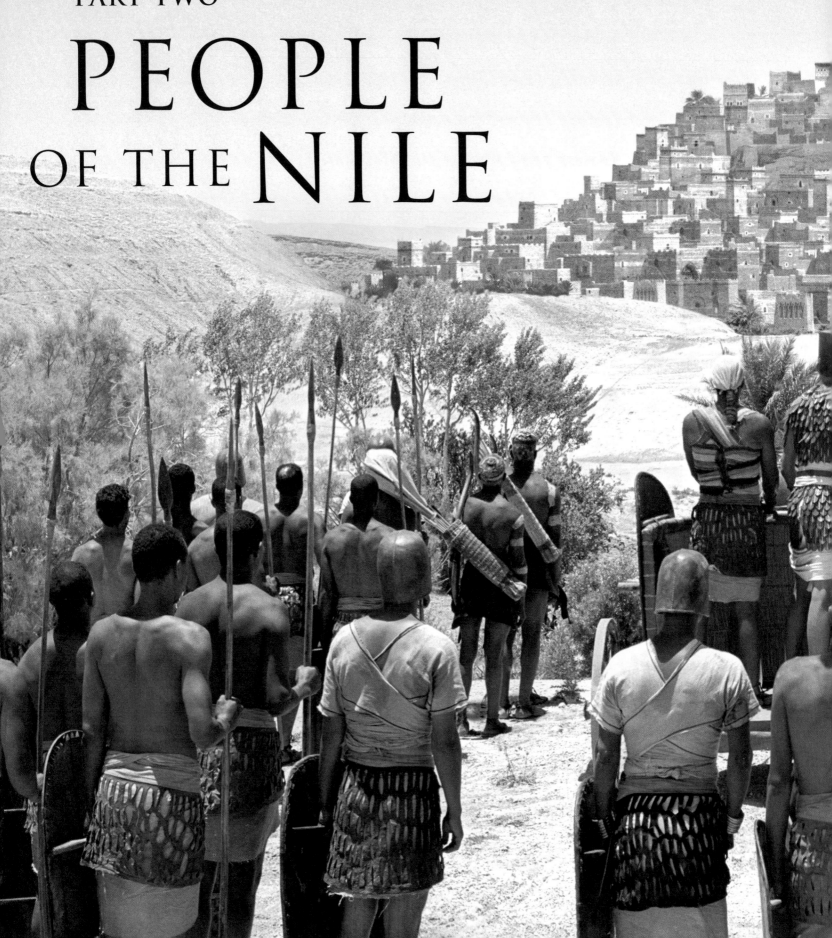

PART TWO

PEOPLE
OF THE NILE

THE
BATTLE OF
MEGIDDO

When the pharaoh Tuthmosis III came to power in 1458 BC, he had already been king for two decades. The problem was that he had inherited the throne from his father, Tuthmosis II, but his mother was not that king's Chief Wife and half-sister, Hatshepsut, but a minor concubine called Isis. Tuthmosis II had always been in poor health, and had taken steps to ensure that his only son would succeed him, but Hatshepsut was an ambitious woman who enjoyed considerable power and support in her own right

at the time of her husband's death. When he died, Tuthmosis III was still a child, and for a few years Hatshepsut ruled as the new king's regent, but then, having built up her own power base and appointed ministers sympathetic to her, she took the throne for herself, proclaiming herself the 'Female Horus' – the only time a woman ever claimed the exclusively male title of 'Horus' – and taking over rule of the country in her own right. For good measure, she concocted a story that Amun had impregnated her mother Ahmose, disguised as her father, Tuthmosis I, which gave her claim credence. In addition, she married her daughter by Tuthmosis II, Neferure, to Tuthmosis III, and endowed her with the title God's Wife of Amun. Neferure appears to have died young; the last mention of her is in the eleventh year of her mother's reign.

Having appropriated power, Hatshepsut was represented officially as a man (there was no word in Ancient Egyptian for 'female pharaoh'), with the regalia and even the false plaited goatee 'beard' which was one of the appurtenances of the king. She ruled firmly but well, and the twenty years of her reign were ones of prosperity for the Black Land. She was assisted by a competent administration at the head of which was Senenmut, tutor to her daughter; though of comparatively humble origins, he rose to be Chief Steward of the royal household and the queen's spokesman. Senenmut was also a gifted architect, supervising the construction and placing of the queen's two obelisks at the temple of Amun-Ra at Karnak, the erection of obelisks having hitherto been exclusively a male ruler's prerogative; but then, Hatshepsut was only the fourth queen in the history of the empire, the first having been the shadowy Queen Merneith in the First Dynasty, the second, Queen Nitiqret at the end of the Sixth, and the third, Queen Sobekneferu, who reigned for four years at the end of the Twelfth. Senenmut also, and most famously, designed the magnificent mortuary temple of Hatshepsut at Deir el-Bahri in the Valley of the Kings.

The position of tutor to royal children was always a powerful one politically, and as it may have been a key rung on the ladder to power for Senenmut, he was proud

Tuthmosis III wears the royal *uraeus* and *nemes* (headcloth) in this statue from the time of his reign.

The funerary complex of Queen Hatshepsut at Deir el-Bahri is directly aligned with the Temple of Karnak on the East Bank.

of it, and images of him frequently show him with the infant Neferure in his care. Senenmut's relationship with the queen was one of great intimacy, which they made no secret of, leading some scholars to have speculated that he was in fact the girl's father. His own tomb is also at Deir el-Bahri, where he lies with several companions, and the carefully mummified carcasses of a little mare and a dog-headed baboon, probably pets. The ceiling is an elaborate map of the heavens, which suggests that Senenmut, who probably died in the same year as the queen, 1458 BC, counted astronomy among his other interests. There is no doubt that he was a capable and intellectual man, and that the reign of Hatshepsut owed much to his efforts. The monuments of the period are light and elegant, in the same style as her mortuary temple.

Among the events of the reign commemorated in the temple is an expedition to Punt, in which the king and queen of that country are depicted, the latter extremely obese, perhaps as a result of illness, perhaps because of a tradition, still current in some African cultures, that obesity was a symbol of wealth. The expedition to Punt for

trade was a highlight of the reign, which was a peaceful one, though during it Egyptian hold on provinces in Syria-Palestine weakened.

Tuthmosis III, who spent his time out of power engaged in military training and pursuits, conducted campaigns on behalf of the throne, despite his aversion to Hatshepsut. It's fair to surmise that he was biding his time, and also protecting, as far as he could, his future interests. He was a soldier first and foremost, and his rule of thirty-three years would see him emulate and surpass the exploits of his grandfather, Tuthmosis I. Egypt would experience dramatic territorial expansion and at the end of the reign would enjoy unquestioned and unchallenged lordship over its neighbours.

When Hatshepsut died she was probably in her early fifties, and although there is no evidence to suggest that her end was hastened by Tuthmosis, the fact that her principal adviser, Senenmut, died at the same time indicates that Tuthmosis was by then powerful enough to take what was rightfully his and rid himself of the clique which had protected the interests of his usurper. Later in the reign, he caused her royal cartouches to be erased from monuments, but the blotting out of her name was by no means thorough, which has been of great cultural and historical benefit to us.

Hatshepsut did not leave a particularly healthy country behind her. As he took the throne in the one-thousand-year-old city of Thebes, Tuthmosis also took stock of the Black Land. Internally, all was well, but there was trouble in the territories annexed to the north, in Syria-Palestine. Taking advantage of Hatshepsut's lack of interest in affirming her military might there, local princes had formed a loose coalition under the Prince of Qadesh, a descendant of the Hyksos and based in Qadesh, a powerful city far to the north, in modern Syria, to free themselves of their Egyptian overlords. Putting their rebellion down seemed to the young king to serve two purposes: the first was the obvious one of reasserting Egyptian interest in the area, with its important trade routes; the second was to use war as a means of asserting himself as king: Hatshepsut had not been unpopular, and although he was the undisputed heir, he knew that he had to put his stamp on the monarchy.

As pharaoh, the young man (he was in his mid- to late twenties when he ascended the Golden Throne) was subject to a series of daily rituals which were designed to set him apart from and above all others. His morning toilet would probably have begun with a bath, after which he was dried with towels embroidered with his cartouche. Then almond and lotus oil were rubbed into his back and limbs to protect him, and through him, his people, from the powers of darkness. He would then have been robed, first with a crisp white linen kilt and then a linen tunic, while gold armlets were fixed on to his wrists, kohl applied as eyeliner, a black wig placed on his head, and on it, a golden circlet or coronet, the process transforming him into a god-king.

Now, at the outset, he had to face the threat posed by the Prince of Qadesh and his Mitannian and Canaanite allies – an alliance, according to the Egyptians, of no fewer than 330 princes. That number is probably an exaggeration but we do know that the Prince of Qadesh controlled an area around Qatna, and that he shared a border with the Kingdom of Tunip, with which he was in alliance. It is possible that Qadesh and Tunip were acting as loyal vassals of Mitanni, a great rival power to Egypt. (The two powers would confront one another eleven years later and Mitanni would suffer defeat.)

The Egyptians had not forgotten the invasion of the Delta by the Hyksos kings just over a century before, and the shock it dealt. But they learned greater military sophistication after the Hyksos, and they acquired a determination not to let their land be invaded again. They knew very well how tempting a prize Egypt was to outsiders, with its great mineral and agricultural wealth; but they also had an inborn sense of their own superiority, which had been shaken but not extinguished by the Hyksos. Now it seemed that the 'vile' and 'wretched' Asiatics were on the warpath again, and the Prince of Qadesh was making rapid progress southwards.

Tuthmosis' first task was to swell the ranks of the standing army by a recruitment of the peasantry, free of their commitments to the land because at the time of year in question the harvest was done. He also appointed a young scribe, Tjaneni, to act as historian of the

RIGHT: The wings of the god Horus – wrapped across the pharaoh's chest in this ceremonial costume – were believed to give divine protection.

LEFT: The Prince of Qadesh's coalition of Canaanite and Mitannian forces threatened the fledgling rule of the young pharaoh Tuthmosis III.

RIGHT: Tuthmosis III offers prayers to the god Amun. According to mythology, Amun was father to the pharaohs.

campaign. Every pharaoh understood the power and importance of words, and for the Ancient Egyptian middle and ruling classes, writing was a route to eternity, the literal sense of hieroglyphs being 'the god's words'; and in the words of one instruction book aimed at scribes, 'a man perishes, his body is dust, all his family are laid in the ground. But it is writing that makes him remembered.' Tuthmosis did not waste any time. An inscription informs us that he took power on the tenth day of the second month of winter in the twenty-second [regnal] year. Mobilization began immediately and it took two months to muster an army and, ultimately, station it at Memphis.

ONE MORNING SOON AFTER Tuthmosis had begun his preparations for war, three men were fishing from a reed boat on the Nile not far from Thebes. As they hauled in their nets a good catch of perch spilled out in the bottom of the boat around their feet. Fishermen were not held in high regard in Ancient Egypt, and the upper classes didn't eat fish, but to the poor it was a welcome and plentiful source of protein within easy reach. The fishermen, naked but for simple loincloths, were pleased with their catch, especially the youngest, Ahmose. He scrambled ashore to take the baskets of fish the other two men – his father and uncle – passed to him from the boat.

Nine-tenths of the population of the Black Land lived along the narrow fertile strip where the Nile cuts through the North African desert. Most of the people were peasants tied for life to land that belonged to the king, to major landowners and to the temples. The main concern of their lives was the success of the harvest, and what little food they could grow privately, together with what game and fish they could catch. It hardly ever rains in Middle and Upper Egypt: the only source of water is the Nile, worshipped as Hapy, god of the flood, a bearded, pot-bellied man with pendulous breasts and a headdress of aquatic plants. Cultivated fields and stands of date-palms reach down to the banks of the river, and stretch away from it as far as the irrigation canals dug by the peasants can reach. Water was first hauled into them from the river by simply filling pots, but by the Eighteenth Dynasty the *shaduf* had been introduced,

Peasants like Ahmose provided the army with a reserve force of potential conscripts.

with its long wooden pole attached to upright supports. One end of the pole had a counterweight, the other a bucket: by this means water could easily be lifted from a lower to an upper level. The *shaduf* was widely used until modern times, when it began to be replaced by engine-

to the sand. She rescued it and flung it back, catching him on the chest. In mock anger he set off after her as she ran away behind the little mud-brick houses, catching her there and rubbing noses with her.

Their days of courting, however, would soon be over.

Officials kept records of the population, which were used to conscript young men and replenish the army with able-bodied fighters.

driven pumps. Another water-raising device, the Archimedean Screw, attributed to the great scientist and thinker Archimedes (287–212 BC) was later adopted in some places.

Ahmose the fisherman was still unmarried, though he had a betrothed, Nefer, a girl from his village one year his junior, and also relatively old still to be unmarried. Now, settling by the riverside to gut the fish with a flint knife – flint was sharper and cheaper than copper or bronze – he caught sight of her as she sat with two older women stripping the leaves from palm fronds and gathering the tall spines into bundles. He stood up and waved, picking up the largest fish to show it off. Playfully, he threw it up the bank to her, while the others looked on, laughing. Nefer failed to catch the fish at first, and it fell, still flapping, on

This was the time of year when the harvest was at an end. Peasants might expect to be called up for work on any one of a number of building, quarrying or irrigation projects during the following season of drought, but this year the arrival at the village jetty of a small falcon-ship, or naval boat, containing four soldiers and a scribe, indicated a different sort of pressgang. It is impossible to say whether or not rumours of the impending war would have reached the Nile villages, but the river was the main artery of the country and vessels sailed up and down it all the time, so that it is not inconceivable that Ahmose might have had some idea of what the soldiers' arrival portended.

The scribe and his detachment arrived at the door of Ahmose's house and, producing a list, began to talk with the older men. The scribe was a local official, one of

SCRIBES

Scribes were the bureaucrats, the civil servants of Ancient Egypt. The profession was a coveted one and required special training in scribal schools, often attached to temples or to the palace itself. The profession of scribe was well paid and often passed from father to son, as was the case with most professions in Ancient Egypt. The availability of papyrus, a plentiful and cheap source of writing material, and the skill of literacy, did much to make Egypt the highly ordered and organized society that it was. Scribes, who worked as taxmen, accountants, historians, social-workers, administrators, personnel officers, and so forth, took pride in their inky fingers. They are often depicted with pens tucked behind their ears, and in so-called 'block' statues, their knees drawn up to their chins, or sitting crosslegged with a roll of papyrus spread open before them.

In the army of Tuthmosis III, scribes served two functions. There were those like Tjaneni who performed the functions of war-reporter and propagandist, and there were those who were in charge of the logistics of the army – supervising everything from food to arms distribution, and helping the officers in communicating strategy to the various units. Scribes would have fulfilled the roles of quartermasters and recruiters, and may have been involved in mapping and intelligence-gathering, though there is as yet no concrete evidence for these functions.

Above all scribes were used in the administration of the tax system and the allocation of 'wages'. To this end much of their work at scribal school involved applied mathematics.

Training was arduous. In addition to having to master mathematics, scribes had to be conversant with over 700 hieroglyphs. Much of the learning process was by copying texts and acquiring knowledge parrot-fashion. Many a young mind must have wandered, and evidence has survived of doodling on ostraca. But inattention was severely punished by beatings: one schoolteacher describes punishing a child for laziness with a hundred lashes, and a well-known text advises that 'a boy's ears are on his back: he only listens to the man who beats him'.

Boys would enter school at about five years old, and stay until they were fifteen or sixteen. Classes would have taken place in the open air and the students had 'slates' to write on – a wooden board covered with a thin layer of plaster which could be wiped clean and renewed as necessary. As they progressed, they would move on to papyrus. Pens were made from another reed – *juncus maritimus* – and scribes chewed one end to form a fine brush. Red and black inks were the colours chiefly used, deriving from ochre and soot or carbon. The cakes of ink were bound with gum and moistened with water for use. They carried their materials in a palette that also contained a water-cup.

Religious texts had to be learned by heart, as well as civil service lists of common tasks and duties. Included in the curriculum would be geometry, grammar, good behaviour and ethics, as well as, for some scribes at least, foreign languages, the most commonly taught being Akkadian, the lingua franca of the time. A basic primer, Kemyt, was in use for over one thousand years, a testimony in itself to Ancient Egyptian conservatism. It is the world's oldest text-book.

Scribes were required to know over 700 hieroglyphs, which they began to learn from the age of five.

whose duties was to keep a note of all able-bodied men in his district who were eligible to be drafted for any state duty. Ahmose and his younger brother stood a short way off, fearful of what this might mean, but already knowing that one or both of them might now expect to be forced to leave their home for many months.

Nefer was also nearby, and as soon as she realized what was going on, she pleaded first with her prospective father-in-law to intercede, and then with the scribe to show mercy to this particular man, her future husband.

Men conscripted into the army could expect to be taken from home for months, if not years at a time.

But the scribe merely smiled and the soldiers laughed as they held her back from him.

The scribe approached Ahmose with his list and looked the young man and his brother up and down. The brother was dismissed. The scribe crooked his finger at Ahmose.

There was nothing to be done but obey. Sadly, Ahmose gathered up his few possessions – a goat-hide to carry water, his shaving kit, a spare loincloth and some bread and dried fish – and packed them in a coarse linen bag. With a soldier standing close by to make sure he

didn't run for it, he said goodbye to his family and to Nefer, who pressed an amulet into his hand – a blue *wadjet*, 'Eye of Horus', pendant to protect him. The young couple clung to each other for a moment, hoping that this would not be for the last time or even for long, and then one of the soldiers tugged at Ahmose's arm. The scribe and his party had selected four other young men for service from this village, and Ahmose now joined them as they all made their way with hanging heads to the moored falcon-ship.

By 1458 BC, the rebels had reached the fortress-city of Megiddo, about seventy kilometres south-west of the Sea of Galilee, commanding the key trade routes of northern Palestine. The aim of the rebels was to create a united front to end Egyptian dominion over their princedoms. Here they planned to rally their forces before moving on towards Egypt itself, but they were nervous of how much information Tuthmosis, an untried enemy, had already gleaned about them through his spies. Through their own, they knew him to be a much more militaristic pharaoh than his predecessor, and that he was gathering an army with the intention of confronting them. They were confident of their own might, however, and may have decided to let the Egyptians march up to meet them. They calculated that the Egyptians would be tired after the long desert trek, and that they could more easily be crushed away from home, with only long lines of communication to connect them to the Black Land.

Meanwhile, in September of that year, Tuthmosis moved his army up through the country to the north-eastern frontier fortress of Tharu. Here he received the most recent intelligence from his spies; and it was here that his scribe and chronicler, the young Tjaneni, began his war diary: 'Now, at that time, it happened that the Asiatic tribes, the people who were in Sharuhen, and from Yeraza to the Marshes of the Earth, had begun to revolt against His Majesty ... '

Among the conscripts recuperating after their march up to Tharu was Ahmose. Ahmose had been allowed to keep his amulet, and he clutched it as he looked around

fearfully. He had received only the most basic training, and now found himself further than he could imagine from his village, which he had never left before, all but alone, save for a few fellow-villagers, and not having the least idea where he was.

Ahmose and his fellows received their first real rations at Tharu: porridge, bread and beer. But there was a lot of jostling in the queue for everyone was dusty, dirty, impatient and tired. Ahmose stepped back into the man behind him, a tough-looking Nubian trooper who immediately and angrily shoved him forwards, causing him to spill his beer and drop his bread. Ahmose stooped to retrieve the loaf as a regular soldier who held a rank roughly equivalent to our non-commissioned officers

yelled at him. Ahmose knew he was expected to be a man, but he felt close to tears.

As Ahmose found a space to hunker down and eat his dinner, as far as possible from the burly Nubian who was still glaring at him, two of Tuthmosis' young generals – for he had replaced all those in power under Hatshepsut with his own people – Yamunedj and Djehuty, were in the armoury, inspecting the bows and arrows they had ordered for themselves, their bowstring-drawing hands already sheathed in special soft leather gloves. Satisfied, they went to join Tuthmosis. The king was already surrounded by his senior officers. Although Hatshepsut's reign had been relatively peaceful, it was an exception. The Eighteenth Dynasty had been dominated by warrior-

Ahmose arrives with the other conscripts at the fortress of Tharu in northern Egypt.

pharaohs, and as a consequence had seen the development of a military elite, a new professional class in
Egyptian society. Indeed, under Tuthmosis III, whose
reign was a series of campaigns, the officer class, enriched
by the spoils of war, would dominate for a time the upper
reaches of Egyptian society.

Now, sure that every eye was on him, the king drew his
own bow. It was said that no-one else had the strength to
draw it (and perhaps this is the father of the story of
Odysseus' bow in Homer's *Odyssey*). He aimed at a copper
target, specially made for him because the power of his
shot was too much for an ordinary straw one. Then he
loosed the arrow. It went straight through the target, which
sang in the wind. His officers roared their approval. Unlike

Napoleon, Tuthmosis could – and needed to – demonstrate his personal prowess, as well as his skill at strategy.

Ahmose, meanwhile, had finished his meal and, along
with the other conscripts, was sitting crosslegged on the
sandy ground listening to the admonitions of an officer
who was addressing them. He couldn't take in what was
being said. He looked around, at the high red walls of the
fortress, at his fellow-soldiers, at the Nubian who seemed
to have taken against him, and clutched his talisman,
thinking of Nefer. He felt very homesick.

This army had taken months to recruit, and every man
counted. The equivalent of a modern NCO spotted
Ahmose's wandering gaze and hit him with a baton.
Ahmose turned to catch the NCO's eye.

ARMY LIFE

There was no formal uniform in the army during the time of Tuthmosis, but a standard issue loincloth and tunic, with a hide shield and a spear or short stabbing sword. Regular soldiers had armour made of lozenges of leather sewn together, and the elite charioteers, the crack cavalry of the day, armed with powerful bows, were the envy and admiration of all the troops.

A large compound was laid out beside the fort to accommodate the army, and thousands of men would have been milling around in it, rubbing shoulders with donkeys, the army's pack-animals. The donkeys were absolutely crucial to the success of Tuthmosis' campaign, and supplies were worked out with minute precision, since Tuthmosis had a desert to cross to the north. The donkeys would carry wheat and barley and fresh water.

Even a small army of 10,000 men would require 20 tonnes of grain and 95,000 litres of water a day. The logistics of organizing such supplies were daunting, but the scribes were equal to the task, having highly developed mathematical formulae for just such an eventuality.

Officers required a more sophisticated diet, and a limited number of goats and cattle were also among the livestock in the baggage trains.

A standard Egyptian military camp was a large rectangle, protected by a fence of round-topped, leather-covered, metal-studded shields. The king's own tent would be in a smaller compound of its own at the centre of the larger one, and senior officers had their own tents; but for the ordinary troops there was no protection beyond a coverlet made of reed matting.

Once they were registered, conscripts would be allocated their rations. As Ancient Egypt was a society without money, economics followed the principles of a sophisticated barter-system. Soldiers were paid, according to their rank and experience, in food; but the food was often represented by a wooden ration token in the shape of the loaf for which it could be exchanged as needed. These tokens to all intents and purposes

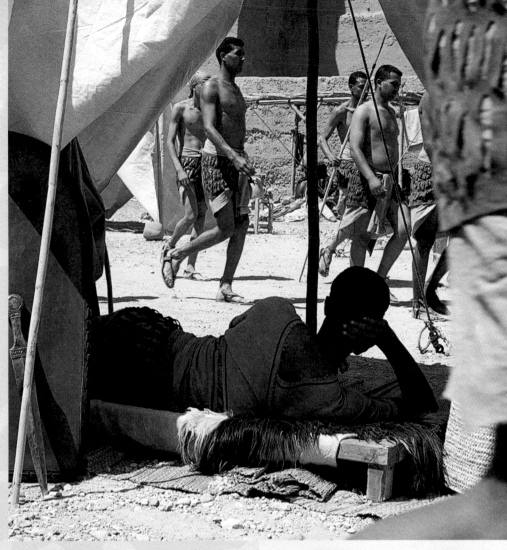

served as money or, more accurately, vouchers. By their means the administrator-scribes could keep track of supplies and regulate them accordingly. Soldiers could probably expect ten loaves a day (they were smaller than modern ones), supplemented by three jars of beer, and, exceptionally, two units of meat and three cakes.

OPPOSITE, TOP RIGHT: Even conscripts like Ahmose were well-trained to fight at garrison army camps. No Egyptian soldier went into battle physically unprepared.

OPPOSITE, BOTTOM RIGHT: Horses were valued as noble animals used for charioteering. They were far too valuable to be used as beasts of burden.

INSET RIGHT: Logistics were the key to any army's success and scribes kept track of everything.

Once the lecture was finished, Ahmose and his companions from the village hoped to have a little time to themselves: it was late afternoon, and the sun hung heavy in the west, bathing the camp in red light. But the NCOs had decided to organize a wrestling match or two, and whistled the men up for them. One of the cornerstones of military training, which would continue here at Tharu, was wrestling, the basis of hand-to-hand combat. All sport and most games ultimately derive from military training, and it seemed that Ahmose was not going to have a moment of relaxation after all. Worse was to come: a circle formed round him and into it was pushed the big Nubian, called Nakht. Nakht was possibly nineteen years old and almost twice Ahmose's size. But Ahmose was wiry, and knew all about quick movements from his skills as a fisherman.

The two men circled each other, looking for a hold. Ahmose's instinct was to avoid the Nubian, hoping to trip him up at least, for he knew that there were no holds barred, and that a contest could end with the knockout or serious disablement of one of the fighters. He also knew that Nubians were considered to be the best wrestlers of all. From the cheers and catcalls it was obvious that Nakht was thought to be one of the real toughs in their squad, and Ahmose was terrified. Nevertheless, he knew he had to see it through.

Nakht had a longer reach, and soon threw Ahmose to the ground. Ahmose knew how to roll out of trouble, however, and sprang back to his feet. He took another fall or two, and then, angry at last, but still in control, dropped to grab his opponent's ankles and threw him heavily, pinning him to the ground before he had a chance to recover – winning the bout. Horrified at his victory, he stood over Nakht, tentatively holding out his hand to pull the bigger boy up. After just a moment of tension, Nakht grinned broadly, reached out his own hand, and let Ahmose help him rise. Once on his feet, he grabbed the younger boy round the waist and heaved him up on to his shoulders, whirling him round as the other soldiers bellowed their approval.

So a friendship was made. But the time for such activities as wrestling for training would very soon be over.

Nakht and Ahmose battle it out. Wrestling was a popular sport and helped create lethal soldiers.

I N THE SEASON OF *Shemu* (Spring) 1548 BC the army left Tharu and marched north into Palestine. This is how the scribe, spin-doctor and war correspondent Tjaneni related it:

> Year twenty-three [of Tuthmosis' reign, counting from when he officially came to the throne as a boy]: first month of the third season. On the fifth day, we left this place in might, in power and in triumph to overthrow that wretched foe, to extend the boundaries of Egypt, just as his [the king's] father Amun-Ra had commanded.

There were no maps, as far as we know, for the area into which the army was advancing, though they must have known where their goal lay through information they had gleaned from their spies. Scouts were also sent ahead to assess the situation. These scouts were among the few Ancient Egyptians to ride on horseback: horses were generally reserved to draw chariots in pairs. It should be remembered that horses, even now, so long after their introduction at the end of the Hyksos period, were still a precious resource.

Tuthmosis would have been carried ahead of his army in a litter, protected from the sun. His scouts and spies would have returned to him from their forays into Palestine with messages inscribed on clay tablets carried in leather pouches, concerning not only the disposition of the enemy's troops, but also indicating landmarks by which to guide his army to their goal.

Accompanying the pharaoh would have been his boon-companions, men who, according to tradition, had been brought up and educated with him. They held coveted positions of power, and their closeness to the king meant that they could enjoy rich rewards in the form of land, slaves and gold. For ordinary soldiers there were no such incentives, though looting was tolerated after a victory. The scribe Tjaneni confines himself to describing the exploits of the leaders, and doesn't go into detail about

Tuthmosis III reviews his troops before the decisive battle of Megiddo.

Tuthmosis looked to Amun for protection, and anointed his generals with scented oil to shield them from harm.

homeland. Egyptian armies included large numbers of foreign mercenaries. Conscripted men may have been tempted to desert, but punishments for desertion were harsh and meted out to the deserters' families, who were forced into hard labour for life.

At last the army arrived at Yehem, about twenty kilometres south of Megiddo. It was now, as Tjaneni tells us, 'the sixteenth day of the first month of the third season' in 1457 BC, and two months since they had left Tharu. The army had passed Gaza, where they spent only one night, and Joppa, which resisted the Egyptians and was taken after a brief siege which General Djehuty stayed behind to conduct. (The story goes that Egyptian soldiers were smuggled into the city in baskets – a conflation or possible originator of the stories of the Trojan Horse and Ali Baba.)

The army's daily rate of march latterly had dropped to eight kilometres a day. At Yehem, about 120 kilometres north of Gaza, they camped after a ten-day march; for the first time in many days they had a chance to fill up their canteens with fresh water and bathe their battered bodies and injured feet. It was here that spies returned to confirm the reports that the enemy had gathered at Megiddo. Yehem was the most northerly point of current Egyptian influence.

In his tent, Tuthmosis gathered his generals round him to discuss the final advance. From Yehem there were three possible local caravan routes. The longest led north to Jokneam, below Mount Carmel, and to the north-west of Megiddo itself. Another route led east to Taanach, eight kilometres to the south-east of Megiddo. These two routes were the safest, but there was a third which led directly to Megiddo. However, this third approach was through the Aruna Pass, so narrow that in places it is barely ten metres wide, and because of rockfalls there would scarcely be room in other places to get the chariots through. The steep sides of the pass also made it particularly vulnerable to ambush. The discussion over what route to take was recorded by Tjaneni. Tuthmosis was determined to take the Aruna route, but his generals demurred, Djehuty pointing out, 'How is it, that we should go upon this narrow road, while they tell us that the enemy is waiting for us there, holding the way. Won't our vanguard be

conditions for the average trooper, but he does mention that the army advanced for the first part of its journey north at an impressive twenty kilometres a day or more. They would have needed to keep this pace up while crossing the waterless Sinai, or 'Ways of Horus' as they called it.

The experience of the ordinary soldier is conveyed in a letter written to his son at home by an anonymous scribe, warning him against a military career:

He is called up for Syria. He may not rest. There are not clothes, not sandals … His march is uphill through mountains … He drinks water every three days; it smells foul and tastes of salt … His body is ravaged by illness … his body is weak, his legs fail him … He is worn out from marching … Be he at large, be he detained, the soldier suffers … He dies on the edge of the desert, and there is none to perpetuate his name … He suffers in death as in life.

The march through Sinai would have taken its toll on the infantry, and illness and disease would have always been a greater cause of death than combat. To die away from home was a terrifying prospect because for an Egyptian to have a chance of reaching paradise he or she would have to be buried within the sacred borders of the

WEAPONRY

Weaponry to begin with was limited to the simple bow and arrow, the spear, the battle-axe and the mace. Arrows and spears would originally have been tipped with flint heads. Maces were heavy stone clubs attached to wooden handles. Another early weapon was the throwstick, looking not unlike a boomerang, though it isn't certain that it performed in the same way. Soldiers had no armour, but wore a belted kilt. By the Middle Kingdom they at least had shields, and axes and spears were developing into more sophisticated weapons: the heads of weapons were now made of copper.

Around 1650 BC Egypt was successfully invaded from the north by a group of Asiatic kings known to us by their Greek name of Hyksos, who established themselves as rulers for about one hundred years. The reason for their success was their vastly superior weaponry, and the military innovations they bequeathed to Egypt were a crucial legacy. The most important was the horse-drawn chariot. Hitherto the Egyptians had used donkeys as agricultural beasts. The horse was unknown, as was the speedy chariot. It consisted of a light wooden or basketwork frame (electrum was used for ceremonial or regal vehicles) and it rested on two wheels of four-to-six spokes, about a metre in diameter. The chariot was drawn by two horses and carried a driver and a warrior, who was armed with a spear, shield and bow. Chariots were highly mobile and versatile, and could easily be manoeuvred to surround or confuse a slower foe,

or be used for darting attacks. Horses were never ridden alone, except perhaps by scouts, but the chariot-cavalry, inherited from the Hyksos, became the elite force of the Egyptian army of the New Kingdom. Not only did it revolutionize war, it gave dashing social status to the young soldiers – the *maryannu*, 'young heroes' – who manned it. The word is Indo-European, and may derive from the chariot-owning nobility who formed the upper class among the Hurrians, who came from near the Tigres river. Horses were only ever used by the rich, and the royal chariot enjoyed such status that gods were allotted to the protection and maintenance of its various components.

Along with the chariot came the much more powerful composite bow, a dagger, and an early form of short sword. Ordinary soldiers began to enjoy the benefit of body-armour consisting of bronze plates attached to leather or heavy linen surcoats, and although helmets were still some way off, the king affected a new blue crown, the *khepresh*, which was occasionally associated with the art of war. At the start of the New Kingdom the standing army consisted of two divisions of 5000 men. A few years later, Rameses II had doubled that number. There were fifty chariots to each division, and the ability to handle horses well was the highest attribute a man could have.

The fortress of Tharu was a place where weapons were manufactured. Smithies turned out bronze battle-axes, swords and spearheads. Bowmakers were less in evidence, for it took a year to make a new composite bow, and they had to be continuously mass-produced by a factory of craftsmen to keep the huge army and, above all, the charioteers, supplied. The best composite bows were made from imported wood and horn, and bound together with fish-bladder glue. Fletchers, however, were busy making arrows, and those used by the charioteers were bronze or ivory-tipped and made-to-measure, as were the bows, in accordance with the user's strength, stature and length of arm. Arrowheads varied in size, weight and material according to the preferences of the bowman and the nature (if hunting) of the prey.

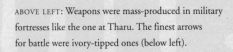

ABOVE LEFT: Weapons were mass-produced in military fortresses like the one at Tharu. The finest arrows for battle were ivory-tipped ones (below left).

INSET: The Egyptians survived without the chariot for one-and-a-half thousand years. It was not until the invasions to the north at the end of the Seventeenth Dynasty that chariot technologies were adopted from the Syrians.

FAR LEFT: Infantrymen were simply equipped with knives, spears and leather shields.

ambushed while our rearguard is still in Aruna?' The argument carried weight, and Tuthmosis hesitated, but didn't waver: 'I swear, as Ra loves me and my father Amun praises me, I will march on the road to Aruna. If any of you want to follow these other roads, then go. But those who wish to can follow me. If I were to do otherwise what would these men of Qadesh think? "His Majesty is afraid of us!" That is what they would think.'

None of the generals abandoned Tuthmosis, and it is clear that he was speaking rhetorically. The whole story may be apocryphal, since similar tales are told of other heroic pharaohs. But Tuthmosis was aware of the gamble

he was taking. The following day at dawn the army mobilized and set off on the twelve-kilometre uphill march to the town of Aruna, on the southern slopes of the Carmel range and at the head of the ravine, which was itself about ten kilometres long. The king himself rode in his chariot at the head of his troops as they entered the valley: 'His Majesty swore, saying: "None shall go forth before me." He went forth at the head of his army himself, showing his way by his own footsteps; horse behind horse, His Majesty at the head of his army.'

The march through the pass took twelve hours, and every step of the way the army was at risk of ambush.

Tuthmosis III led his own troops into battle.

The Prince of Qadesh rides towards Megiddo with two of his allies.

Progress was slow, since the men often had to manhandle the chariots over rocky sections, and the pack-donkeys had to pick their way carefully. Once or twice, stones tumbled down, dislodged from the rocks above, but Tuthmosis' gamble had paid off. He had taken the riskiest route, but it was the one the enemy least expected him to take, and no ambush here had been prepared. The enemy had merely posted scouts as a precaution, and had gathered the main part of their force at Taanach, whence they believed the Egyptians would most likely launch their attack. A northern detachment was positioned at Jokneam. When the Aruna scouts saw the Egyptian army,

they hastened back to the Prince of Qadesh at Taanach to report. But by then it was too late for him to redeploy in time to stop the Egyptians, and Tuthmosis' army emerged from the ravine unhindered and unscathed. As Tjaneni writes, 'By the time the vanguard had reached the end of the pass, the shadow had turned, and when the seventh hour was turning, measured by the sun, His Majesty arrived on the banks of the brook of Qina, to the south of the city of Megiddo.'

By now, the enemy forces had withdrawn into the city. The Egyptians pitched their camp, and the order went out: 'Equip yourselves! Prepare your weapons! For we shall advance to fight the wretched enemy in the morning.'

Megiddo, strategically and commercially important, was not being fought over for the first or the last time. Another battle there, many centuries later, would cause the city to be commemorated in the Bible as Armageddon; and in the First World War, 3500 years later, it was captured by the 1st Viscount Allenby, who took the city's name as his title. He was inspired by Tuthmosis III's strategy when planning his assault. By first light on the day of Tuthmosis' battle, the Asiatic army had drawn up its lines outside the city, facing the Egyptians. Tjaneni describes the scene:

Tuthmosis' troops, including Ahmose, prepare to charge against the enemy. Spears were mostly hurled at close quarters because of the fear of an enemy returning the thrown weapon. ABOVE: Egyptian military standard. The standard bearer held a commanding military position with two hundred men under him.

FORTIFICATION

Year twenty-three, first month of the third season, on the twenty-first day, the day of the feast of the new moon. Early in the morning the command was given to the entire army to move. His Majesty rode out in a chariot of electrum, arrayed in his weapons of war, like Horus, the Smiter, Lord of Power; like Montu of Thebes; while his father, Amun, strengthened his arms.

The feast of the new moon was auspicious for Tuthmosis, who favoured the cult of Khons, the god of the moon. But the war-god Montu would be at his elbow as well, as would Reshef, a Syrian war-and-thunder god whom Tuthmosis had appropriated as his own protector. 'The southern wing of His Majesty's

Fortification was understood and practised from the beginning – the city of Memphis was said originally to have been surrounded by massive white walls, from which it took its original name – by the legendary King Menes. Temples and towns were fortified as a means of protection; only later were fortresses built to defend frontiers. In time the border with Nubia was policed by permanent garrisons housed in a series of fortresses. To the east and west at least, the desert provided a pretty effective deterrent to invaders. But the protection of trade routes and colonial interests led to a complex system of fortification having been developed by the time of the New Kingdom.

Syrian archers take up their positions on the battlements of Megiddo.

army stood on a hill south of the brook of Qina. The northern wing stood to the north-west of Megiddo. His Majesty was in their centre, with Amun as the protection of his limbs.'

Before the battle, Tuthmosis anointed his generals with scented oil to protect them from harm, and even among the ranks, the officers anointed the men. Soldiers beat their shields with their battle-axes, chanting a war-cry as the battle-horns sounded and they started their advance on the enemy. Ahead and to either side, the chariot squadrons fanned out, their bowmen firing into the massed infantry of the Asiatics. Both armies lumbered towards one another, finally meeting and joining in hand-to-hand combat, hacking and slashing with sword

Hand-to-hand combat was where battles were lost or won. This is where a young soldier's training would pay off.

Brute strength was the key to survival in battle at close quarters.

The enemy retreats back into the city
as the Egyptians gain the advantage.
The Prince of Qadesh escapes with his life,
hauled up onto the battlements,
while others are not so fortunate.

OPPOSITE: Looting of the battlefield
held its own rewards.

and axe. 'Then His Majesty prevailed against them at the head of his army … And when they saw His Majesty, they fled headlong to Megiddo in fear, abandoning their horses and their chariots.'

It can't have been as easy as Tjaneni would like to have us believe, but the Asiatic ranks certainly did break in disorder and the men retreated to the city in such disarray that they left many valuable weapons, chariots and horses abandoned on the field of battle. So fast was the retreat that the gates of the city had been closed even before the Prince of Qadesh and a large part of his army had got back in. From the walls, cloth ropes were hastily lowered to them: 'The people hauled them up, pulling them by their clothing, into the city; the inhabitants having closed it against them and lowered clothing to pull them up.'

As the Asiatics clambered up the walls, the Egyptians hurled axes and spears at them, or shot at them with fire-arrows. The Prince of Qadesh got back into the city safely, but the field belonged to Tuthmosis.

Both Nakht and Ahmose had survived the battle, and now they and their comrades-in-arms stood amongst the dead and dying, adrenaline pumping through them and filled with the euphoria that comes with the knowledge of having survived a great danger. Among the dead, they were quick to notice officers and nobles who had fallen wearing the finest armour and jewelled and golden collars, helmets and armlets. Knowing that these spoils would be all they would have to show for their travails, the Egyptian infantrymen soon forgot all discipline and fell to looting and plundering. So distracted were they that the defenders of the city were able to open the gates once more to let some of their remaining stragglers in. Tuthmosis was furious. 'Now, if only the army of His Majesty had not given their heart to plundering the things of the enemy, they would have captured Megiddo at this moment.'

WARFARE

There was no standing army for much of Ancient Egypt's history, though from early on the king was surrounded by a small, elite professional troop of bodyguards. At times of war, armies were levied from the population and young men from the villages were pressganged into service. It is tempting to speculate that, in the early days at least, wars were simply not fought at seed-time or harvest, but military service would have been one of the duties peasants would have been called to by *corvée*, along with building and quarrying duties, for example. Soldiering was certainly not regarded as an attractive profession if the description given in the Satire on Trades is anything to go by.

> Come, let me describe to you the condition of the soldier, that much tormented one. He is taken when yet a child to be imprisoned in a barrack. A searing blow is dealt his body, a rending blow is dealt his eyebrows. His head is split open with a wound. He is laid down and beaten like papyrus and battered with castigation ... His bread and water are upon his shoulder like the load of an ass, his neck having formed a ridge like that of an ass. The vertebrae of his back are broken whilst he drinks of smelly water and halts only to keep watch. He reaches the battle: he is like a plucked bird. He proceeds to return to Egypt: he is like a worm-eaten stick.

Garrison duty was generally dreaded by conscripts since it meant months if not years (a single tour of duty could last up to six years) of boredom and deprivation at outposts fraught with danger and far from home. Surviving fragments attest to this. One soldier is described as being sent to the garrison of Kharu, 'having left his wife and his children, his clothing is skins and his food is grass of the field, like any head of cattle'. Another, an officer, writes home from a coastal garrison where he has been sent to perform construction work:

> I am dwelling in Damnationville with no supplies. There have been no people to knead bricks and no straw in the district. Those supplies I brought are gone, and there are no asses since they have been stolen. I spend the day watching the birds and doing some fishing, all the while eyeing the road which goes up to Djahy with homesick longing. Under trees with no edible foliage do I take my siesta for their fruit has perished. The gnat attacks in the sunlight and the mosquito in the heat of noon, and the sand-fly stings – they suck at every blood-vessel. If ever a jar of Kode wine is opened and people come out to get a cup, there are 200 large dogs and 300 jackals, 500 in all, and they stand waiting constantly at the door of the house whenever I go out, since they smell the liquor when the container is opened. The heat here never lets up.

By about 2000 BC local governors appear to have been in the habit of running their own private brigades, and national campaigns may have made up their armies by combining these into a larger force. By the Twelfth Dynasty there seems to have been a small professional army, or at least a professional officer class capable of training recruits in time of need.

Professional soldiers were very often of foreign origin, either slaves who had been enabled to buy their freedom by enlisting, or mercenaries who, attracted by the high standard of living in Egypt, wished to remain there. In the Late Period, the Egyptian army and navy depended very much on Greek and Phoenician soldiers and sailors.

ABOVE: Nubian soldiers played a crucial role in the Egyptian army for centuries.

ABOVE: The New Kingdom saw the birth of mass warfare.

BELOW: A lightning-quick chariot charge was designed to break the enemy front line and strike a psychological blow.

Tjaneni points out that not all the plundering was random. Valuable assets like horses would be official booty. 'The victorious army of His Majesty went around, counting their spoils. We captured their horses, their chariots of gold and silver. Their champions lay stretched like fishes on the ground.' However, no amount of plunder could compensate for the lost opportunity.

Scribes were detailed to make lists of what had been gained, and soldiers made their way over the battlefield chopping one hand off each of the fallen enemy, despatching the mortally wounded. The hands were gathered in baskets and brought back to a unit of scribes, who were thereby able to make a tally of those killed.

Six stallions, a chariot wrought with gold, its pole of gold, belonging to the enemy; a beautiful chariot, wrought with gold, belonging to the Chief of Megiddo; 892 chariots of his wretched army: total, 924 chariots; a beautiful suit of bronze armour belonging to the foe; a beautiful suit of bronze armour belonging to the Chief of Megiddo. 340 living prisoners. 83 hands.

LEFT: The army of Tuthmosis III could advance at an impressive twenty kilometres a day or more.

ABOVE: The severed hands of slaughtered enemies collected for counting. In this way the Egyptians could record the numbers of enemy killed.

Tuthmosis reproached his generals for not maintaining better discipline: 'Had you captured this city, I would have given the god Ra this day because every chief of every country that has revolted is in there, and because the capture of Megiddo is the capture of one thousand cities!' But it was too late to do anything about it. The army would pay the price for its greed by settling down to a long siege. There would be no early homecoming for them now. A palisade and earthworks were built and, during the siege, part of the Egyptian army ravaged the surrounding countryside, ranging as far north as Galilee, sacking several small towns and enslaving the local population. They captured 38 local chiefs and 87 of their children as well as 2000 slaves and their families. Booty from these mini-campaigns was impressive:

> ... flat dishes of costly stone and gold, a large two-handed vase of Kharu work, miscellaneous dishes and drinking vessels, three large kettles, eighty-seven knives, gold and silver rings, a beaten-silver statue, six ivory, ebony and carob-wood chairs, with six footstools, and six large tables of ivory and carob-wood. A sceptre-shaped staff of carob-wood wrought with gold and costly stones belonging to the enemy; a statue of the enemy (? Prince of Qadesh) wrought with gold, the head of which was inlaid with lapis lazuli. Bronze vessels and large amounts of clothing ...

For many of the Egyptian soldiers there would be no homecoming at all. In the ancient world, more soldiers died of their wounds after a battle than died fighting, succumbing to shock, loss of blood and wound infections leading to tetanus and gangrene. Doctors and surgeons were skilled in setting broken bones, in amputation and in cauterizing wounds, and through the study of animals and the processes of mummification the Ancient Egyptians had a good working knowledge of anatomy; but levels of hygiene were low and risks of infection high. Honey, however, was known to be a natural disinfectant, and it was used to dress wounds. Surgeons knew that their knives had to be red-hot to cauterize wounds, but they did not know that in heating them they were also sterilizing them. Linen bandages were used, held together with resin, and the Egyptians even invented a form of sticking-plaster. Wounds were stitched using thorn or bone needles and string. Burns were treated with a mixture of mother's milk (with its antibiotic properties), gum and ram's hair, and the treatment was reinforced by invocations to the gods.

Among those being treated in the medical tents was Ahmose, who while looting on the battlefield was hit in the head by a stone fired from a slingshot by a Syrian on the ramparts of Megiddo. Head wounds were the most common injuries sustained by Egyptian soldiers, who were not all equipped with helmets at this period. For this a doctor would apply a piece of raw meat to the wound in order for its blood-clotting agents to stanch the bleeding. Ahmose had also been tied across his chest to a post to keep him immobile and from injuring himself. Things were not looking good for Ahmose, and when Nakht caught the doctor's eye he knew that his friend was not expected to live. Reaching out to Nakht, Ahmose pressed his amulet into the Nubian's hand, whispering a few words – a last message for Nefer. Then his head fell forward.

Ancient Egyptians were not especially good at siege warfare, and it took the entire summer – seven months – to force Megiddo into submission. At last one day – in December in our calendar – the gates opened as the women of the city prayed and lamented on the ramparts. The children of the leaders of the rebellion emerged, dirty, scared and hungry, carrying swords, jewels, longbows, necklaces: 'Then the enemy [the Prince of Qadesh] and the chieftains who were with him sent out to My Majesty all their children, bearing many gifts of gold and silver [and] all their armour and weapons of war.'

The surrender of the children was an acknowledged gesture of defeat. These would be taken back to Egypt as hostages and brought up as Egyptians, returning as adults to Palestine to rule dutifully in the pharaoh's name. The rebels themselves would be bound to pay tribute and allowed to return to their cities, though stripped of all their goods and sent home – the ultimate humiliation – on the backs of donkeys. Throughout his reign Tuthmosis would keep them in submission by a series of almost annual campaigns.

The final booty from the battle was enormous. The Prince of Qadesh and his allies surrendered eighty-four of their

The children
of the defeated
enemy chiefs emerge
from the besieged
city as a symbol
of its surrender.

children, who had probably been sent north for safety before the battle. There was a vast number of horses – 2041 mares, as well as 191 foals, the 6 stallions already mentioned by Tjaneni, and an unnamed number of colts. Such a large addition to the home breeding-stock would have been of enormous value. The Egyptians also took 200 suits of armour, 502 bows, 7 wooden tentpoles with silver inlay, 1929 'large cattle', 2000 'small cattle' and 20,500 'white small cattle' (sheep or goats). Among other goods the scribes listed furniture, clothing, vessels of metal and stoneware, and 'walking sticks with human heads', which may have been like the ones found in Tutankhamun's tomb, one of which had a carved, bearded Syrian head as its handle.

At last the king returned to Thebes in triumph, and in due time the defeated princes came to pay homage and their dues.

Tjaneni chooses to give the last words of his account to the defeated Prince of Qadesh: 'Never again will we do evil against Tuthmosis, may he live forever our lord, in our lifetimes, for we have witnessed his power. Let him only give breath to us according to his desire.'

Those members of his army who had survived could return to their own homes and take up the pattern of their lives again. Nakht kept his promise and returned the *wedjat* amulet to Nefer, who dressed in the grey of mourning and cast ashes over her head.

SOURCES
FOR THE
STORY OF
'THE BATTLE
OF
MEGIDDO'

The main source of our knowledge of the battle of Megiddo, one of the earliest and most important campaigns by warrior-pharaoh Tuthmosis III, is an account preserved in the form of a carved inscription on the sixth pylon of the temple of Amun at Karnak. (Another version of the text was placed on a *stele*, which was erected on the southern border of Tuthmosis' territories – as a reminder to possibly restive Nubians of his might – at modern-day Gebel Barkal in the Sudan. It is now in the Museum of Fine Art in Boston, Massachussetts.) The account of Megiddo is of core importance historically as it is the first extant detailed description of a battle we have.

This method of celebrating military victories (in which propaganda demanded that the Egyptians were always shown to be unequivocally triumphant) was common throughout the civilization of Ancient Egypt, though few as complete as this have come down to us. We do not know who actually carved the inscription, since artisans and craftsmen were not regarded as deserving individual recognition (a tradition which continued in the majority of cases down to the Renaissance in Italy). We do, however, know who was responsible for the diary – or official campaign journal – on which the inscription is based. This in itself is rare, for even scribes, though regarded as important officials of the administration, usually remained anonymous. The scribe was viewed in the composition of society as the conduit of absolute, pharaonic truth, which brooked no comment or question.

This particular scribe was a young man when he followed the Megiddo campaign of Tuthmosis III, and went on to enjoy a brilliant career, ending it as a general. We know his name – Tjaneni – from a biographical inscription on his tomb (number TT74 in one of the private cemeteries near the Valley of the Kings) that was discovered in the nineteenth century.

Tjaneni kept his campaign journal whilst actually in the field. His role, though similar to that of a war reporter, had more to do with glorifying the might of the pharaoh and belittling the enemies of Egypt than with strict reporting. In that sense perhaps not much has changed, since war journalism traditionally bears a favourable bias towards the side it is reporting. However, the description does show the young and relatively inexperienced king arguing with his generals over strategy, showing some emotion (rare in Ancient Egyptian annals), and vulnerability, though the king inevitably triumphs over doubts, and his instincts and gambles pay off triumphantly.

The final version, recorded on a leather scroll rather than on papyrus (for extra durability) was placed in the temple of Amun as part of an archive known later as the Annals of Tuthmosis III. Tjaneni's connection with the inscription on the temple pylon mentioned above is put beyond doubt by certain passages from the 'biography' in Tomb 74:

I followed the good god, the ruler of the truth, the king of Upper and Lower Egypt, Tuthmosis III … I saw the

The sixth pylon at the Temple of Amun at Karnak has taught us most of what we know about the Battle of Megiddo.

important to point out that the characters of the common soldiers, including our hero, Ahmose, are not authentic historical entities, though their actions and experiences reflect truthfully the experiences of Egyptian foot soldiers of the time, drawn from other contemporary accounts and fragments. For significant periods during the long history of Ancient Egypt there was a permanent standing army composed of professional soldiers but, at times of war, extra infantrymen would be drafted from the peasantry, as depicted here.

Of the officers and senior figures mentioned in this story, most were real people and participated in the events described. Generals Djehuty and Yamunedjeh, according to inscriptions on their tombs, accompanied Tuthmosis on the campaign. Though they are not mentioned by name in the Megiddo text, it is reasonable to assume that, following their own funerary 'biographies', they were indeed present.

All other details, from clothing to architecture, from ceremony to romance, are drawn from authentic contemporary sources.

victories of the king, which he made in all foreign countries … no foreign country existed, which could survive it. I was there [and] recorded these victories, which he had made over all foreign countries, [and] put [it] in writing, as they occurred.

The story of the battle of Megiddo within this chapter is closely based on authentic historical material, and any additional input is based on sound academic guesswork or the synthesis of what we know to have been general custom in Ancient Egypt. For clarity, however, it is

TOMB ROBBERS

The Twentieth Dynasty (1186–1069 BC) was not a distinguished one. Rameses III has been considered the last truly great pharaoh, and his eight successors, all called Rameses, paled by comparison.

Thebes, in 1116 BC, was still a powerful religious centre. Across the river from the city, on the West Bank, were the royal necropolises, The Great Place and The Place of Beauty: the Valley of the Kings and the Valley of the Queens. The pharaohs no longer lived at Thebes, but they were still buried here, and work on a pharaoh's tomb began as soon as he ascended the throne. The Theban necropolis-complex had its own workforce and ancillary workers, and was governed by its own mayor. In 1116, the mayor was an official called Pawero. His principal responsibility was the security of the royal tombs, and he was as ambitious as he was greedy.

Eastern Thebes, site of the great temple-complex dedicated to Amun, had, during a long period in the Eighteenth Dynasty, been the capital of the country, and was still effectively its religious centre, and its population was large, around 50,000. It also inspired great affection in those who lived there; as one inhabitant wrote: 'What do they say to themselves in their hearts every day, those who are far from Thebes? They spend the day dreaming of its name.'

Almost as ancient a foundation as Memphis, Thebes bore its title of Southern Capital proudly, although the south was now administered on the pharaoh's behalf by a vizier, at that time Khaemwese, the highest official in the district, and a man known as much for his arrogance as his administrative short-sightedness.

Thebes was dominated by the priestly class and by an aristocratic elite. It had always been a prosperous city, but now it was a city under strain. A series of bad harvests had depleted the granaries, and the price of wheat had quadrupled. The economy was further shaken by

Tomb builders plaster the walls of the pharaoh's burial chamber.

worries about Libyan depredations in the west. It was not a good time to be poor in Ancient Egypt.

References to the 'desert dwellers' occur in a diary which records events in the third regnal year of Rameses X, *c.* 1105 BC. The diary describes how in that year, the gangs of skilled workers living in the village of Deir el-Medina in the Valley of the Kings, and engaged on the excavation and decoration of the royal rock-cut tombs there, were idle during practically all the 'third month of the [harvest] season'. Fear of the 'desert dwellers' is given as the specific reason for this on days 6, 9, 11, 12, 18, 21 and 24 of that month. Such reports had been coming in for at least a decade. The Libyans were evidently roaming through Upper Egypt, but although they seemed like a frightening presence to the isolated and relatively unprotected workmen's community of the kings' tombs, there is no record in the diary of any violent clashes or military intervention. It's also worth noting that although the Egyptians were aware of the Libyans, life on the east bank of the Nile at Thebes – the city of the living, in other words – went on much as normal, even on the dates when the proximity of 'desert people' is noted. But Rameses XI, the last and one of the longest-reigning kings of the dynasty, had to deal early in his reign with renewed incursions from the north and west; and the period of his rule was further troubled by a rise in the independence and power of the priesthood of Amun at Thebes.

It was a time when there was a highly significant spate of thefts from the tombs of the great. Among the poor, and living in a humble quarter huddled against the city walls, was an unskilled quarry worker of Kushite descent called Amenpanufer. His work involved cutting stone at a quarry serving one of the mortuary temples on the West Bank. He qualified neither for a residence in the skilled workmen's village, nor for any of the other benefits

BELOW: An artisan painter colours the hieroglyphs traced onto the plaster wall of a tomb. Among the tomb builders, different painters had their own individual jobs. Senior painters would provide delicate outlines of hieroglyphs that their junior colleagues would colour in.

ABOVE: Amenpanufer had none of the valuable skills of the royal tomb builders. He was an ordinary labourer in one of the city's quarries.

MUMMIFICATION

The Ancient Egyptians realized that in trying to provide the best possible care in the afterworld for their dead, by giving them a room, they had also separated them from the one thing guaranteed to preserve dead bodies: sand. Since the preservation of the body was all-important, but at the same time there could be no question of returning to simpler burials with little room for grave-goods, some remedy had to be found.

The connection between sand and desiccation: that desiccation was a means of immediate preservation, was not made until early in the First Dynasty, from which period evidence of the first attempts to preserve a body by artificial means

have been found. The first mummies were simple and not very effective, consisting largely of wrapping the corpse in many layers of linen bandage, and it was not until towards the end of the Third Dynasty and the beginning of the Fourth that internal organs began to be removed and buried separately; and the linen bandages were soaked in resin which, when hardened, would at least retain the form of the body they wrapped. Underneath, the tissues rotted away. In time there were improvements, such as the replacement of resin by plaster, more easily mouldable and giving a more lifelike effect.

As time passed, the art of mummification reached great heights of sophistication, and even by as late a period as the fifth century BC, when it had declined considerably, Herodotus can give us

ABOVE: Embalmers prepare for the process of mummification. To the Egyptians the heart, not the brain, was the source of human wisdom, memory and emotion. As it was felt that the heart could reveal a person's true character, even after death, the organ was left in the body during the mummification process.

RIGHT: The mummy of a young adult man found at Thebes. His arms, legs, fingers and toes have been individually wrapped in the resin-soaked bandages which cover his entire body. The eyes, eyebrows and mouth are painted on the wrappings and the hair is left exposed. This dates from the Ptolemaic or Roman period, after 305 BC.

FAR RIGHT: Blood was drained from the cadaver as moisture had to be completely removed from the body in order for its preservation to be successful.

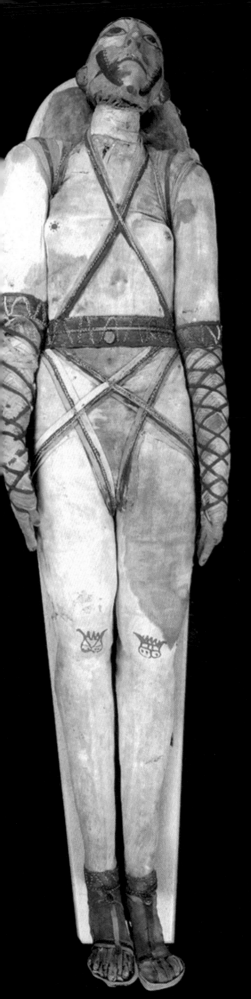

a detailed and vivid description of three levels or classes of embalming. Much of what he describes is coloured by the careful methods of the New Kingdom, whose traditions were still remembered even if the processes by Herodotus' time had become simplified.

FIRST-CLASS MUMMIFICATION

The 'first-class' treatment Herodotus tells us about was accorded to the god-pharoahs. When Hatshepsut died her body was accorded full honours. It was laid out first in the *ibu* – the place where it was purified – then the *wabet*, open to the north and south, so that the north wind could blow through it and remove the unpleasant odours, and where the process of embalming took place, then the *pernefer*, or 'Place of Beauty', where it was decorated and made to look as lifelike as possible, and finally in the *sekh*, a tent erected on an alabaster plinth before the tomb, where the final preparations were made.

This lengthy process involved the removal of all the organs but the heart (believed to be the seat of the mind) and the kidneys (which were too difficult to reach). The brain, regarded as an organ that existed merely to keep the sinuses clear, was softened by the introduction of oils, and then removed through the nostrils after the ethmoid bone had been broken, by means of a long copper hook. Once the organs had been removed, the body was covered in natron (a naturally occurring salt largely consisting of sodium carbonate and bicarbonate, which was mined in great quantities), and dried out for forty days. The cavities of the body vacated by the organs were later packed with resin-soaked pads of linen to bulk them out and give a lifelike appearance to the corpse.

The whole process of a fully-fledged mummification took seventy days. This period, which marked the time between death and burial, which also meant rebirth, may be a reflection of the seventy-day period when the Dog Star, Sothis, vanished, eclipsed by the sun. Its reappearance marked the beginning of the Egyptian year.

SECOND-CLASS MUMMIFICATION

'Second-class' treatment consisted of the injection of cedar oil up the anus, which was then sealed

while the body was subjected to the same natron treatment. Later, the anus was unplugged and the oil released, bringing with it a large quantity of dissolved internal organs, though quite how oil would have the quality of dissolving organs is uncertain: perhaps it served simply as a medium for carrying out tissue which had decayed naturally. This treatment also seems to have been used on at least some of the sacred Apis Bulls (see p. 232).

THIRD-CLASS MUMMIFICATION

In the third-class treatment, the body was simply washed, the inside cleansed 'with a purgative' which isn't identified further, desiccated with natron, and then (though Herodotus doesn't mention this) wrapped in linen.

Writing later still, in the first century BC, Diodorus mentions three classes of mummification, offered at different prices. He also says that the embalmer's profession was one handed down from father to son. The body should be kept whole: that was imperative; but if a part was missing – a finger, for example – it could be replaced with a wooden model. Many later mummies, mainly from the Ptolemaic and Roman Periods but a few dating back to Rameses II's reign, were coated with imported bitumen, an expensive product probably having some mystical significance: black was the colour of the soil and of resurrection.

There seems to be no doubt that the art of mummification reached its peak in the New Kingdom. Details of the techniques used are still unclear. Embalming was a secret art and no written contemporary accounts have yet surfaced.

which they enjoyed. His home was a single-storey mud-brick terraced house in a narrow, twisting street by the city walls. Here, where the rubbish piled up in the streets as people swept it out of their houses, and there was no rain to wash it away, and where the donkeys were seldom groomed thoroughly, the flies were a plague. In the tiny squares, into which the streets occasionally debouched, little markets sold bread, wheat, cloth, fruit and beer. In the year 1116, the bad harvests were to

blame for lack of trade, and food was in ever-shorter supply. Some of the poorest people had already been reduced to eating boiled papyrus reeds.

Amenpanufer was on his way home. He was a worried man. At twenty, he was already the father of three children, and now his wife was about to give birth to their fourth. He loved them dearly and prayed to the goddesses Taweret and Hathor that this birth would be as successful as the others, but he did not know how he was going to keep

Amenpanufer's wife was extremely lucky to survive the ordeal of bearing four children, especially given the unsanitary conditions that poor people lived in and the lack of medical care.

them all in food. Or rather, he did; but it was a risky business. He had had one narrow escape already, and he didn't know if he'd be as lucky a second time. With another child, he'd have to take further risks. But, he thought, why shouldn't the poor living benefit from what the rich dead couldn't – and obviously didn't – use? He eased the weight of the burden he carried in a leather bag under his tunic.

He could hear the yelling before he reached his wooden door and smiled quickly at sympathetic neighbours clustered in the street near it. Pushing it open he ducked under the low lintel and entered his dark front room, and, pausing only to kiss the image of Bes, god of the hearth, which stood in a niche, ran up the stairs to the roof where his mother sat with her grandchildren in one corner. In the other, in a hastily erected reed hut, his wife squatted over the two bricks her feet were balanced on, supported by a hefty midwife whom he knew from the previous three times. Seeing him, she waved to him to pick up the clay beaker of beer on a low stool next to her. He knew what to do. He put some crushed poppy seeds from the bowl next to it into the beaker, and held it to his wife's mouth. The poppies would alleviate the pain. She drank greedily, then turned her face away impatiently and urgently as the next contraction came. The north wind blew, indicating Hathor's favour. Amenpanufer thanked the goddess silently for having watched over his wife. But he also knew that it was through his own efforts and risks that he could afford the midwife and the poppy-seed. It was good that so many of his trusted neighbours were engaged in the same business. But you had to look after your own when the economy slumped.

Amenpanufer's wife was lucky to have survived to the age of eighteen with four successful pregnancies behind her; and Amenpanufer and his wife could themselves expect, if they were lucky, only another dozen or so years. There is evidence of very few older people among the poor. At thirty-five, Amenpanufer's mother was an exception.

He unslung his bag and, exchanging a glance with his mother, placed it in the corner by her, as she slapped the curious children away from it. Crouching down, Amen-panufer upended it and tipped its contents on to the ground. There was a golden-winged scarab set with lapis

A new-born baby would be washed with warm water until the flow of blood in the umbilical cord had ceased and it could be cut with an obsidian knife. The placenta and the cord were placed reverentially to one side. In the case of the working-classes they would not be dried and saved to be buried, one day, with their owner, as was the habit of some members of the nobility.

A typical birthing scene would have women reciting incantations to the Seven Hathors who presided over the birth, and who would predict the nature of the child's death. A child born on the twenty-third of the month would be killed by a crocodile; on the fourth by fever; on the fifth by love. Lucky children were born on the ninth day of the second month of *Akhet* – they would die of old age. Even luckier were those born on the twenty-ninth day of the same month: they would die 'well-respected'.

But if the baby were to live at all, and most didn't survive infancy, it would need to be protected from want and disease; a protection which only material well-being, however modest, could supply.

lazuli, a jasper amulet of the *djed* pillar, two electrum fig-urines of the goddess Neith, and three toys, all modest: a linen-and-wood doll, a boat, and a leopard whose wooden jaws could be made to snap open and shut with a string. These he gave to his children. The rest he gave to his mother, who wrapped them individually in linen rags.

them for use in the afterlife. But the workers who pre-pared their tombs had noticed how little use the dead appeared to make of them after all. Amenpanufer had joined a gang of tomb robbers. Gold and silver were melted down; jewellery could be broken up; and there were plenty of channels through which these things

Amenpanufer had to be careful about how much he showed off the little luxuries his sideline allowed him to afford, but at a time when great wealth and corruption sat side by side with poverty, he and several of his friends had lost their respect for authority, and for the wealthy dead who slept on the West Bank. There were rich pick-ings to be had on the other side of the Nile. By this time in the history of Ancient Egypt, anyone with enough money could buy a decent funeral, and be buried in a tomb with all their fine possessions and jewellery around

could be sold back to the living upper classes. It was remarkable how few people seemed to worry about divine retribution, and even people on Amenpanufer's level had come to realize that divine retribution some-how never seemed to come. In any case, he was prepared to run the risk; and he was far from alone.

Nothing that had for so long been represented as sacred now daunted these tomb robbers; the traditions of two millennia carried no awe or religious significance for them any more. After the first step had been taken, and

LEFT: Amenpanufer hides a stash of stolen grave-goods, wary of telling even his friends of the lucrative sideline he had found.

the sky had failed to fall in, there seemed to be no reason not to continue. However, the gangs did not always form an easy fellowship, and it was not unusual for one to betray another in order to save itself.

Taking the linen bundles from his mother, Amenpanufer went downstairs to the back room of his house,

own gardens and looms; but plenty of men came to trade, and even in the economic slump some business still went on, for things were not that bad for everybody. One woman had ducks in baskets for sale, another traded honeycakes. A man with a dirty-looking sack of grain was arguing over a bolt of linen with a

Thebes was a busy commercial town where anything could be bought and sold, including stolen goods.

beyond which was the kitchen-courtyard, and hid them behind a loose mud-brick in the wall. Then his wife's increased howls brought him back to the roof. Soon afterwards, the midwife was holding up a slippery new young son, whom Amenpanufer's mother washed with warm water until the flow of blood in the umbilical cord had ceased.

The next morning, Amenpanufer made his way to one of the markets. These markets were generally run by women, who produced everyday goods from their

tough Libyan woman whom Amenpanufer knew slightly. The man was wasting his time, he knew. However scarce grain was, the woman wouldn't give a bolt of good linen for the dirty and no doubt rotten produce he had in his bag.

Amenpanufer made his way across the market and round a corner into a side alley whose whitewashed walls were bare of windows. Turning another corner, he came upon a small beer-shop that looked closed, but he went inside anyway. In the gloom at the back a man

The Chief of Police examines the stolen goods Amenpanufer has to sell.

was sitting at a low table. Amenpanufer went over to him and sat down on the stool opposite him. He had brought his leather bag with him, and from it drew the linen bundles. One by one the other man opened them, looking at each item briefly but carefully before rewrapping them.

Amenpanufer, although he knew it wasn't necessary, could not resist looking over his shoulder from time to time at the door. Four years earlier, he'd been caught with goods from one of his first robberies, from the tomb of the Theban king Sobekemsaf II. No-one knew much about him, but the tomb he lay in with his wife Nubkhas wasn't secure and the break-in had been easy. Sobekemsaf must have been important. They'd called him 'The Great' when he'd been in power five hundred years earlier. It had been a close call for Amenpanufer,

and he'd only escaped the fearful punishment that was the fate of all tomb robbers (though so few were ever caught it seemed worth the risk) by bribing a scribe, Khapmope. He'd let things cool down and then gone back to tomb-robbery. He'd got used to the extra income and couldn't do without it now. Anyway, he imagined himself safe. He was trading with powerful friends. The buyer across the table from him now was called Bakwerel, a man with a badly deformed face: a deep white scar crossed the right side of his face from forehead to mouth, and the right eye was white and blind. Bakwerel had got the wound years earlier, fighting a tomb robber. Now he had seen the sense of the business, and gone into dealing in grave-goods himself. But now he was also head of the Medjay – he was the local Chief of Police.

HIGH ON THE WEST BANK of the Nile was the village of the skilled tomb workers of Deir el-Medina, tucked away amidst the rugged cliffs of rock in which the pharaohs of the New Kingdom, their families and the nobility, had been buried, and dominated by the pyramid-shaped peak of Mount El-Qurn. Among those buried here were Tuthmosis III, Rameses II, and the king whose resting place, discovered three thousand years later, would revolutionize Egyptology: Tutankhamun.

In 1116 BC, work on the tomb of Rameses IX had been in progress for ten years. The work was carried on under conditions of great secrecy, for the rock-cut tombs were designed to deter grave-robbers, and were separate from the owners' mortuary temples. The great pyramid burials which had been favoured in the Old Kingdom

had proved to be too much of a target for despoilers, and by this time only a plain doorway cut into the rock marked the burial places of the kings and queens.

Inside the tombs it was dark, and the plastering of the walls and the drawing and subsequent painting on them had to be illuminated by copper reflectors which channelled sunlight a certain distance down the corridors. But beyond that oil lamps were used. Working in a dusty, airless atmosphere, the artisans suffered from bronchial and respiratory complaints, and their eyesight was damaged as they created, in poor light, works of great beauty designed to be seen by no one but the dead. Blindness was something greatly feared, though medical treatment for failing eyesight did exist in the form of a lotion of honey and ochre, applied to the eyes with a vulture's quill as a dropper, and kohl. Honey is antiseptic,

ABOVE: The Medjay in charge of security of the necropolis site on the West Bank of Thebes were largely of Nubian origin.

LEFT: On the walls of the royal tomb, Pentaweret adds the final touches to a portrait of the pharaoh Rameses IX.

Twentieth Dynasty, one scribal post was passed down through six generations of the same family, for example.

Over sixty men would work in two gangs, each responsible for one side of the tomb. In a country where the river played the central role, it seemed natural that the workforce should be organized like a boat's crew, the port and starboard groups each working under a captain, their overseer. Among the skills deployed were those of plasterer, who covered the excavated walls of rock with a smooth surface for the designers to draw the scenes that would entertain the dead in the afterlife, replicating life as it went on, had always gone on, and always would go on in the Black Land – scenes which would then be coloured by the painters. Also working there were carpenters, sculptors and stone masons, and all of them were backed up by a support team supplying them with food and water and fresh oil for their lamps. The lamps smoked, and as the smoke stung the eyes of the painters, they added salt to the oil, which reduced the smoke but also the brightness of the light. It was however the lesser of two evils.

The architectural plan used in building Rameses IX's vast tomb still exists. By 1116 the main corridor stretched one hundred metres into the relatively soft limestone rock. Excavation was only ever hard when the workers struck veins of flint, which ran in layers through the limestone. But the initial excavation of a tomb never seems to have taken more than a year.

Once the walls had been plastered, work was divided along a grid by snapping a string dipped in red paint against the walls, in order for working drawings to be scaled up as they were transferred to the walls. The process of finishing a tomb could last more than fifty years, though final preparations were hurried along if the tomb's intended occupant died before it was ready, and some were completed with almost indecent haste. Most of the men who worked on these monuments would not expect to see the end of their work: even with their privileged lifestyle – they were exempt from any other duties and their incomes were more-or-less guaranteed, but they would be very lucky if they lived to be forty.

In 1116, the food shortages had led to the failure of

ochre reduces inflammation, while kohl protects the eye. Less attractive remedies for eye troubles included the application of 'tortoise bile' and 'water from a pig's eyes'.

There was a great sense of camaraderie in the small and closely-knit community. Even though their life-expectancy was not long, they were proud of their craftsmanship and the position they held in society as a result of it, and their sons succeeded them in their professions, starting their apprenticeships early. Employment connected with the king's tomb was generally passed from father to eldest son, with the nominal approval of the vizier of Thebes. During practically the whole of the supplies to arrive on three occasions. Each time the workforce had felt confident enough of their value to the state to go on strike until the wages they were due – usually received in advance – were paid. When times were good, the workmen of Deir el-Medina were paid, chiefly in grain from the royal granaries, on the twenty-eighth day of each month, in advance. They also received vegetables, fish, and wood for fuel, which were supplied by a specially detailed community of peasants. The village had its own service support industries as well: washermen and potters, water-carriers and fishermen. Two junior scribes looked after all the artisans' administrative and private paperwork. Doctors cared for their health. There were also soothsayers, and 'wise women'. Donkeys were rented out to woodcutters and policemen and, as the Nile was so far away, the water-carriers, poor themselves, would also rent donkeys from the wealthier villagers in order to transport water to the village. The village, whose modern name is, as we have seen, Deir el-Medina, was in antiquity called – perhaps in hope – 'The Place-of-Truth'. The name was to acquire an ironic ring. By 1116 BC, the village had been in existence for about 450 years.

The artisans were valued employees of the state and no-one expected them to work unreasonable hours. Their working day was limited to eight hours, though in practice this meant longer working days in summer, when the hours of daylight were longer. At the height of the Egyptian summer, the eight-hour working day was actually nine hours and twenty minutes. Hours were measured with 'shadow-clocks' – a device in which the shadow of a horizontal raised bar fell on another bar fixed at right-angles to it, which had regular markings on it, as the sun crossed the sky.

Though they were valued, the tomb workers were not entirely trusted, and they were supervised by two other groups of state employees: scribes, and the mainly Nubian Medjay police force. The scribes assessed and supervised the daily progress of the work, and they were also responsible for security. The royal tomb-builders knew some of the greatest secrets in the country. They knew not only where the bodies were buried,

but also where the grave-goods, constituting great treasures, were placed.

At the start of every working day, tomb-builders had to draw their tools from a central store (copper chisels and other implements would in any case have periodically to be resharpened, though copper has the quality of becoming hardened by use). Each evening, the workers would have to hand their tools in again, when they would be carefully weighed, and details noted on flakes of limestone by the scribes. Tools were checked in and out so that they could not be used in tomb robberies, and every day the names and the number of men working on the tomb were carefully noted as they entered the building works, and again as they left. There was no chance of anyone loitering. And the village was sufficiently far away from the tomb to prevent the workers from returning there, except on their two days off at the end of the eight-day working week.

The scribes of course were open to corruption themselves but the Ancient Egyptians had a system of watching the watchers. Failing to resist the temptations offered by corruption carried its own risks – though naturally there were always plenty of people willing to take the chance, especially at a time of insecurity and economic depression. Each artisan as he joined the village community did have to swear an 'oath of office', by which he undertook to keep an eye out for and report anything suspicious taking place in the necropolis. This had the effect of creating an atmosphere of mutual suspicion among the villagers, though many rebelled against it and, indeed, formed their own, self-interested alliances.

The workers kept their own tools in the village, and worked there on private commissions and on their own account. They created their own modest but well-crafted tombs by the village wall, presided over by Hathor, their favourite deity. Many of the villagers used their spare time to build furniture and make funerary goods. There was an increasing demand for grave-goods in Thebes. In the Old Kingdom, only the pharaohs and the nobles could afford grand burials; but by the time of the New Kingdom, with the rise of middle-class literacy and affluence, the once-exclusive *Amduat – The Book of What Is*

In the Underworld – was available to all but the peasantry. Coffin-texts were mass-produced, with blanks left for the purchaser to fill in his or her own name. The village craftsmen created little collectives, pooled their resources, and sold what they produced in their spare time on their own account, thereby as much as doubling their incomes. But for some of them even this was not enough, and in times of hardship, when prices were high and wages either low or in arrears, it was difficult for the men to resist the temptation of the wealth buried right next to them.

At the end of the working week the tomb builders walk home to their purpose-built village in an isolated valley.

One of the senior scribes on duty at Rameses IX's tomb at the time was called Harshire. Harshire was an honest man and it is possible, in the light of events, that he was working for Paser, the senior mayor of Thebes whose jurisdiction covered the East Bank, though notionally Harshire was answerable to Pawero, the city official. Harshire had noticed some collusion between Pentaweret, the head painter of the starboard crew, and its captain, Userkhepesh. The men were too often together, and although Harshire had not as yet seen or found anything to constitute evidence sufficient to bring

to the attention of Vizier Khaemwese, whose office embodied the local high court, he continued to watch. He had been considering recommending to Mayor Pawero that one or other of the men be switched to the port crew, when one particular evening he saw Pawero himself, flanked by two policemen, talking to Pentaweret and Userkhepesh. This in itself was nothing unusual, as the mayor made routine visits to the tomb and spoke to the senior workmen about progress. However, Harshire had noticed that Pawero had been in conversation with the head painter and captain of the starboard crew quite frequently lately, and on this particular evening, he noticed something he might have missed had he blinked: a small leather bag passed between the captain and the mayor, disappearing under the mayor's ample tunic in a trice, while the two Nubian policemen seemed to be studying earnestly some detail in the rockface nearby.

A single path connected the Valley of the Kings to Deir el-Medina, and it was guarded by Medjay: a brigade of as many as 120 of them manned the valley and the village, two policemen to each worker. There were guard-posts at the entrance to the village as well as at the entrance to the valley construction sites, which acted as checkpoints for the workmen and their families every time they passed them.

The village itself consisted of sixty-eight flat-roofed houses, each about forty square metres in area, and tightly packed together in a grid system of alleys contained by a thick perimeter wall. Much of the village has survived, and with it much of the detritus and cast-off ostraca of the people who lived there: from these informal remains, including letters, receipts, journals, records of lawsuits, laundry lists, popular hymns, quotations from literature and sketches and cartoons, we have learned an enormous amount about the way of life of ordinary Ancient Egyptians. Many of the cartoons have a strong satirical edge, depicting officialdom and the law as vicious, stupid and brutal: in one series, a boy is shown caught by a cat policeman and a mouse judge, who beat him. In yet another, a judge is depicted as a donkey.

Pentaweret the painter strolled past the guards at the gate to the village, waving at them as he was written in,

for everybody knew everybody and the police staff were seldom changed. Nevertheless one had to be careful.

Pentaweret kicked up some sand idly as he walked down the narrow main street in the cool of late evening, looking forward to his dinner and very happy, despite the usual nervous flicker, that the increased size of his chest hadn't been noticed. Lamplight glowed through the small windows of the terraced houses as he passed, and the stars and moon in the clear sky bathed the street in an electric blue glow.

In one of the tiny squares he stopped to buy a drink from a water-seller, meeting at the spot with Userkhepesh. The two exchanged a few words over their drink, but Harshire, listening in shadow round the next corner, heard nothing but commonplaces. Then the two men went their separate ways, and Harshire made for his own quarters, wondering what course of action to take.

Pentaweret pushed open the door to his house and went in to find his children in the main room, playing

The painter Pentaweret, one of the privileged tomb builders who succumbed to the temptation to steal from the rich tombs.

The houses of Deir el-Medina were built to a standard design with a kitchen courtyard behind the main living area.

Many of the villagers were literate and their surviving notes and letters give us a detailed picture of life in Deir el-Medina.

with their toys. He greeted them warmly, and admired the cartoon his older son had drawn on a flake of limestone of a monkey stealing figs from an orchard. He called out to his wife, who emerged from the kitchen courtyard with a cup of wine and a plate of bread. Pentaweret sat down and ate and drank, and asked 'what's for dinner?', rather hoping for lamb stew and beans in oil, his favourite. He looked over his younger son's copying exercises, and corrected one or two hieroglyphs.

Many of the villagers were literate, and thousands of written notes, sketches and work journals have survived to give us a vivid picture of their lives. They worked hard, but holidays and festivals gave them frequent extra days off, and they had time and leisure to think of themselves as individuals, which was not the norm as far as the mass of the peasant-farmer population was concerned. We know for example from local records that fathers were even granted paternity leave. Their free time allowed them, as has been mentioned, to make objects for their own tombs, and even take special commissions

to supplement their income. But that was not enough. A good standard of living enables a person to think of an even better one, and Pentaweret had become involved in a black economy which enabled him to augment an already privileged lifestyle.

For some time he had been able to smuggle works of art destined for the tombs of the dead back from their supposedly last resting-places to the land of the living. These objects came from older tombs in the vicinity of his work which had been excavated secretly by colleagues, or from the very tomb he was working on. Today, he had managed to wrap around his chest a golden pectoral ornament, which he now quickly unbuckled, dropping it into the linen sack his wife held ready for it while his children's attention was distracted by the arrival of their nurse with their supper. Privacy was unknown in Ancient Egypt, and both husband and wife knew that children were as quick at seeing anything as their tongues were to wag. The older son, Pashedu, was already, aged eight, in on the game. His brother Userhat, two years younger, could not yet quite be trusted.

Pentaweret wasn't alone. His family was one of several in the village that had organized themselves into a cartel, plundering the tombs of the West Bank, and in such a small community, they, having power, held sway. Nevertheless they had to be constantly on guard, so when there was a knock at the door soon after they had eaten, Pentaweret and his wife Takharu were on the alert for a moment. But the knock had after all been coded, and certainly wasn't imperious, so when the painter undid the wooden pegs which served as locks to his front door and swung it open, he wasn't surprised to see his friend, the captain of the starboard team, Userkhepesh. He came in quickly, turning sideways to admit the basket he was carrying slung over one shoulder. It was heavy and it was evidently a relief to him to drop it on the floor before removing the rough linen cloak that had concealed it. Userhat had already gone to bed on his mat-mattress on the roof, dreaming in the garlic-aroma'd smoke of his own and the neighbouring kitchens. Pashedu was still awake and, with his father and 'uncle', took the cover off the basket. On top were what they expected, a few bags of dried beans and wheat. Underneath, a crop of a dozen or so gilded and jewel-encrusted figures of mummies: these were *ushabtis.*

Pashedu and his father sorted the haul out and wrapped individual items in linen as soon as Userkhepesh had taken his leave, after the traditional offering of bread and salt, and after the customary checking of the goods had been done. Then, as Takharu began to fret about security and bedtime, but quite aware at the same time of the necessity of the business, Pentaweret and his son put the packages into two large donkey panniers, filling each about two-thirds full. They then dragged the baskets upstairs to the roof, passing each over the low parapet wall to their neighbour, a woman whom we will call Imentet, who with the boy and the man carried the baskets over the rooftops to another lower parapet on the thick wall not far from the gateway to the village, where, below them, the two Medjays on guard were intent on a game of Twenty-Squares. Pashedu gave a long, low whistle into the darkness to his right, and immediately a man whose feet were bound in linen came along the wall,

softly leading a donkey whose hooves were equally bound. They made no sound on the wind-driven sand which covered the rocky pathway just beyond the village wall. Imentet and Pentaweret lowered the baskets down to the man with the donkey, who hitched them quickly

either side of the animal, which staggered in the way donkeys do, quietly and patiently under the weight. Having covered the baskets with soiled laundry, the donkeyman and his beast then made their way back to the track from the village through the long defile to the river, where, posing as a washerman serving the Place-of-Truth, he took a ferry over to the East Bank, where friends and a welcoming black market across all classes were willing to entertain them.

But that particular night, as the police guards nodded over their board game, the scribe Harshire, needing more proof for his already nascent suspicions, had himself, with two spies, observed what had been going on. And now he decided that he would take action. It seemed to him that he had discovered enough proof of tomb-robbing in the very Place-of-Truth, and now he decided to report his

Pentaweret shows his wife his haul from the tombs of the Valley of the Kings.

Paser, playing *senet* with his son, receives the news of Harshire's arrival.

suspicions. He knew that according to the chain of command he should first have told his immediate superior, Pawero, the mayor of the West Bank; but for whatever reason, he took his findings instead directly to Pawero's superior, Paser, the mayor of East Thebes, soon afterwards. In doing so, he set in train a series of events which would prove to be the undoing of the poor quarry-worker Amenpanufer, and would ultimately lead to the exposure of a wider world of corruption, which, however, seems to have proved resilient to his investigation.

P ASER WAS PLAYING a game of *senet* with his oldest son in the courtyard of his house in the grand suburbs of Thebes when his personal body-servant appeared to announce the arrival of a visitor who required an immediate audience. Paser glanced at the slip of limestone on which the visitor's name was written and told the servant to admit him. Deliberately botching his next move, so that his ten-year-old son would win, he smiled at the boy and pushed his chair away from the low table on which the board-game had been set up, standing to receive his guest. The boy, realizing that this was business, allowed himself to be taken into the next room by another servant, who returned immediately, removing the board-game and replacing it with a jar of Kharga wine, bread and salt.

Paser was a pious and conscientious man, a nobleman who was attempting to pass on to his son, through the board-game, a sense of respect for religious tradition, since the *senet* reflected the journey from our present life to that of the hereafter. The ancient game itself had been depicted as one played by a man against death:

something which we recognize as the game of chess played against death in medieval history.

The visitor was Harshire. He came in quickly, huddled in a cloak. Pausing only to sit down and accept the traditional bread-and-salt offering placed before him, but not touching the yellow wine, the scribe told Paser what he knew. Having heard the news, Paser, the next morning, discreetly ordered more of his own men in place on the West Bank, to begin an investigation.

But Paser was not the only one to have spies, and news of what he was planning reached Pawero only a few days later, as he was hunting duck with throwsticks (Pawero's were carved in the shape of snakes) on the banks of the Nile a few kilometres downriver. At first he was stunned, then furious. On the one hand, it would not look good on his record if it were found that tomb-robbery had been going on to any great extent in the West Bank; but on the other, Pawero may have been involved in it himself. That was certainly Harshire's suspicion, though he does not seem quite to have had the courage or the evidence to name Pawero to Paser.

Meanwhile, Pawero knew that he had to take diversionary action, and quickly. In fact, the way he now behaved seems to indicate strongly that he was collaborating with the tomb robbers of the village. The first thing he did was arrange a meeting with Bakwerel, the Chief of Police, who was involved in dealing in stolen grave-goods. Both men were in unassailable positions, but only if they could distract the attention of any investigation before it got too close. In order to do that they had to meet trouble halfway, and they had to find a scapegoat. Both men knew that Paser was a conscientious, pious and just man. But the vizier, Khaemwese, was less so: what was more, the vizier was a man whose vanity could be flattered, and who was significantly less intelligent than Paser. To ensure that attention was deflected from them, Pawero and Bakwerel needed to get Khaemwese involved, since he outranked Paser. Their scapegoat therefore needed to be a sufficiently serious offender to get the vizier concerned in the investigation. And they had just the right man.

Bakwerel knew all about the bribe that had changed hands between Amenpanufer and the scribe Khapmope four years earlier, after Amenpanufer and his gang had despoiled the tomb of Sobekemsaf II and his wife, Nubkhas. The violation of a royal tomb was a crime of the greatest gravity; Khapmope would testify to save his own skin, and nobody would believe Amenpanufer against the word of such a man as Bakwerel.

Amenpanufer was sitting at home with his new baby on his lap, discussing names for him with his wife. To the Ancient Egyptians, a person's name was of paramount importance, inextricably bound up with his personality and his fate, so the choosing of names was a matter of no small importance. But this child's fate was soon to be decided: fatherless, the little family would barely stand a chance without a source of income. As the baby's tiny hand clutched Amenpanufer's thumb in a strong, experimental grip, there was a pounding on the street door, which immediately burst open to admit a squad of Medjay led by Bakwerel himself.

Despite the imploring tears of his wife, and the frightened cries of his mother and his other children, one of whom clung to his legs, two policemen seized him and dragged him into the street and off towards the city centre. Another two stayed behind to search the house, and came up with enough trinkets to make a case, though Bakwerel had brought a bag of stolen amulets and figurines to make sure. The family was left under guard. It was the sixteenth day of the First Month of Inundation.

Vizier Khaemwese, called upon to conduct Amenpanufer's interrogation in person, crossed the hall towards a side chamber where the quarryman was to be brought to him. The vizier was the most powerful Egyptian outside the royal family, and answerable in Upper Egypt only to the pharaoh. His responsibilities ranged from the organization of tax-collection to the management of finances, building works and the administration of the law. He was the embodiment of Egyptian justice. In stealing from a king's tomb, Amenpanufer had committed an act not just of theft but of sacrilege. The kings of Egypt became gods when they died, and the security of their lives in the hereafter, which was disturbed by any

The vizier Khaemwese
interrogates
Amenpanufer.
Amenpanufer's
confession was
rediscovered over
3000 years later.

violation of their graves, was tantamount to disrupting
the security of the nation as a whole. To despoil such a
tomb and to disturb the corpse of the god-king was to
break the cycle of life, and could bring down chaos and
destruction on the Black Land. Such an act also showed
a dangerous lack of respect for the status quo, something
which the Egyptian establishment was anxious to preserve at all times.

Khaemwese's task was to establish Amenpanufer's innocence or guilt – not that the process would be much more
than a formality – and the Ancient Egyptian justice system
had its own efficient and straightforward way of settling
such questions: torture, principally in the form of beatings
or twisting the victim's limbs with a stick, though castra-
tion and other physical mutilation, such as the cutting-off
of the nose and ears, were also sometimes employed. This
was an accepted part of the interrogation process. Amenpanufer was lucky that he alone bore the torment; frequently the relatives of the accused and even witnesses
were tortured as well. It rarely took long to extract a confession, and, as always, scribes were on hand to record it.
In Amenpanufer's case the court report has survived and
in it we have a rare opportunity to hear the authentic voice
of a member of the Ancient Egyptian working class.

By the fourth day of the investigation, Amenpanufer
had made a full confession to the thefts from the tomb

ABOVE: As part of the investigation
the vizier is taken to inspect the royal tombs
on the West Bank of the Nile.

RIGHT: The tomb desecrated by Amenpanufer
and his accomplices belonged to Sobekemsaf,
a pharaoh buried over 500 years earlier.

of Sobekemsaf and his wife, and to its desecration. In
accordance with the law, the court now visited the scene
of the crime with the accused. Khaemwese travelled in a
litter and was accompanied by Pawero and Bakwerel,
together with other officials, while police guards dragged
Amenpanufer along in their wake. From a distance, the
painter's son, Pashedu, watching from the Place-of-
Truth, saw the procession as it made its way into the
cliffs of the West Bank. Conveniently, Sobekemsaf's five-
hundred-year-old tomb was outside the Valley of the
Kings, and a long way from the current site of Rameses
IX's tomb and the workers' village. Satisfied that the
investigators were turning away from the village, the boy

turned to go back there himself, when suddenly he froze. There on the path in front of him was a yellow scorpion. They were a constant menace in the village, and tomb workers were frequently incapacitated as a result of stings. But for the Ancient Egyptians these creatures represented something far worse than their very painful but not by any means always fatal poison. They were seen as agents of chaos, sent to disturb the divine order of things. They were harbingers of ill-luck. A scorpion-charmer was permanently resident in the village.

Amenpanufer's guilt was quickly established: they had his confession and the formal expedition to the tomb confirmed that it had indeed been violated. But Pawero wasn't satisfied and, to reassure the vizier that all else was well on the West Bank, he took him on a tour of inspection to some of the tombs (selected of course by Pawero) in the Valley of the Kings, to demonstrate to him that they were intact. Khaemwese took his word for it, and, the investigation concluded, the party returned to Thebes for the trial of Amenpanufer.

In the meantime, Paser had written to the pharaoh in Memphis, demanding an independent investigation at the highest level; but in doing so he went over Vizier Khaemwese's head. This was a serious breach of protocol and would not endear Paser to Khaemwese, something which Pawero, the minute he heard about what Paser had done, turned to his own advantage. He had no intention of letting a commission from Memphis arrive and start stirring things up; indeed, it was essential for his own career that he avert such a visit.

He wrote at once to Khaemwese, in mock innocence and concern, telling him what Paser had done: 'I am unable to make any sense of these grave accusations, but it would be a sin for me to keep silent. I am therefore reporting these charges to you, which the mayor said that he would report directly to the pharaoh our lord.'

Pawero had judged his man perfectly. Khaemwese's reaction to his letter was probably a furious one. He seems to have been more concerned with the insult to his authority than about Paser's actual allegations against the villagers, and the last thing he wanted was for the pharaoh to be brought in over his head. The tomb-

Amenpanufer in court four years after his crime. The law caught up with him eventually.

robbing investigation now gathered wider political connotations, and the trial of Amenpanufer, about to take place, would carry an important sub-text with it: every official not in Paser's camp would want it to spell the end of any investigation into tomb-robbery so conclusively that Rameses IX would not think it necessary to react to Paser's letter – might, indeed, think him overly zealous or to be overreacting. When the High Court gathered for the trial in the Temple of Karnak, a centre of administration and law as well as a sacred religious site, there was more than the usual amount of tension in the air.

THIS WAS NOT A TRIAL in any modern sense however, but a formality: a public confession, and the elite of Thebes were there to hear it, each wearing the ostrich-plume pendant symbolic of Maat, the goddess of Truth and Order. Standing before the court were Amenpanufer's accomplices in the robbery of four years earlier, rounded up as a result of his confession and tortured into making confessions of their own. There were eight defendants in all, herded into a dishevelled

group to one side of the hall as Nesamun, the Royal Scribe, made the introductory speech which listed all the accusations against the principal accused, Amenpanufer. Seated along one wall, other scribes busily recorded every word.

At last it was Amenpanufer's turn to make his statement. He began, as was customary, with an oath: 'If I speak falsehood, may I be mutilated [in the nose and ears] and be sent into exile to the Land of Kush.' Nesamun now required him to 'name the thieves who were with you'. And the quarryman began his confession:

'I was employed ... with ... other stone-masons, and I fell into the habit of robbing the tombs in company with the stone-mason Hapiwer, son of Merenptah ... the carpenter Sethnakht, the stone-cutter Hapiro, the farmer Amenemhab, the carpenter Irenamun and the water-bearer Khaemwese, and with the boatman Ahay: in all eight men. We went to rob the tombs as we usually did ... '

In the course of what followed Amenpanufer described in detail how the men had taken a boat across the river at

ABOVE: Vizier Khaemwese presides over the trial in the Temple of Karnak.

RIGHT: Harshire and Paser await the outcome of Amenpanufer's trial.

night, and hidden it among the reeds on the West Bank, before climbing up to the unguarded tombs. They were well-organized and experienced robbers, and each had a skill to contribute to the task in hand. The tomb of Sobekemsaf was unlike those they had broken into hitherto, though they gained access by chiselling in from the back using their own tools which they had brought with them from their homes. When rock proved too tough for the chisels, or it was too time-consuming to cut through with them, the robbers lit fires against the face and heated the stone, then throwing water on it so that it shattered – a trick every quarryman knew. They penetrated the tomb from the back, partly to avoid detection, but perhaps also to avoid the curses warning people away carved over the door of the tomb. In view of their total lack of respect for the contents of the tomb and even the corpse, however, the latter precaution seems less likely. Whatever the reason, some careful surveying had to be done to make sure they judged their point of entry correctly.

Once inside, the robbers had lit torches and fumbled their way through the inner chambers of the tomb. This was evidently the richest they had ever attempted, and they were overawed at the wealth of goods they saw laid out before them: furniture, wooden chests, shrines, chariots, bolts of fine linen, statues of the gods. Above all they found the sarcophagus and mummy of the king himself, and although Amenpanufer refers to him formally as 'this god' in his confession, the robbers were no longer so awestruck as not to break into the coffin:

'We opened the sarcophagus and coffin, and found the noble mummy of this king equipped with a falchion; a large number of amulets and jewels of gold upon his neck, the headpiece of gold upon him. The ... mummy of the king was completely bedecked with gold, and his coffins were adorned with gold and silver inside and out, inlaid with all kinds of precious stones.'

Robbing tombs was not just
a crime but was considered sacrilege
and punished accordingly.

LAW AND ORDER

Law was enforced in the name of the goddess Maat, who represented Truth, Order, Morality and Ethics. Justice was administered in the most serious cases from the royal court, but in the majority of cases through regional capitals, the capitals of the administrative districts, and smaller courts.

Torture was often employed as a means of getting at the truth once a suspect had been arrested and the case was under investigation, though police as we understand them did not – at least until the Roman Period – have more than a peace-keeping function. Police were the agents of government, but criminal and forensic

tomb-robbery, would include a senior foreman whose reliability was accepted, as well as officials and administrators of the local government. There were many cases that would be heard in a kind of small-claims court, these largely being over debts, estate boundary disputes, and so on. Punishments varied. Corporal punishment was common, and could be severe, up to 100 or even 200 strokes of the cane. More serious offences could merit branding, sometimes on the forehead, and cutting of the flesh. Dismemberment has been recorded, and the cutting-off of noses and ears was not uncommon. Sentences of hard labour in special camps and

investigation were not exact sciences. In Thebes, suspects were taken to the riverbank, to a building called 'The Place of Examination', which probably had a fearsome reputation. Suspects were deemed guilty until proven innocent and had to begin any statement they made – even if under duress or as the result of torture – with a disclaimer that could bring further punishment on their heads: 'If I speak falsehood, may I be mutilated/exiled', was a common form of words for this.

Magistrates of a local court varied from sitting to sitting but, in the case of an investigation of

ABOVE: Thebes appears not to have had a permanent courtroom, and Amenpanufer's trial took place in one of the courtyards of the Temple of Karnak. The Egyptian word for a court is *kembet*, literally 'a corner', reflecting the impromptu nature of courtrooms.

exile were also available to the courts, though capital punishment could only be carried out with the consent of the pharaoh. It should, however, be remembered that the nature and administration of the law varied in the course of Ancient Egypt's long history.

It was no surprise that Amenpanufer and his companions wanted to take the opportunity, despite the risks, to share in the advantages the rich had and kept to themselves even in death. There may have even been an element of anger, for some tombs were not only looted but smashed up – a deliberate act of defiance. In the case of some tomb robberies, the thieves had used the torn-off limbs of the mummies as torches, or even whole mummified children.

They took Sobekemsaf's body out of its mummy-case and undid its linen bandages to get at the amulets they knew would be wrapped closer to the corpse to protect it.

'We collected the gold we found on the noble mummy of this
god, together with his amulets and jewels, which were on his
neck, and [that gold on] the coffins in which he was resting ...
We took ... articles of gold, silver and bronze and divided
them amongst ourselves ... and we set fire to the coffins.'

The reason for the last act was not vandalism but to get the gold leaf which covered the wooden mummy-cases to melt. Once solid again, it could be scraped up and sold on the black market. The booty from the night's work was good:

'Twenty *deben* of gold fell to each of the eight of us, a total
of 160 *deben* of gold [about 14.5 kilogrammes], the
fragments of furniture not being included. Then we
crossed [back] over to Thebes.'

CANOPIC JARS

The principal organs in Ancient Egyptian burial culture were stored separately in four jars, known to archaeologists as canopic jars, which were buried with the mummy. Each originally bore a stopper in the shape of a human head, though by the later Eighteenth Dynasty the stoppers had acquired different heads for each body part: that of a man, Imsety, linked with Isis and the south, for the liver; an ape, Hapy, linked with Nephthys and the north, for the lungs; a jackal, Duamutef, linked with Neith and the east, for the stomach; and a falcon, Qebehsenuef, linked with Serket and the west, for the guts.

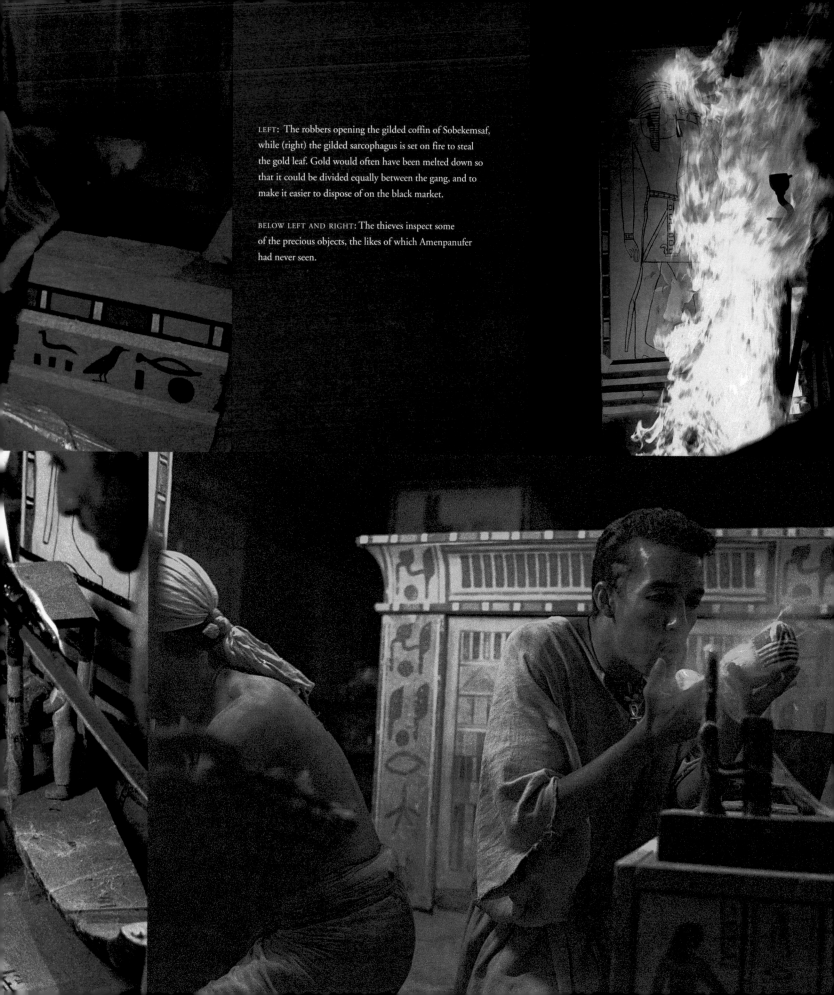

LEFT: The robbers opening the gilded coffin of Sobekemsaf, while (right) the gilded sarcophagus is set on fire to steal the gold leaf. Gold would often have been melted down so that it could be divided equally between the gang, and to make it easier to dispose of on the black market.

BELOW LEFT AND RIGHT: The thieves inspect some of the precious objects, the likes of which Amenpanufer had never seen.

What Amenpanufer came out with was alarming: he spoke of the officials he'd bribed, and added that the robbery for which he and his companions had been tried was by no means the only one, nor were they the only people engaged in the crimes, nor had the robberies by any means ceased:

> 'Thus I, together with the other thieves who are with me, have continued down to this day in the practice of robbing the tombs. A great many others from here steal from them as well, and they are as good as partners of ours.'

All this was duly recorded, and now at least the matters Paser had brought up could not be swept under the carpet. Nevertheless he knew that he had made an enemy of the vizier; and Pawero was as slippery as he was clever.

For Amenpanufer, silent at last, there was no future left at all. With his companions he was taken the following day and dragged at the ends of ropes out of the town to a site on a knoll a little way to the south. On the way his despairing wife had managed to fight her way through the jeering crowd that lined the route to reach him for long enough to press a little clay *ankh* amulet into his hand, which he took, though he barely noticed her. Badly beaten and bleeding, he knew that he was on his way to face the cruellest death the Egyptians had devised, reserved for the most heinous crimes. His body would be disfigured so that it would not be any use to him in the afterlife: a fate in itself worse than death for it would condemn him to become a ghost, belonging forever nowhere. There would be no grave at all for him.

On the little hill eight new sharp wooden stakes, each about three metres long, had been embedded in the ground. Near them were older ones, supporting what looked like rags wrapped around blackened and

Amenpanufer had seven accomplices, including two carpenters, a stonemason and a boatman. These skills were all useful in their work as tomb robbers.

Amenpanufer
being led away
to his execution.

stinking lumps of meat. This was the place of impalement. Death would be agonizing beyond imagination.
Each man was lowered slowly onto the sharp point of a
stake inserted into his anus. The executioners then let
go and allowed gravity and the victim's own weight to
do the rest. When it was all over and the crowd had
dispersed, before the dust had even settled, the vul-
tures would perch on the men's shoulders and begin
their feast with the eyes.

Amenpanufer's last extempore confession did have an
effect. A year later, the vizier was obliged to launch a massive investigation to clear up the tomb robberies that had
continued on the West Bank. Pentaweret the painter and
his family, together with Userkhepesh the captain and his,
and most of their accomplices, were arrested and tortured,

and each of the ringleaders among the artisans eventually
shared Amenpanufer's fate. A purge of the city of Thebes
itself took place at the same time. Grave-goods were found
in the houses of people of all ranks; even the wife of the
Fourth Priest of Amun was found to have in her possession
stolen jewellery and furniture. Gold, silver and bronze, as
well as precious oils, jewellery and fine linen from graves
were discovered in places many kilometres distant from
Thebes, showing the extent of the black market network.

But the mayor of East Thebes received no thanks for
this clean-up. Paser seems never to have recovered his
position, for he disappears from the records soon after
Amenpanufer's trial. Vizier Khaemwese took much of
the credit, as did the man he put in charge of the whole
operation: the mayor of the West Bank, Pawero.

SOURCES
FOR THE
STORY OF
'TOMB ROBBERS'

This story, like that concerning the twins (Chapter Nine), enjoys very full source material. At the end of the 1840s or beginning of the 1850s (the precise date is still unclear), a hoard of papyrus documents, largely consisting of law reports, was discovered by treasure-hunters on the west bank of the Nile near Luxor. As was often the case with discoveries of this kind, involving people whose motives were purely profit-led, the papyri were divided up amongst the finders, and even in some cases torn in two in order to make the most money possible from their sale. During the second half of the nineteenth century they were sold to representatives of various European museums and institutions, avid for Egyptiana and often in stiff competition with one another. Among these establishments was the British Museum, whose collection is almost unrivalled; but only a gradual process of international research and detective work has permitted the full story to come to light.

Among the most important documents relevant to this chapter is the Abbott Papyrus, named after Dr Henry Abbott of Cairo from whom the papyrus in question was purchased for the British Museum in 1857. This papyrus tells the story of the tomb robberies from the point of view of the two local mayors involved, Paser and Pawero, and gives details of their feud over the tomb-robbery investigation. The document is essentially an administrative report of the court case and a narrative of the evidence compiled by the official commission prior to the trial. Some Egyptologists believe that the text is not disinterested, but written primarily from Pawero's point of view. It reveals that the writer had access to Pawero's private correspondence, and certainly Pawero emerges from it better than does Paser. Salient points from the document include the following:

(Day 18): On the orders of Khaemwese and Pawero, a commission is sent to the West Bank of the Nile – i.e., to the Valley of the Kings – to examine the tombs of the kings. They find that all the tombs are intact, except that of Pharaoh Sobekemsaf. On Pawero's orders, arrests are made.

(Day 19): The tomb workers cross the river and celebrate in front of the house of Paser. There follows a brief description of the exchange between Paser and the workmen. Paser claims that Harshire has revealed to him five serious charges against the tomb workers.

(Day 20): Pawero sends a letter to the vizier, which contains a more detailed account of the argument between Paser and the tomb workers, and begins: 'Copy of the document which Pawero … placed before the vizier concerning the words which the Mayor of Thebes spoke to the tomb workers … Deposition of Pawero, Prince of the West: "I met the royal butler … Paser, the Mayor of Thebes, was with him, standing quarrelling with the tomb workers."'

(Day 21): The court sits to try the accused for tomb-robbery. At the trial the vizier denounces Paser for supplying false evidence.

Ancillary documents from the same original hoard were subsequently collected, including the purchase by the British Museum in 1872 of a further papyrus describing the interrogation of Amenpanufer and his being beaten with sticks. This was obtained from Selina Harris, whose father had been a regular visitor to Egypt. Another related papyrus was bought by William Thyssen-Amherst, First Baron Amherst of Hackney. Now in the Pierpoint Morgan Library in New York, it is a fragmentary document that nevertheless contains half a court confession detailing a tomb robbery. The second half of this papyrus was uncovered by the curator of the Egyptian Collection at Brussels, Jean Capart, in 1935, when he was invited to examine a small group of antiquities which King Leopold II had bought in the course of

various trips to Egypt in the previous century. Capart found the document inside a small wooden figure of a scribe called Khay, where it had been placed to increase the value of the statuette. Crucially, it identified Amenpanufer unequivocally as the man who had plundered the tomb of Sobekemsaf, completing the confession in the Amherst-Pierpoint document, additionally recording that he had bribed his way out of prison four years earlier, and his statement that tomb-robbery was wide-spread. This document, the Leopold Papyrus, is now in the Musées Royaux d'Art et d'Histoire in Brussels.

Further papyri from the same hoard, subsequently collected by the British Museum, add to the story, including an

The Abbott Papyrus is a unique document that contains the details of an official commission gathered prior to the trial of Amenpanufer and his accomplices.

account during his trial by one Thewenani, a tomb worker accused of robbery, of his memory of witnessing the execution of Amenpanufer thirty years earlier: 'I saw the punishment which was done to the thieves in the time of Khaemwese. Is it likely that I should go to seek out this death?' Some Egyptologists believe that this memory, still green after thirty years, is evidence of the cruelty of Amenpanufer's end by impalement. Two further fragments, comprising one original, describe the arrest of other villagers a year after Amenpanufer's trial.

MURDER
IN
THE TEMPLE

PSAMTEK I (664–610 BC) was effectively the first king of the Twenty-sixth Dynasty. Ruling from his home city of Saïs in the Delta, he proved to be an able king, gradually freeing himself from the shackles of his Assyrian overlords. He also managed, if not to neutralize, at least to reduce the power of the priesthood of Amun at Thebes, which was in any case weakened after the withdrawal of the Nubian pharaoh, Tanutamani, to his homeland, where he died in 656 BC. (For more on this see pp. 92–3)

It was Psamtek's ambition to reunite the country under him. The power of the priesthood was a major obstacle to this, but because it was powerful, the new pharaoh had to proceed cautiously. As a first step, he dispatched one of his most able and ruthless aides (and cousin by marriage), a man named Petiese, with a detachment of Libyan mercenaries, to the town of Teudjoi (now el-Hiba), in Middle Egypt, on the banks of the Nile, about 250 kilometres south of Saïs, and an important cult-centre of Amun. Teudjoi had a large and wealthy temple, which administered the extensive religious landholdings in the area.

The town, a largely agrarian community owing its existence to temple business, was surprised by Petiese's arrival, in force, with two falcon-ships and 250 foreign soldiers in unfamiliar red leather uniforms. Petiese's orders were to take over the town and the temple in Psamtek's name, and to do it quickly and discreetly: there would be no way of stopping the news reaching Thebes but Psamtek wanted as little force and bloodshed as possible.

As the Greek sailors lowered the masts, Petiese led one platoon of his men straight to the temple, through streets thronged with anxious faces. The rest of the soldiers sealed the town. The temple, an imposing mud-brick and stone structure on a mound abutting one of the city walls, was the largest building in the town by far, and easy to identify. Petiese marched straight in between the high pylons of the gatehouse and into the first courtyard, where the priest and his attendants were waiting. There was a remarkable similarity between the two men: both were elderly, perhaps fifty years old; each had the face of one used to command, with a hawk-nose and a down-turned, imperious mouth. But the priest had only to glance at the fifty tall men with drawn swords who had immediately formed a broad semicircle around his white-robed, shaven-headed companions to realize that

Petiese arrives in Teudjoi with Libyan mercenaries employed by the new regime. As the pharaoh Psamtek I tightens his grip on the kingdom, members of the new regime grab key positions of power across the country.

Petiese with the
young priest his
soldiers had beaten.

resistance would be useless. He would have to accept he
was to be replaced by Petiese himself.

Neither he nor the rest of the priests could do anything to defend themselves. If they wanted to maintain
order and continue to enjoy the privileges they had, as
well as avoid any sacking of the town, they could do
nothing but accept the new state of affairs. Thus, all
was accomplished, as Psamtek would have wished, with
the minimum of violence. There was only one serious
incident. A young priest, not out of his teens, had been
caught making his way down to the river. The soldiers
who'd arrested him had quickly beaten a confession out
of him – the boy wanted to get on board a south-
bound ship to warn Thebes. When they'd heard that,
they'd beaten him up some more, and only the timely
arrival of Petiese had prevented them from finishing
him off. Nevertheless the boy, whom we will call

Samut, had some cruel whiplash marks across his back
and an ugly gash on his face. Petiese had him brought
to his own ship, where he personally washed the
wounds clean. The last thing he wanted was to start his
career as head priest here by antagonising the locals. He
knew it would be an uphill struggle to win over the
priests in any case.

The details of this story come down to us from
Petiese's own great-great-grandson, 150 years after the
event, when the descendant, reduced to poverty, tried to
revive a court case that had been dragging on for most of
that time, over the inheritance of Petiese's title. Even in
Petiese's own time, though, the tale was one more concerned with greed, political manoeuvring and tragedy
than success, whether spiritual or material.

Petiese finished bathing the boy's head and stood up,
leaving him to the doctors with strict instructions that he

RELIGION

Egyptian religious belief was a very different thing from anything we experience today. Ordinary people did not partake in the daily rituals associated with the chief gods, and their humble beliefs were centred more on local deities and the gods of love, protection and childbirth, such as Hathor, Bes and Taweret. They could, however, petition the grander gods, usually by means of a votive stela, which would be offered at a shrine such as those that existed at the workmen's village of Deir el-Medina in the Valley of the Kings.

People believed in the gods that were manifested in the crocodile, the hippo and the snake, and sought to propitiate them. Most gods, even 'sophisticated' ones, had animal attributes, though as time went on they were represented increasingly as animal-headed humans rather than as the animal itself.

It took a long time for the national religion of Ancient Egypt to formalize itself into a more-or-less stable pantheon worshipped consistently everywhere. The main gods, if we exclude the early ones associated with the creation of the world (see p.47), are Osiris and Isis (Osiris presiding over the underworld as the principal god of the dead) and their siblings Nephthys and Set. Set attempts to destroy Osiris but fails; later he engages in a feud which stretches across eternity with Osiris' son Horus. Horus is associated with the sun, and the sun-god has many forms, all of which may be regarded as versions of the same god. Each sun-god had his own 'family' of local importance. Amun was the sun-god of Thebes, his wife was Mut, a vulture-goddess, and their son was Khons, god of the moon. At Memphis, the chief god was Ptah, whose wife was Sekhmet, the lioness-goddess, and their son was Nefertem, god of the blue lotus.

A sun-god was the principal god, whatever name or form he took. But there were other gods equally important to Ancient Egypt, not least in the maintenance of order, since these were not embodiments of primal forces such as day, night, the sun, the river, storms and so on. These were gods who represented concepts or accomplishments. Maat was the goddess of truth; Thoth was the god of writing (and, by extension, administration). Before entering the afterlife, a dead person was

arraigned in the Hall of Truth, having to make before Maat what was called a 'negative confession' – a denial of all the evil deeds one might possibly be charged as having committed over the course of a lifetime. Maat sat in one pan of a set of scales; the deceased's heart was placed in the other. The scales were held by Anubis, while Thoth stood by with his scribe's palette, recording the proceedings. Nearby crouched the beast Ammut – 'The Devourer' – part crocodile, part lion and part hippo – ready to swallow the heart of anyone not deemed fit to pass on to paradise – the Fields of Iaru – which Ancient Egyptians saw as an agricultural heaven, with massively tall grain and unending fecundity.

If the heart was found wanting, Ammut would devour it. This meant that its owner would be transmuted into an evil spirit which would bring bad luck or illness to the living, and be hated and feared by them, existing alone and in constant solitary and reviled struggle with gods and men. If on the other hand the heart did balance, then the deceased could pass into paradise, to be greeted and welcomed by those who had come before, and enjoy for ever lovely music, unlimited food and drink, moderate sunshine and constant breezes: an ideal version of the land left behind.

During the extraordinary sixteen-year reign of the Eighteenth-Dynasty pharaoh Akhenaten, all the gods were abolished in favour of the Aten, a deity who had long existed but who was now elevated to the position of the one and only true god, perceived as the life-giving warmth of the sun's rays. Whether Akhenaten was the first thinker to postulate monotheism, or whether it was a political move to break the power of the priesthood is unclear; but it is interesting that after Akhenaten's early death his name was obliterated and all the gods he had banished returned.

LEFT: Bes, the god of the hearth, protector of the home.

RIGHT: Leopard skin was worn by Sem priests, who assisted at important ceremonies such as the Opening of the Mouth ceremony and funeral rituals. Leopard skin was also worn by some of the high-ranking priests of Amun in the New Kingdom.

be cared for. Then he went back ashore to meet the local mayor, dispose his troops, and arrange for his lodgings until he could have a house built for himself. In the meantime he had his belongings brought ashore. He would send a message to Psamtek back in Saïs by the next royal boat sailing north.

P SAMTEK I WAS AN able diplomat. He knew that he would not be able to destroy the priesthood, but he thought he could see ways of bringing them to heel perhaps without their even realizing it. In 656 BC, learning of the death of Tanutamani the last Nubian pharaoh far to the south, and aware that the power of Assyria was beginning to wane, he decided on his next move.

At last feeling confident enough publicly to declare himself 'King of Upper and Lower Egypt', in his ninth regnal year Psamtek I also secured for his daughter Nitokris (Nitiqret) the succession as God's Wife of Amun at Thebes, arranging for her to be adopted by Amenirdis II, next in line for the position following the present incumbent. Each God's Wife was a virgin, but had to adopt (i.e., nominate) her successor before her own reign was over. The act of Nitokris' adoption is recorded on a great stela originally at Thebes which tells how she set off for that city accompanied by a large flotilla commanded by the General and Chief of the Harbour, Somtutefnakht, who was also ruler of Herakleopolis.

In the royal progress to Thebes, Somtutefnakht acted as Psamtek's viceroy, and the appointment shows the subtlety of Psamtek's diplomacy. To have gone himself might have looked too triumphalist, too like the beginnings of a takeover. But Somtutefnakht was not just anybody: he was married to the pharaoh's sister. Still, he came as a diplomatic visitor only; Psamtek did not want to alarm the local secular administrative chief, Mentuemhat, whom he hoped to win over to his side. This time there would be no crude replacement tactics, as had happened at Teudjoi. And if there should be any danger of Nitokris' being regarded as an unwelcome interloper, she came with a kind of dowry for Amun: vast endowments of land owned by the crown in Upper

Egypt; and boatloads of food, drink and treasure from Lower Egypt. The whole event had all the trappings of a done deal. There seems little doubt that by accepting Nitokris, the College of Amun and the Civil Authorities were also – ultimately – prepared to accept Psamtek: though the length and nature of negotiations that went on before her arrival are unknown.

Psamtek also showed by this strategy that he was prepared to wait, not to rock the boat. He would not have his daughter jump the queue, and during the time she was in Thebes, the priesthood would get used to her, so that when she acceded to the post, her acceptance should be seamless. By this symbolic manifestation of his power at Thebes, Psamtek dealt the death-blow to any further Nubian aspirations in Upper Egypt, not that they were now any more than nominal. By his ninth regnal year, Psamtek had to maintain friendly relations with a still-dangerous Assyria. Nevertheless, he had control of the Delta, and Somtutefnakht, Lord of Herakleopolis, not fifty kilometres north of Teudjoi, was his loyal ally.

We know from the Theban adoption stela that Nitokris was welcomed with enthusiasm at Thebes, and there was no reason for the local bigwigs to think that Psamtek would be any less of an absentee monarch than Tanutamani, who hadn't been there for the last eight years of his life, or the Assyrian king, who never settled in Egypt. Psamtek intended nothing of the sort but was still prepared to wait, even allowing Mentuemhat's son Nesiptah to succeed his father as civil administrator. Nesiptah stayed in office for fifteen or sixteen years. And Nitokris' major-domo, Aba, was not from Saïs, but was a local man.

Patience paid off. In due course Nitokris became the God's Wife, holding the office throughout the remainder of Psamtek I's long and generally peaceful reign, as well as that of his successor, Nekau II. In his first regnal year, 595 BC, Psamtek II, Nekau's successor, had Nitokris adopt his daughter Ankhnesneferibre, as her successor. In this way royal control in the priestly College of Amun was perpetuated: Ankhnesneferibre succeeded in 584 – in the reign of Psamtek II's successor, Apries – and held office for sixty years. She assumed the title First Prophet of Amun on her succession, and this strengthened her authority at Thebes. Eventually she passed her power on in turn to her own adopted daughter.

PETIESE SPENT ELEVEN YEARS in Upper Egypt, doubling the revenues from temple lands to the pharaoh, but the source of his wealth remained Teudjoi. Through his wife, he managed his private house and estates. Most of the priests appeared to have come round to accepting him, even Samut, now a man of thirty. There was no military presence any more; though Petiese was severe, he was not cruel, and he had found that a little leniency in the small things brought people to a quick accommodation with the new regime, as long as they were free to go on with their own lives.

And the rituals continued. In the temple, every morning, as on every morning since time immemorial, the image of the god Amun in his shrine was awakened, bathed, anointed, fed and dressed. Petiese, who,

although a usurper, was no unbeliever (such a concept did not exist), daily performed the rites observed by his predecessor.

The offerings made by Petiese and his fellow-priests ensured the continued goodwill of the god towards his chosen land. But Petiese had a statue to himself erected within the temple precincts. It showed him kneeling with a figure of Amun in front of him, the whole standing on a plinth with an inscription listing his titles. Petiese asserted his right to twenty per cent of the revenue from the temple's estate. This was something new, and a reward for loyalty from the king. All priests enjoyed a percentage of the temple estates, but Petiese was getting *twenty times* more than anyone else. One wonders if Psamtek knew, or if by then Teudjoi was too much of a backwater to matter to him. Either way, Petiese's greed would be his undoing. Although the priests tolerated his rule because they had to, they felt no loyalty, respect or fondness for their chief priest. But,

The sanctuary of the god Amun was the most sacred part of the temple of Teudjoi.

PRIESTLY RITUALS

Religion at the state level was something controlled and run by the class of priests, but they were also administrators and the religion they pursued was tied up in the day-to-day administration of the state, as well as with the early-established and deeply felt belief in and cult of the afterlife. The principal purpose of religious ritual was to underpin the stability and essential immutability of the state.

Priests did not move among the people or use religion as a means of comfort or coercion. The temples were not open to the public and only at times of festivals were the images of the gods paraded for people to see. At the same time, gods could be asked for favours (especially by the pharaoh, who went from being associated with the sun-god to becoming his embodiment on earth), and reproved if they did not grant them.

Priests were obliged to observe certain injunctions, such as wearing white, keeping their bodies and heads shaved and always clean, avoiding women, at least during certain ritual times, and maintaining the daily 'awakening' of the god in his sanctuary, as well as sending him to his rest at night. Priestly offices were highly coveted positions, because of the power and prestige of the temples. There were many categories of priest, and most served the temple part-time, typically for one month in three, while maintaining other professions the rest of the year. All priests were paid a ration of the temple's daily food and drink offerings which the god 'ate' in essence, leaving the real comestibles for his servants. There was no strict rule of celibacy for the priesthood, and though there were no women priests from the time of the New Kingdom, female officiants in the guise of dancers, musicians and 'sealers of doors' were present in the temples.

The daily ritual, alluded to above, was the most important; indeed, it was deemed imperative if the world was to be kept turning. Every morning, the officiating priests would purify themselves, wash with water from the sacred lake (a man-made rectangular pool, and a feature of every major temple), replenish the libation vessels with water from a sacred well, prepare the oblations

and carry them to the temple. Meat offerings were roasted, with spells recited for every step of the cooking process. Then, by torchlight in the dark confines of the temple and clouds of incense, the morning song would be sung and the doors to the inner sanctuary where the image of the god resided would be thrown open to wake the Divine Presence. The chief priest divested the god of yesterday's robes, presented him with myrrh, washed him and anointed him with precious scented oils before dressing him in new clothes and offering him the food that had been prepared. Similar rituals of attention to the god were performed at noon and at dusk; but the dawn ritual was the most important.

Religious offerings were part of a strict daily routine for priests that included shaving their bodies, paring their nails, chewing natron, wearing clean linen garments (no wool) and papyrus sandals (no leather). Priests washed twice a day and twice at night, they couldn't eat fish or beans and they had to re-purify themselves after sex.

even though most of the soldiers were gone, the priests still didn't feel confident enough to rebel.

Through his loyalty to the king and his astute management of Teudjoi's vast estates, Petiese, now in his forties, was one of the richest men in Egypt. In the decade or more since he had taken control, he'd doubled the revenue flowing from the local temples of Amun into the royal coffers, and his seat at Teudjoi had become a minor power-centre of its own.

He had built a huge villa for himself and his family, surrounded by high and stout mud-brick walls, just outside the town. There the north wind could cool the house, while water transferred from the Nile supplied the fishponds and supported a lush garden surrounding the house and its central courtyard. His wife had borne him four children: a daughter, Nitemhe, first, and then, as if in compensation, three sons. Nitemhe was already of marriageable age – the mid-teens – but Petiese hesitated, still unsure of the right husband for her. His relationship with his children was formal rather than warm, but that was his nature, rather than typical of Ancient Egyptians. He saw in his sons his future, the care of his old age, and his life-insurance. But being the man he was, Petiese also wanted to deploy his daughter profitably.

At last, in 649 BC, he settled on his choice for her. The prospective husband, Horodj, son of Peftu-ubasti, was a junior priest who came originally from Thebes. Petiese had met him a year earlier near Oxyrynchus (modern Pemze), where Horodj had been sent to collect taxes from temple lands during the annual cattle count. His ancestors had been high priests at Teudjoi. Like so many professions in Ancient Egypt, although all were open to those with talent and determination enough, priesthoods were usually passed down from father to son. Petiese reasoned that if he married Horodj to Nitemhe, he would establish his *bona fides* for his heirs, much as pharaohs

Priesthoods were hereditary positions.
As Horodj's ancestors had been priests
in Teudjoi, Petiese saw him as a suitable
husband for his daughter.

had done in dynastic marriages. Petiese was a usurper; but if his daughter married a man of the priestly stock of Teudjoi, all would be well in the future. Even so, he did not revert to any other earlier traditions, and kept control of twenty per cent of the estate's income. This would fall in turn to his daughter and son-in-law, who would, together with Petiese's sons, supply the material comforts of his old age.

A contract of marriage was agreed on, and the families of both parties to it gathered in Petiese's mansion at Teudjoi. Nitemhe may not have been keen on the idea of marrying someone so much older, but she had no choice. At least she would be protected materially. The Ancient Egyptians had no religious marriage contract; it was on the simplest level just a question of a man and a woman saying to each other, three times, 'I marry you'; there wasn't even any need of witnesses. In practice, however, and certainly in the case of marriages where considerable property was involved, a contract protecting both parties was drawn up. The next question was the succession, if possible male. Nitemhe was almost certainly still a virgin at the time of her marriage to Horodj. He would probably have been aware, as he took his bride to bed, of the advice of a well-known papyrus of 'Admonitions': 'Love your wife ardently, feed her and clothe her. Fragrant oils are good for her body. Make her happy all her days; for she is like the field that brings profit to its owner.' After the marriage, Horodj took on many of the duties that Petiese had fulfilled for so long.

Petiese was beginning to feel that the time had come for him to hand over power. Without waiting for his daughter to become pregnant, or to see if his first grandchild would be a boy, he seems abruptly to have opted for retirement, summoning Horodj to him out of the blue and announcing, 'I have asked the pharaoh to allow me to leave his service. I am an old man. I am tired. I can't endure any more.' His plan was to leave Teudjoi in Horodj's hands and return to Thebes, where he had property interests, with his wife and sons. Horodj, who had learned from his father-in-law not to trust the local clergy, apparently replied, 'Don't let the priests know this, they are rascals.' But Petiese, secure in his power,

reassured Horodj that if anything went wrong, he had only to send word to the pharaoh.

And so the old administrator made his preparations for departure. This was not the best of news for Nitemhe, recently married, and, as she had discovered, to a man for whom she had no feelings. The thought of being left in this provincial town, with its indifferent people, made her feel completely isolated, and already she felt the cold breath of loneliness on her neck. What would she do without her family?

Her father assured her that her misgivings were unfounded, even though she went so far as to beg him to take her with them. The fact was that Petiese genuinely believed that he was giving his daughter the best possible life: but he was a man who thought that real happiness could only be the associate of material gain.

The morning came for the family to embark. Petiese went aft to the deck-cabin soon after the Greek sailors had cast off, but Nitemhe stood and watched until the boat had disappeared round a broad leftward curve of the Nile. Only her mother seemed to be on deck watching her too; but as the sun shimmered on the water and deceived the eye, Nitemhe could not even be sure of that.

ABOUT SEVENTEEN YEARS passed. In that time it does not appear that Nitemhe saw her family again, although, as river traffic was frequent and efficient, and neither side of the family was lacking in funds, it seems likely that visits were occasionally paid and reciprocated. During those seventeen years Nitemhe grew from a girl of fifteen to a woman of thirty-two, and, after four years bore her husband the first of two sons. Theirs was not the easiest of relationships, and had not Nitemhe brought such benefits with her, Horodj might have divorced her for being barren long before.

Nitemhe must at least have come to an accommodation with her husband, for they were still together and had built up, through their own private house and estates, a sizeable secondary business, which Nitemhe ran. Like most aristocratic ladies, she was in charge of the 'home farm' while her husband looked after the

MAGIC

The Ancient Egyptians lived in a world they believed to be watched over by remote gods, but inhabited by local gods and demons, who had to be accommodated and sometimes mollified, but some of whom could also be controlled to further one's own ends. Most people, except perhaps the most sophisticated, had a firm belief in magic and forms of sorcery.

Magic could be invoked to protect, to heal, to take revenge, to encourage love and to seek wealth. Evil always had to be shown to fail: thus malignant animals, such as male hippos, were always depicted well below their real size in relation to a human – too small to do any real harm. In certain texts, animals whose image had a hieroglyphic function were deliberately left incomplete – a bird without its legs, for example – so that the animal in question could not 'become alive'. And magic played an important role in protecting the dead in their journey from the tomb to the Fields of Iaru.

Amulets were worn by all classes of people to ward off evil in all its forms: the best-known to us are the *ankh* and the *wedjat*, or Eye of Horus. This was Horus' left, or lunar, eye (the other was the sun), which had been torn out or damaged by Set during one of the many conflicts that occurred between the two gods. Thoth restored the eye, thereafter known as the sound eye, which is what *wedjat* means. There were many other amulets, including the scarab, and small gold images of the gods, but all were needed in the unremitting struggle to keep the forces of evil at bay. They were especially important in the hours of darkness, when the sun entered the Boat of Night.

We have seen how the Seven Hathors presided over the birth of a child. Seven was a number charged with significance in Ancient Egypt, and the Seven Hathors had their evil counterparts in the Seven Arrows of Sekhmet, the lioness-headed goddess who in a sense mirrored Hathor but who was not simply evil; one might liken her to the

Hindu goddess Kali. The Seven Arrows, however, always brought evil fortune, often in the form of infectious disease; and they were powerful weapons in the hands of an adept magician. But, under control, they could be used as a defence, for example in warding off the Evil Eye. Many gods were worshipped because the creatures who represented them were in real life animals which had to be propitiated if they were to do you no evil: the scorpion, the jackal and the snake, the hippo, the crocodile. Flat, curved wands of bone or ivory, carved with images of the gods, were used as protective devices.

The Ancient Egyptians believed deeply in the significance and value of names. It was thought that if an enemy knew all your names he could have power over you. Thus, most people had a secret name known only to their closest family.

Cursing or execration was often associated with figurines or red pots. Execration texts would be written on the pots or models, which would then be smashed: foreign and domestic enemies were often subjected to this treatment. Love charms involved a similar sort of sympathetic magic.

The *wedjat* or Eye of Horus. Amulets such as these were worn as protection against evil.

BIRTH AND CHILDHOOD

Pregnancy and birth were surrounded in mystery. The mother and child had to be protected from a variety of demons, particularly female ghosts, and this was effected, among other means, by the use of ivory or bone apotropaic 'wands'. These would be carved with images of the gods and goddesses associated with maternity, the home and childbirth: Taweret, Heket, Bes, Hathor and Horus were the most commonly invoked. Stillbirths were common, as was the death of the mother in childbirth; and infant mortality was high, as children were prey to a number of diseases.

There were practical measures taken at the beginning of life: oil rubbed on to the mother's skin prevented stretch-marks and, it was believed, facilitated pregnancy and there was even a means of predicting what gender your baby would be: 'You shall put wheat and barley into purses of cloth. The woman shall pass her water on [them] every day. If both sprout, she will bear. If the wheat sprouts, she will bear a boy; if the barley sprouts, she will bear a girl. If neither sprouts, she will not bear at all.'

Nursing could take some years. In the 'Instructions of Ani' these words occur: '[Your mother's] breast was in your mouth for three years.' Breast-feeding was believed to be a kind of birth-control, in that as long as a woman was feeding her child, she would not conceive again. Upper-class women employed wet-nurses. Twins are rarely alluded to and may have been regarded as freakish at some stages in Ancient Egyptian history. Male children were more highly prized than female, but all were adored. The pharaoh Akhenaten who had, as far as we know, only daughters, had himself depicted with them and his Chief Wife in scenes of unmistakable domestic bliss.

Children dressed in miniature versions of what adults wore. The male children of the better-off were educated, but girls received little or no formal education. As many middle- and upper-class women ran their own businesses, it is fair to assume that they were at least numerate.

For the middle- and upper-classes, literacy was a vital part of life, and although education was

Amon-Hir-Khopshef, son of Rameses III, with his 'side-lock of youth'. This wall painting is from his tomb in the Valley of the Queens near Thebes.

generally reserved for the upper echelons of society, Ancient Egypt was a meritocracy where men of humble origins (women had less opportunity) could rise to great heights. The army in the later dynasties was a particularly good route to follow.

In wall paintings, children are depicted as little adults, though pre-adolescents are often shown wearing the 'side-lock of youth', a long plait worn usually on the right side of the otherwise shaven head. This side-lock was cut off when a child reached its early teens, and the child then passed immediately into adulthood. The side-lock of youth pervaded all periods of Ancient Egyptian history, though it was commonest during the Old Kingdom.

Children enjoyed toys: examples have survived of balls, whipping-tops, throwsticks, skittles, 'jacks', dolls, toy furniture and animals. Many games are also shown, involving dancing, athletics and acrobatics, as well as leap-frog, tug-of-war, arm-wrestling and juggling. Other games appear to be early versions of blind-man's-buff, cops-and-robbers, grandmother's footsteps and so on.

priests and the management of the temple, its rituals and estates. A great house such as the one run by Nitemhe was a commercial enterprise in itself. A true daughter of her father, she proved herself an able businesswoman. The surplus food and cloth produced by the household was traded up and down the Nile by the family's agents, under Nitemhe's supervision.

Her sons, known to us as Ibi and Karem, were now eleven and thirteen years old. Egyptian children of either sex, as far as we know, had their heads shaved except for a plaited lock of hair dangling from the right-hand side of the skull. Once maturity was reached, as was now the case for Karem, the time came for the cutting-off of the side-lock. This indicated that the child had reached adulthood – puberty was not a transition recognized by the Ancient Egyptians – and had to take his proper place in society, even though his schooling might not yet be over.

The ceremony of removing the lock was domestic and painless. A minor priest came to the house and muttered a few formulaic incantations, while Nitemhe took a clean bronze knife and cut the lock off close to the skull. A barber stood ready to shave the remaining tussock of hair clean to the scalp. Karem would then be ready for his first wig, which was another sign of boyhood passing.

Another rite of passage, however, would then face Karem for, at the time, the circumcision of boys was current in local society. Certainly the sons of priests seem to have been circumcised as a matter of course. A junior priest would briefly anoint the boy's penis with cedar oil and withdraw, as the senior officiant severed the foreskin with a flint knife. The bleeding skin would then be quickly stanched with linen bandages soaked in honey.

The boy's coming of age and the changed political situation in Teudjoi were the twin triggers that led the priests to take action against the family of Petiese. The balance of power was shifting. Psamtek's patience had paid off, and years of diplomacy, coupled with the acceptance of his daughter Nitokris as God's Wife of Amun, had led to a solid alliance between Thebes and Saïs. But this undermined the privileges Petiese's family enjoyed at Teudjoi. Here, Psamtek was prepared to make concessions. This was not a major centre of power, and the

Soon after they reached puberty, boys were considered men. There was no concept of adolescence: rather, they were expected to be grown-up and full members of society.

pharaoh was prepared to see the priests take back their power there if they wished to.

But all this was sub rosa. In the meantime, when not carrying out their duties in the temple, the priests managed the estate and the ancillary royal estates held in the pharaoh's name. The majority of the harvest was collected by the temple and then redistributed: one part to the court; one part to the temple for its own maintenance and for the income of its priests. In Ancient Egyptian society at this time, the temple in general was the clearing-house for the country's wealth. Some land was leased out to peasant-farmers, who paid one third of their harvest as rent; priests also had their own tax-free plots, carved out of the temple lands. There were at Teudjoi four shifts of twenty priests, each shift on duty at the temple for three months at a time. Outside their periods of duty, they had secular work: they were farmers, or administrators, or businessmen. But the temple held them together.

By the thirty-seventh year of Psamtek I's fifty-four-year-sovereignty, the pharaoh had reached a binding accommodation at long last with the priesthood at Thebes. The priests at Teudjoi, having bided their time for so long, now saw no need to remain under the control of Petiese's family. Meanwhile, Horodj and his family seemed to be blissfully unaware of the changing political focus which was leading to an erosion of their power. They continued to lord it over the people of Teudjoi. Every year at harvest time, the temple contin-

muning with the gods. But contact with the locals, except at the official level, was minimal.

THE TIME FOR HARVEST had come around once more, and, as was customary, Nitemhe officiated at the feast of Renenutet, the cobra-headed goddess of plenty, the Lady of the Fertile Fields, who ensured an abundant harvest, and wealth for the year ahead. She was the snake who destroyed the pests that threatened the crops: 'Renenutet is in all things. Every-

RIGHT: Offerings to gods not only took place in the great temples. Family houses had their own domestic shrines in courtyards.

ued to collect all the produce of the land around the city, and every year the family of Horodj, by far the richest in the district, continued to take their twenty per cent share. The family seems to have been unaware of or indifferent to the resentment which they increasingly aroused, entertaining and generally living the high life. Karem had a team of horses and a chariot, and Ibi, the younger son, was already being trained to ride. The food on the table at Horodj's home was of the best quality; after all, food and drink were one more way of com-

thing will be brought forth by the million for everybody in whose granary there had been dearth. The land of Egypt is beginning to stir again, the banks are shining wonderfully. Wealth and well-being dwell with them, as it has been before.'

Fertility was also about children, who were part of the abundance of nature, and the goddess Renenutet was their special protector. At her annual feast, children played a special role and assisted in taking down the old corn dolly that had been placed over the granary

ABOVE: Priests were employed at temples to care for the cult statue of the deity. The god was thought to have daily needs for clothing and food, which it was the priest's job to tend to.

to protect it during the past year and replacing it with a new one. The old one was then thrown on to a fire, taking with it, as it was consumed by the flames, all the evil and bad luck it had absorbed during the last twelve months.

There was another snake in the Egyptian cosmos: Apophis, the destroyer. Apophis was a great serpent who lived in darkness and daily tried to devour the Boat of the Sun at sunrise and sunset, when the skies were stained red by the blood of the defeated reptile. The priests at Teudjoi may well have invoked Apophis to bring down the overweening sun of the house of Petiese. Execration rituals existed, by which a model of the enemy could be smashed or buried or otherwise cursed. Many spells of this nature have survived, of which the following is an example:

> This spell is to be recited over an image of Apophis drawn on a new sheet of papyrus in green ink, and over a figure of Apophis in red wax. See! His name is inscribed on it in green ink ... I have overthrown all the enemies of pharaoh from all their seats in every place where they are. See! Their names are written on their breasts, having been made of wax, and also bound with bonds of black rope. Spit upon

them! To be trampled with the left foot, to be fallen with the spear and knife! To be placed on the fire in the melting-furnace of the coppersmiths ...

Not long afterwards, the priesthood of the Temple of Amun at Teudjoi decided that at last it was time to take action to throw off these secular and usurping overlords who had for so long deprived them of their power and one-fifth of their income. Perhaps it was witnessing the coming-of-age of Karem, and with it the prospect of another generation of oppressors, that spurred them into action, or the recognition that Petiese's power in Teudjoi had been weakened by the strengthening of bonds between Thebes and Saïs. Either way, the traditional priesthood had reached a point of no return: they would take back what was rightfully theirs, if they could. It would be a matter for history to judge if they had chosen their moment wisely or not.

Samut was one of the ringleaders; and once the matter had been discussed, the decision to take action met with no dissent. When a plan had been agreed on, it was set in motion without delay. Samut engaged the services of three young priests, who were prepared to arm themselves with clubs and set up an ambush in the corn store.

RIGHT AND OPPOSITE: Corn mummies were ritual figures stuffed with a mixture of earth, sand and barley. For the Egyptians, they represented the annual cycle of renewal and rebirth, and were associated with Osiris – the god of resurrection. The destruction of the previous year's corn mummy was thought to bring about a good crop in the coming harvest.

That same night, perhaps aware that something might be afoot to threaten her children, Nitemhe invoked a spell and drew a circle round the beds of her sons with a wand dedicated to Renenutet. The Ancient Egyptians believed that the time of sleeping left them vulnerable; but there were spells to ward off the demons who might pour poison into sleepers' ears. Children were believed to be the most open to attack from other demons who might come to kiss, steal or kill them. Circles drawn round the bed with a connected charm were designed to protect the sleeper.

The harvest wasn't yet completely gathered, and

LEFT: The Temple of Amun in Teudjoi. Temples were not only religious centres: they were the treasuries of Egypt and the headquarters of administration and justice.

BELOW: The priests of Teudjoi conspire to murder the grandsons of Petiese.

son to go to the temple in his father's absence and fulfil the task. It was, after all, a formality, and had been for more than a quarter of a century.

So it was that, on a morning soon after, Horodj went down to the quay and boarded his private boat to cross to the estates on the other bank. In the meantime, the chief steward of his house had organized five donkeys, bearing empty panniers and under the command of a houseboy, to accompany Karem and Ibi up to the temple to collect what was their due.

They made an early start to avoid the worst of the sun, and despite the recalcitrance of one stubborn ass, they reached the courtyard of the temple by the second hour of daylight. Karem was nervous, very conscious of the responsibility placed on him, and yet still feeling very much like a child. Some of these priests had been his tutors, after all, and had not been afraid, on occasion, of giving him a good thrashing if he'd neglected his lessons. That morning, the place seemed much quieter than

Horodj still had to claim the remainder of his share. Once it was ready to collect, however, he found that he had pressing business in the neighbouring villages of the estate, on the other side of the Nile. Thinking that the responsibility of making the collection would be a good new test of manhood for Karem, he instructed his older

usual, though the boys noticed a pile of sacks of grain apparently stacked ready for them in one corner.

Leaving the donkeys with the houseboy near the gate of the courtyard, they approached the sacks uncertainly, calling out as they went. They were close to the pile when Samut emerged from the colonnade behind them, in company with half-a-dozen other priests. Samut had always struck fear into the boys: he was a strict teacher and his scarred face was the stuff of nightmares in their childhood. Summoning up his courage, Karem asked where the grain was that was his family's due. Samut smiled grimly, and answered that they could collect it as soon as their own dues had been paid. He gave a signal with his hand and from behind the sacks the three young priests emerged, armed with their clubs. Hemmed in, the boys could do nothing but run towards the inner confines of the temple, with their assailants in pursuit. Samut and his companions followed, ignoring the houseboy who, hastily tethering the donkeys, followed his masters at a discreet distance.

Karem and Ibi must have known there was no way out of this trap, but they fled instinctively. Now at last they found themselves cornered before the sanctuary of the god himself. Short of dodging past their pursuers and finding their way back to the first courtyard, they had no hope. Ibi was beginning to whimper. Karem took his hand and drew the small bronze dagger at his side. If he was now deemed to be a man, he would at least die like one. The three priests closed in while, from a distance, Samut and the others watched. The first blow knocked the dagger from Karem's hand. The second caught Ibi on the side of the head. Then the clubs fell thick and fast.

It took no more than three minutes to send the boys to the Boat of Night. Unobserved behind a lotus-column, the houseboy watched only for the first thirty seconds before fleeing out of the temple and down the hill, back to his master's house, to raise the alarm.

Hardly had the houseboy arrived back at the family mansion to report to the steward what had happened than orders were given to close the gates and barricade

'Then the young priests drew out their staves from the grain and surrounded the two sons of Horodj. They fled into the temple, but the priests ran after them. They caught up with them at the entrance to the shrine of Amun, and beat them to death.'
From Rylands Papyrus IX.

Petiese arrives
to enforce the
Pharaoh's will.

them. Those house servants trained to bear arms manned the walls, while another houseboy was sent down to the river to take a boat across and carry word to Horodj. Nitemhe sat with her elbows on her knees, put her knuckles in her mouth, and rocked, comforted by her children's nurse, the midwife who had brought them into the world.

It did not take long for word to reach Horodj, and he immediately drew the worst conclusion possible from the tale the boy told him. Quickly he ordered his men to get his boat ready, and sent word to the local Chief of Police who deployed a detachment of soldiers. By nightfall a police guard was set up around Horodj's house, but he himself did not return. Instead, he had made for Thebes, fearful for his own life, perhaps, or aware that he could exert no power over the priests, aiming to alert his father-in-law, who could command greater influence. But it was a round trip of six days.

While her husband was away, Nitemhe, barricaded inside her house and not knowing what the next move from the temple would be, heard that her sons were definitely dead. A stalemate seems to have existed during Horodj's absence, the priests taking no further action and the police content to secure the mansion without doing anything more. But several days later Horodj returned, bringing with him a detachment of soldiers and his father-in-law, now well struck in years, but still a commanding presence.

Petiese immediately took matters in hand, ordering a search of the temple, which the police, backed by the soldiers, duly carried out on his authority. It didn't take long for them to round up the three murderers, together

with Samut and his wife and son, and other renegade priests who had fled the temple, but only as far as their estates nearby. Why there had been such a long stand-off is unexplained: perhaps the priests had sent their own delegation to Thebes, and had been waiting for orders concerning how to proceed. Either way, Petiese was back in command at Teudjoi now.

The Ancient Egyptians believed that the act of murder was an offence against the natural order. It was punishable by death, on the command of the pharaoh. A search of the temple precincts soon turned up the bodies of the two boys, which had been thrown into a disused storeroom. Petiese had them brought out on wooden litters, wrapped in linen to deter the swarms of flies. The linen was impregnated with scented oil to disguise the smell of rotting flesh. The litters were immediately taken down to

the river's edge, where a Place of Embalming had been erected. The embalmers set to work, their nostrils stuffed with scented linen pads, and with linen bandages over their mouths.

Meanwhile the priests were brought into the main courtyard of the temple, to stand before a tribunal headed by Petiese. The priests knelt before him, knowing that it was within his power to see all of them executed. On the other hand, they knew that if Petiese did not show mercy, that would scarcely help his master the pharaoh's political cause in Thebes. Formally, therefore, they begged Petiese for clemency.

Petiese, a veteran politician, knew exactly what he must do. Trying to avoid his daughter's and his son-in-law's faces, and banishing from his heart all personal consideration of what he had lost in terms of descen-

his power was gone: 'This man put his heart to set this city in the pharaoh's service. This tablet records all his good deeds and his priestly offices. He who harms it will lose *his* sons, his flesh will burn, and his name will be lost for eternity.'

Soon afterwards, Petiese made preparations to return to Thebes. Despite her pleas, he once again refused to take his daughter with him, and left her with her husband in their empty mansion at Teudjoi, to continue their uneasy relationship with the priests of the temple there.

Petiese was a faithful servant of his king, who was con-

LEFT: The Chief of Police was a paramilitary office, and he could deploy soldiers to help catch the murderers.

dants, he listened to their plea calmly, and then gave his judgement.

> The good deeds that I have done in this town, I did not do for your fathers, but for Amun. These priests who killed my boys, I have the right to demand that justice be done. But … with the blessing of Amun, I will let them go. I will not cause a thing to be done to you on account of something that is past … Is it right to ask Amun to kill these priests and let the town be destroyed?

Nitemhe collapsed in tears in her husband's arms, but even Horodj recognized the expediency of Petiese's action. On the national level, the death of his sons was the result of a local feud that could not be allowed to undermine the settlement reached between Saïs and Thebes.

The boys received a quiet funeral, though all honours and rights were accorded them; and Petiese had a further inscription cut into the base of his statue in the temple, emphasizing his family's right to their twenty per cent of Teudjoi's estates, and adding a warning – a final vainglorious action, highly characteristic but showing how

demning his family to a living hell. He believed that his steadfast loyalty to the king would ensure the security of his family at Teudjoi forever; but he was too blinkered or too unimaginative to see that fidelity is a disposable asset in the game of power. Petiese died before the end of the reign of Psamtek I. His sons continued to serve the throne throughout the Twenty-sixth Dynasty.

We don't know the ultimate fate of Horodj and Nitemhe: Petiese's eldest son became head priest at Teudjoi; but, within another generation, the priests there once more rose against the patrician's family, a revolt that over

the next 150 years led to conflict, protracted lawsuits, and ultimate ruin, both for the city and for Petiese's heirs. Petiese's statue was eventually defaced and thrown down into the Nile, and his great-great-grandson, reduced to poverty, finally committed to paper the whole bitter story of his family's rise and fall. By the time he wrote it, the Persians had invaded Egypt, and the rule of the country by true natives of the land was over forever. The priesthood of Amun, however, retained its wealth and power for another 300 years.

LEFT: The priests kneel before Petiese, begging for his mercy. Libyan mercenaries, known as the Machimoi, stand guard around them. Answerable to the mayor, they maintained order by bringing guilty parties to justice, and were not viewed as a hostile body but as guardians and protectors of the community.

SOURCES
FOR THE
STORY OF
'MURDER IN
THE TEMPLE'

This story is to be found in one of nine texts discovered at el-Hiba (the ancient town of Teudjoi), on the eastern bank of the Nile in Middle Egypt. It was purchased locally in 1898 by the traveller and explorer Lord Crawford, and found its way into the John Rylands Library in Manchester in 1908. Rylands Papyrus IX is almost the only text we have referring to events in the Saïte period, named after the Twenty-sixth Dynasty (*c.* 664–525 BC), which came from Saïs in the Western Delta. The dynasty ushered in an important phase of regeneration, both culturally and economically. Culturally it harked back to the glories of the Old and Middle Kingdoms one thousand years earlier and more, but reinterpreted the old aesthetics in a way similar to that in which the artists of the Renaissance reinterpreted those of Ancient Greece and Rome. It was a time of general peace and prosperity, though Egypt had by then entered the twilight of her glory years. The story might be better known were it not for the fact that it was originally written in demotic, a form of contemporary business shorthand and difficult to decipher, though published as early as 1909 by the scholar Francis Llewellyn Griffith.

The theme of 'Murder In The Temple' is especially interesting in that the story is told from the point of view of one family. It also provides details of everyday domestic life of the period which appear almost nowhere else. From Papyrus IX we also learn much about the way temples were managed, while the story, of wrongdoing, murder, diplomacy and – if read in its entirety – enormously complex litigation, plot and

counterplot over a period of about 150 years, gives a unique insight into the day-to-day social politics of the time. Rylands IX, or The Petition of Petiese, as it is also known, has been called the single most informative secular text to come down from Ancient Egypt. Ignoring the great affairs of state, it is essentially a family saga in which greed, ambition, offence and petty revolution trigger murder, and following murder an inordinately long lawsuit ensues, which could almost have been penned by Dickens.

The whole story covers a period of time between about 660–413 BC, but the most dramatic events took place in 633 BC. These actions, recounted in this chapter, triggered a long-running feud and battle for legal rights to a percentage of the income created by the temple of Teudjoi. The petition itself begins its story in 513 BC, when a priest called Ahmose appeared in the then down-at-heel provincial backwater of Teudjoi (originally the town had owed its importance to being a strategic site on the river Nile, but those times were long gone). Ahmose had come to claim the percentage due to him from the temple, the right to which came with his office, though he did not live in Teudjoi. But the temple was as run-down as the town, and there was no money to pay the absentee priest. Seeking an explanation, Ahmose interrogated the temple scribe, Petiese, an old man (at seventy, truly ancient for the period), whose rambling account, partly based on memory and partly on family archives, forms the basis of Rylands IX. The story is further complicated by the fact that several family members down the years were also called

Rylands Papyrus IX, which has come to be known as the 'Petition of Petiese'. This important document charts the fortunes of a family with close links to the temple at Teudjoi.

Petiese, and the 'narrator' himself was sometimes inclined to gloss over elements in the story unfavourable to his side of the argument.

Given that the story has its origins at the beginning of the reign of King Psamtek I in about 660 BC, when the first Petiese, great-great-grandfather of the narrator of the petition, turned the fortunes of the temple of Teudjoi round and was rewarded with a share of its profits in perpetuity, subsequent complications are better imagined than described. There is,

however, no denying the stark details surrounding the murder of the grandsons of the original Petiese, whose story, along with that of his daughter and her husband, unfolds here, in the thirty-first year of the reign of Pharaoh Psamtek.

The nub of the dispute lay in the enmity that had grown between the temple priests and the Petiese family. The family had originally enjoyed an income from the temple through offices held in it; when these offices, appointed by the priests, were no longer held by family members (so the

priests argued) the payments should lapse. The family did not agree. However a grey legal area was created when the priests attempted to extend their veto of payment to dues that legitimately belonged to the family, irrespective of the family's tenure of temple offices.

The names of the principal family characters in this chapter are genuine; those of the murdered boys and the priests have been added for ease of following the narrative, and are not named in the original text.

THE
TWINS

THE TRUE PHARAONIC PERIOD had long been over by the time Alexander the Great, aged twenty-four, occupied Egypt in 332 BC, following his successful campaigns against Persia and in Syria-Palestine. The Egyptians, who had for many years endured a succession of Persian rulers, welcomed him as a liberator, and in turn he was careful to earn their trust by respecting their traditions and worshipping their gods, sacrificing to the sacred Apis Bull at Memphis and making a long pilgrimage to consult the Oracle of Amun at the Siwa Oasis, claiming that Amun was his divine father. In return, the still influential priesthood supplied the useful doctrine that the last native king of Egypt, Nectanebo II, who died in 343 BC, had magically taken the form of a snake to impregnate Alexander's mother, the extremely wilful Olympias. This impregnation by a god (for that was what the pharaoh was) authenticated Alexander's claim to the Golden Throne.

In 331 BC, the new pharaoh founded the city of Alexandria on the Mediterranean coast on the western side of the Delta. The city, providing a port for traffic with Greece, was from the outset Hellenistic, both politically and culturally, and would retain its separate identity through the period of Greek rule that was to follow. The shepherds who feature in Alexandrian poetry are from Arcadia, Cos, or Sicily – but never from North Africa.

Alexander was also careful, however, to associate himself with building programmes involving Egyptian temples. The Ptolemaic dynasty that was to follow him constructed some of the greatest and most traditional-looking Egyptian temples to have survived. The colonizers were not slow to adopt local achievements which they recognized as better than their own – for instance, the calendar – though generally they were convinced of their own innate superiority. In turn, Macedonians, Athenians, Alexandrians, Cretans and even Thracians were all lumped together and generally disliked as 'Greeks' by the Egyptians.

Alexander left Egypt the same year, 331 BC, to pursue his conquest of Persia and, beyond it, the whole of the Middle East and western India, marrying Roxana, a princess of Sogdiana whom he had taken prisoner, and

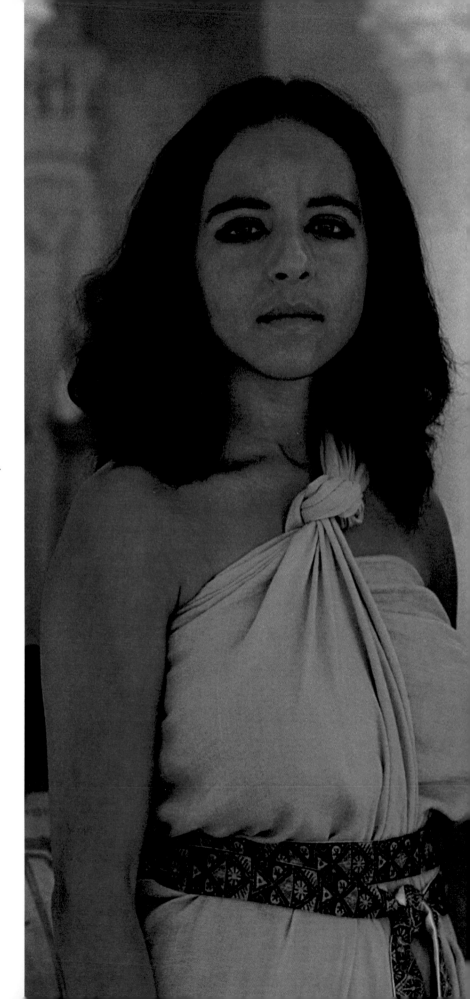

dying in Babylon on his return journey, in 323 BC, four months short of his thirty-third birthday.

On his death, the huge empire was divided between his chief generals or *strategoi*, with Ptolemy taking Egypt. To begin with these men ruled as *satraps*, or governors, on behalf of Alexander's half-brother, Philip Arrhidaeus, reputedly a half-wit, and the dead emperor's young son by Roxana, also Alexander. Ptolemy established his legitimacy with the Egyptians by having Alexander's body brought back to Egypt: there, he performed the traditional rites that a successor undertook concerning his immediate predecessor – by burying him, as Horus had buried Osiris.

Without the cohesive force of Alexander the Great, those who shared his legacy could not live quietly with one another. In 317 BC, Olympias had Philip Arrhidaeus murdered, and both Alexander's widow, Roxana, and son, Alexander, were killed sometime before 305 BC. With the heirs dead, Ptolemy saw his chance of taking the crown of Egypt for himself, and did so by proposing to Alexander's last living relative, a sister called Kleopatra. On her way to Egypt she was murdered by Antigonos, *satrap* of Asia Minor.

With every member of the House of Alexander dead, one-by-one the generals or their heirs declared themselves king of the country they had held guardianship over. Ptolemy did so in 305 BC, taking the name Soter, or Saviour. He thus founded the next dynasty, which was to rule Egypt for nearly 300 years. He himself was a solid and able ruler, reaching the throne in late middle life and abdicating in favour of his son on the grounds of age when he reached eighty in 285 BC. His successors, whose story is more fully covered in Chapter Five, were, by and large, a bloody line, whose habit of in-breeding must have contributed to its overall degeneracy.

In 164 BC, when the tale of the twin girls Tages and

Tages (left in picture) and Taous were twins appointed to mourn for the dead Apis Bull. They were chosen as the embodiment of the sister goddesses Isis and Nephthys, and would devote themselves to the service of the Apis Bull until the death of its successor.

Taous begins, an uneasy alliance ruled, a triumvirate composed of Ptolemy VI Philometor, his sister-wife, Kleopatra II, and his brother, Ptolemy Euergetes II. It was to Philometor and Kleopatra that the twins made the petition, after great wrong had been done them, from which their story is known.

The country was then full of Greek immigrants – the population of Alexandria alone was 300,000 – who lorded it over the local inhabitants. They intermarried with the local population to some extent, especially in the case of retired Greek military personnel who had been given tracts of farmland by the administration as a reward for their service. But they made little attempt to understand the local culture, and on the whole despised it. They were in turn largely disliked by the locals, who reviled them behind their backs, though the Egyptians seemed powerless, despite occasional rebellions, to dislodge them. Some Egyptians, however, sought to better themselves by associating with the dominant nation.

In 164 BC Tages and Taous were probably around thirteen or fourteen years old – not yet married, but easily of marriageable age. They lived in the ancient capital of Memphis with their parents, both Egyptian, Argynoutis and Nephoris, and their older half-brother, Pakhrates, Nephoris' son from a previous marriage, and by all accounts an unappealing character. In 164, Nephoris had been married to Argynoutis for fifteen years. He was prosperous, owning a number of properties in and around the 3000-year-old city, and took good care of his family. Nevertheless his wife and daughters supplemented the domestic income by weaving linen cloth. The girls seemed to have nothing to fear for their future: their father was wealthy enough to be able to provide them with dowries, and their older half-brother, as a male, had enjoyed the privilege of education and would be able to provide for himself. He would doubtless stand to inherit a share of Argynoutis' property, and either live on the income it yielded, or pursue a career in business or the army. We don't know the level of his education, but it is unlikely that he would have become a scribe because that profession – effectively the civil

service of Ancient Egypt – was usually one that passed from father to son.

Nephoris had made a good second marriage, but she was discontented with her lot, bullying Argynoutis' faithful female housekeeper, and showing a marked preference for her son over her daughters. She found that

Apollonios, Ptolemaios' younger brother, who helped protect the twins.

Argynoutis spoilt the girls, for example, with gifts of gold bangles, and sought to keep them in check, especially the livelier and more extrovert – and potentially rebellious – Taous. She was also keenly aware of the better-dressed and generally superior Greek population of the town, and envied them their way of living. They were the new colonials, effectively the ruling class, and dominated the court, the administration and the army.

Every so often Nephoris would order the girls to pile up the bales of linen cloth they had produced so that Pakhrates could load them onto the family donkey. All four of them – mother, son and two daughters – would then set off for the market. Money, in the form of the drachma, was now current in Egypt, at least in the cities where the Greeks held sway, having replaced the old barter system; but prices still had to be settled by bargaining, and although Nephoris had a favourite mer-

chant with whom she dealt, she would not have been above deserting him for another if she failed to agree a price with him. But the quality of the girls' work was good, and so there was rarely a dispute.

However, apart from their uneasy relationship with their mother, and the fact that from time to time Nephoris found it necessary to upbraid Taous for 'dressing up' in swathes of linen destined for sale, there seemed to be few clouds over the life of the little family.

Nephoris' envy and ambition had, however, got the better of her. She had met a Greek soldier called Philippos and formed a liaison with him. He was a robust veteran of about her age, possibly retired with a plot of land, who nevertheless saw in the wealthy and still relatively young woman – though thirty in those days would have seemed far older than it does today – a chance to better himself. As is often the case in colonial societies, in Egypt at the

Divorce was common practice in Ancient Egypt but, as an adulteress, Nephoris stood to lose everything.

FASHION

Garments worn by the Ancient Egyptians have survived in some quantity, as they formed part of the grave-goods, as well as lengths of material stored in carefully folded piles. But garments alone account for only part of the wardrobe which has been preserved. As well as headscarves, robes, tunics, underwear and sandals, the Egyptians wore gloves and even socks on occasion, and this is not to speak of jewellery, worn by both men and women, wigs, and make-up and scents, also used by both sexes.

Linen was the basic cloth, and it was manufactured from as early a date as 5000 BC. The oldest dress known in the world was discovered in a box of rags in the Petrie Museum, London, in 1977 (old clothes were sometimes used as mummy-wrapping) and dates from the First Dynasty.

There were four grades of linen: the cheapest, ordinary everyday type, up to material which only the rich could afford: this was made from flax harvested when the stems were still very young. Some fabrics have been found made from hemp, grass and reeds, and woollen garments were known from at least 3000 BC. Flax could be dyed after the spinning process, and the most common colours were blue, derived from indigotin, red, derived from madder and henna, yellow, from safflower, and green, which came from indigotin doubled-dyed with safflower. Purple and brown were results of other double-dying mixtures.

Clothes were made up by skilled tailors, and embroiderers worked on the finest clothes. They had to be durable, for the Egyptians were a very clean people and had their clothes washed frequently, especially underwear – an essential activity in a hot climate. Examples of clothing have been found bearing either inked or embroidered laundry-marks, and there was a Guild of Washermen, some of whose 3000-year-old laundry lists have survived.

There were two basic kinds of clothing: shaped and wrap-around. The former might take the simple forms of triangles or rectangles, sewn down some or all the edges and fastened with string ties.

ABOVE: This ancient tunic, designed to be worn by a woman, is nearly 5000 years old, probably the oldest surviving article of clothing in the world. It is now in the Petrie Museum, London.

RIGHT: Beauty and cleanliness were important to men and women, and evidence of both manicures and pedicures has been discovered depicted in bas-relief carvings.

One type of dress was made like this, as were loincloths and bag-tunics (a sort of early sack-dress). The latter sort of clothing comprised kilts, skirts, some dresses, cloaks and shawls. The fundamental form of clothing was common to all classes: the rich and the nobility wore garments of the finest linen, however, and owned far more of them. Poor people often wore nothing but a simple kilt or loincloth. Full-length unisex linen garments were also worn, not unlike the modern *djallebiyeh*, whose movement with the wearer encouraged cooling air to circulate.

In Tutankhamun's tomb twenty pairs of gloves were found, some decorated with tapestry. A fragment of leather gauntlet was found in the tomb of Tuthmosis IV. Four pairs of socks were also discovered with Tutankhamun, with a gap between the big toe and the others to fit his sandals. They were of the simple 'flip-flop' type, but the materials used varied from palm-leaf or grass, to papyrus or leather, up to the gold ceremonial sandals worn by the king or queen. Luxurious examples were delicately embroidered or sewn with beads. People removed their sandals in the presence of royalty. Shoes made their appearance in the New Kingdom and were probably an imported idea from the Kingdom of Mitanni, between the Tigris and Euphrates rivers (roughly modern Syria), where they were commonly worn.

Headcloths were worn by ordinary people to protect themselves from the sun, or during messy work such as winnowing. The king is often depicted wearing the formal *nemes*, a large, often striped cover for the head, the best-known example of which appears on the golden mummy-mask of Tutankhamun. Ornate wigs were customarily worn by well-to-do men and women alike. They had the practical purpose of protecting the head and neck from the sun, which the upper classes generally avoided as much as they could. Apart from a brief period in the Fourth Dynasty, and then again during the Late Period, beards were not only unfashionable but a source of revulsion – the kind of thing that signified an uncivilized 'foreigner'.

ABOVE: A simple *nemes* (headcloth), was worn by peasants and farmers for protection from the sun.

time there were many more Greek men than women, and marriages between Greek males and Egyptian females were far commoner than the other way round.

Nephoris and Philippos each had something to give the other, but before they could marry and thereby set the seal on whatever pecuniary bargain they had in mind, a couple of obstacles stood in their way, which they seem to have regarded with as much coldness as ruthlessness.

The first, of course, was Argynoutis. Divorce in Ancient Egypt was generally straightforward and carried no stigma for either party, although in the case of infidelity, especially in earlier times, the woman might expect a harsher punishment than the man. Infertility would have been another common reason for divorce. As marriage was entered into as a private agreement, without official sanction, so it was with divorce; but it was often the case, especially when a marriage between people of property was concerned, that a legal document of some kind was drawn up protecting the property rights either of the injured spouse, the children, or both. It seems clear that Nephoris and Philippos would not have taken the drastic steps they did if a straightforward divorce, followed by a splitting of the property, would have achieved their aim. It may simply have been that Nephoris wanted to have everything; or that without everything Philippos would not have been interested in her. Equally, it may have been that if the adultery had been uncovered, Nephoris would have stood to lose not only her share of the family property, but her original dowry and her reputation as well; and it is clear that Nephoris was sufficiently shallow and vicious to sacrifice everything to her standing and her material well-being. The second obstacle was the twin-girls, who would soon be needing a dowry each, thereby making serious inroads into the family capital.

We do not know exactly how long Nephoris and Philippos had been together before they concocted their callous and simple strategy.

Ancient Egypt was suffused with magic and spells, and incantations and occult recipes existed for every eventuality. There were plenty connected with the art of love,

and many which had to do with getting rid of an unwanted partner: 'Take a mouse and drown it in some water, then make the man drink the water. It will make

him blind in both eyes. Grind the body up with food, and make the man eat it. He will swell up and die.'

But it seems that Nephoris was no believer in the supernatural: she preferred tried and trusted resolutions for the problems which stood in her way. The lovers must have laid their plans and then awaited their opportunity.

Argynoutis liked an occasional drink with a friend. They would sit outside on a clay bench drinking wine from clay cups. On the night that was to prove so fateful

Argynoutis fights for his life with Philippos, the Greek soldier who stood to gain a lot of money by removing him and marrying his wealthy widow.

to him, Argynoutis said goodbye to his friend after perhaps one or two cups too many, and made his way back into the courtyard of his house. The Ancient Egyptians were poor at security, or perhaps they did not generally need it. Doors were usually secured simply with a wooden peg or a bolt. Philippos, who had been lying in wait, quietly entered the courtyard behind Argynoutis, without drawing attention to himself.

The girls got up to greet their slightly tipsy father; but hardly had he entered the house than there was a noise

from the courtyard – it sounded as if someone had knocked over a water jar.

After a moment's hesitation, Argynoutis returned to the courtyard to investigate the noise; it was after all just possible that some animal had created the disturbance. A rudimentary police force existed – the Medjays – but they did not operate regular patrols, nor was there any means of contacting them in an emergency. Argynoutis, who was certainly not backed up by his step-son, was on his own.

As soon as he saw Argynoutis, Philippos lunged towards

him with his drawn sword, but it was dark and despite the wine he'd drunk, the older man was alert enough to side-step his assailant. But the noise and the cries of fear and rage brought the rest of the family out into the courtyard. We cannot speak of Pakhrates' thoughts, but the girls would have been panic-stricken and the mother, no doubt, furious that her lover had failed to make a clean killing and a discreet escape. By now Philippos had succeeded in stabbing Argynoutis in the shoulder, causing

him to flee towards the door to the street. Badly wounded, shocked and frightened, the old man tried to make his escape. There was no one about, and if he cried out for help, no one heard him. If the family lived in one of the richer districts, where the houses stood in their own compounds and were widely spaced apart, this is more than likely to have been the case. Down the street Argynoutis ran, with Philippos now in hot pursuit. He had to finish the job, or everything would be lost.

Tages and Taous would have followed their father, but their mother barred the courtyard door against them, perhaps telling them that such an action would be too dangerous. Perhaps Pakhrates made a show of following, since, as will appear later, the twins, to their ultimate misery, either never distrusted him, or were too gullible and forgiving.

Meanwhile their father had run blindly down a street that led only to the river. He stood at the edge of the black water, well aware of the crocodiles that still inhabited it in large numbers. Gasping for breath and clutching his shoulder, he turned to see Philippos advancing upon him, his sword raised. Preferring the slim chance of life to certain death, he threw himself off the embankment into the Nile.

Philippos was for a moment struck by panic himself: what if the old man got away? As he advanced to the spot where Argynoutis had vanished, and peered out into the darkness, he heard a frantic splashing – then silence. He waited for a moment to be sure, and then sheathed his sword, a smile returning to his face. After all, he thought, to be killed by a crocodile was deemed to be an honourable death by these people; and besides, if there were no body, they would be spared the cost of a funeral.

But although he had lived in the country a while, Philippos was not really conversant with the habits of its animals. Dangerous by day, the crocodile and the fierce male hippos were sluggish and sleepy at night. Argynoutis had not fallen victim to one of them, but had been picked up by a night-fisherman; luckily for him the river was a busy waterway whatever the time of day or night, especially in the region of a major town. But there were probably tears in the old man's eyes as the boat bore him away: he had been shamed and he would not now dare to return home. Was it possible that another factor in his decision not to return was an awareness of his wife's duplicity? It seems odd that he did not go back and summon the support of friends to supplant Philippos and bring him to justice, if only for the sake of his daughters. Perhaps Greeks were just too powerful. Perhaps Argynoutis intended to return and take revenge for his treatment and would have done so, had not another fate overtaken him.

From the petition they later sent to the rulers, it seems that the twins knew that their father had escaped and fled south to his brother's house in the town of Hierakonpolis, originally known as Nekhen but now given a Greek name by the colonizers. However, with no-one to protect them and unable to fend for themselves, they had to resign themselves to staying with their mother and the new head of the household, the Greek Philippos. It was an uncomfortable situation.

We do not know how Nephoris explained away her husband's disappearance or how soon afterwards she moved Philippos in with her. The first obstacle had been removed but the girls remained a problem on account of the dowry they would each expect on marriage, which would eat up one-third of the capital Nephoris had just inherited. She clearly had no intention of letting that happen, but stayed her hand at murdering her children. Instead, she took the extraordinary expedient of simply throwing them out; and again one is forced to wonder what the reaction of her acquaintances and neighbours would have been to such a thing, since no records survive, except for the fact that, by implication, Nephoris did indeed get away with it.

The twins' petition states: 'Our mother took possession of our father's property and cast us out ... We were in danger of dying of starvation ...'

Terrified of what might now happen to them, Tages and Taous made their way to the cloth market, where they went to the stall run by the shopkeeper to whom they were used to selling linen. He greeted them expectantly but was taken aback when instead of cloth they offered him a pair of gold bangles – which had been the gift of their father. Seeing that they were of some value, he decided not to ask any questions, and after some pretence at hesitation made an offer of half-a-dozen copper drachmae for both. Taous was incensed, Tages disappointed at such a low bid and the merchant, knowing that he was getting a good deal anyway, relented to the extent of offering three drachmae more. Glumly, having no other choice, the girls accepted.

By now their first day alone was drawing in, and the sight of an emaciated beggar by the side of the road did

Argynoutis, wounded, flees towards the river.

nothing to encourage them. Starvation was a very real prospect for two young women with no-one to support them and only money enough to last them a couple of days.

Dusty, thirsty and tired, with no idea where to go, they slumped down on a brick bench to take stock of their situation. It was then that Tages remembered an old friend of their father. It was possible that he might be able to help them, and as he lived and worked in the nearby temple-town and necropolis of Saqqara, it might be possible to reach him before nightfall and throw themselves on his mercy. By luck a trader was passing with his camel just then, and told the girls when they asked him that, yes, he was on his way to Saqqara. He would not give them a lift there without being paid, however, and so they parted with one of their precious drachmae. The camel knelt, the girls clambered up, and soon they were heading westwards. Tages reminded her sister that Saqqara was a place where legal redress and restitution could be sought. If they could find their father's friend, Ptolemaios, a Greek by birth, he might be able to help them in their search for justice.

The monument that defined and dominated Saqqara was the ancient step-pyramid of one of the first kings, Djoser, who had reigned during the Third Dynasty, 2500 years earlier. They arrived at Saqqara before dark, and found lodgings without difficulty in a city whose livelihood depended on tourists and pilgrims who wished to petition the gods.

In the temple precincts of Saqqara, pilgrims used to spend the night in dream chambers, opening their minds, as they hoped, to divine messages. To them it was a business of great solemnity and importance, and many visitors to Saqqara spent a night in a centre for dreamers. The 'Corridor of Dreams' was a broad hallway, and off it at regular intervals doors led to small chambers, in each of which a sleeping figure lay on a mat, the head supported by the wooden rest which the Ancient Egyptians used instead of a pillow.

Ptolemaios was an interpreter of dreams. Saqqara had long been a place of pilgrimage for people in search of meaning, and Ancient Egyptians believed firmly in the power of dreams to guide one's life. They called dreams 'revelations of the truth', and saw them as a means by which the gods communicated with human beings. Dream-interpretation had by now become something of a business. Dreamers had to pay for the privilege of using the 'Corridor of Dreams', and if the gods granted them a dream, it would more often than not be couched in terms so symbolic that an expert would be needed to interpret it, for which service another fee was payable.

Ptolemaios was one of five brothers born to a Macedonian veteran called Glaukias. Not particularly well-educated, though he could read and write, at the age of about thirty he had voluntarily taken up a post as a recluse 'in the service of the god'. Why he did so is not known, but it came at a time when the Ptolemies were fighting amongst themselves for control, and the country was going through one of the many unstable and disturbed periods it suffered during the dynasty. Ptolemaios may have entered the temple service as an asylum-seeker.

He had worked in the Serapeum, a vast walled temple-complex on the western side of the city Saqqara, for ten years. He was forbidden by the terms of his job, for he was a temple servant, not a priest, to leave the Serapeum except on special occasions, such as a family wedding, though his day-to-day contact with the outside world was not restricted. This contact was conducted through letters and through his able, younger brother Apollonios, to whom he had been a father since the death of Glaukias three or four years earlier. Ptolemaios may have been either legitimately aggrieved or simply a malcontent. In any event, he was not slow to complain about the ill-treatment he, as a Greek, received at the hands of his Egyptian colleagues. Three times he petitioned the king specifically with complaints about being beaten up by them. Despite every effort made by the Ptolemies, Egyptian resentment of their overlords was never very far from the surface. Apollonios also occasionally suffered beatings.

Ptolemaios, along with a handful of colleagues, found few of their charges yet waking, but as he passed the door of one chamber, the man inside stirred as the sunlight from the window struck his face. Opening his eyes

Ptolemaios' archive of dreams and letters give us an extraordinarily vivid picture of life in the temple town of Saqqara.

and seeing Ptolemaios, the middle-aged man stretched and sat up, holding out a hand to the interpreter by way of asking him to stay. Ptolemaios exchanged a greeting with the man and sat cross legged by his side, laying out his writing palette and his raffia tray full of sheets of papyrus. The dreamer placed two silver coins into the interpreter's hand.

Quickly, before the dream faded, the pilgrim, who had been waiting impatiently for Ptolemaios to settle himself, began to speak: 'A dove seemed to fly out of my hand and I ran after it, saying, I am certainly not going to let it escape. I caught it and put it in my left hand, and I confined it with a palm frond to keep it from escaping.'

As he spoke, Ptolemaios wrote his words down. It was not always easy to interpret a dream and often he had to consult one of the ancient *Books of Interpretation* but it was how he chose to earn a living in a city bustling with willing customers. Animals figured very largely in dreams; but this dream of a dove required some work. Ptolemaios excused himself and arranged to meet the pilgrim later. As he moved away he saw his brother Apollonios approaching him along the corridor. His

DECODING DREAMS

Common dreams involved drowning in the Nile, or having one's teeth fall out, or drinking beer. These were not hard to give a meaning to. And there were others: to dream of a shining moon meant forgiveness; to dream of a large cat meant a bumper harvest. Books divided significance of dreams according to the gender of the dreamer too: 'If a woman dreams she is married to her husband, she will be destroyed; if she embraced him, she will come to grief ... If a man sees himself in a dream eating donkey flesh, good; it means his promotion. Seating himself upon a tree, good; it means the destruction of all his ills. Looking into a deep well, bad; it means being put in prison.'

walk and his expression conveyed a certain urgency, and it was unusual for him to be around so early. Ptolemaios was puzzled and a little concerned, but after a few brief words the mystery was resolved. Still looking concerned, however, Ptolemaios followed his brother out through a gate into the street beyond.

A STREET, WHICH ARCHAEOLOGISTS later gave the name *dromos*, was the main one leading through the centre of the Serapeum. It was paved, and its sides were lined with stalls. At one end stood a Greek temple, while a smaller one jostled for position with the stalls, along with a number of Egyptian and Greek shrines, making a curious mixture.

At the western end of the *dromos*, though, stood the building which gave the whole complex its name: the

Many pilgrims to Saqqara spent a night in a 'dream chamber' and had their dreams interpreted by men like Ptolemaios.

mortuary temple of the Apis Bull, one of Egypt's most ancient animal cults, now transmuted through Greek influence into Serapis. The Bull was also in antiquity the embodiment of the power and fertility of the pharaoh, and had soon become associated with Osiris as well. Serapis – a fusion of the gods Osiris and Apis – was in fact a political invention of Ptolemy I around 286 BC, who wanted to dilute the nationalism that the Apis cult at Memphis had inspired. After the introduction of the new cult of Serapis the Ptolemies rebuilt and expanded hugely the sanctuary at Memphis. The cult was an instant and lasting success, although the Egyptians continued to see the god as Apis, as they had done for over 2000 years, and did not revere him by the name Serapis.

Apollonios and Ptolemaios had now reached their goal. Seated under a yellow-and-red painted awning next door to a beer-seller's shop, were the twins. Having spent the night in a nearby hostel, they had asked the beer-seller where they might find Ptolemaios, and he had sent a boy to Apollonios, who'd heard the gist of their story before hurrying to fetch his older brother.

The girls stood up as soon as they saw their father's friend. Tages stepped forward and took his hands, bursting into tears as she started to tell their story. Apollonios looked at her with feelings of tenderness he did not recognize, and clumsily tried to comfort her as she broke off, while her sister took up the tale. Ptolemaios listened gravely, and at last motioned them to follow him, nodding to his brother to accompany them.

They retraced their steps along the *dromos* until, turning down a side-street, they came to Ptolemaios' modest dwelling. Though Greek, the interpreter of dreams occupied a lowly position in society and was not a rich man. Ushering the girls into his sparsely furnished room with its swept earthen floor, he motioned to a bench covered with a reed mat for them to sit on. Then he fetched them bread and beer and, drawing up a three-legged wooden stool, his one luxury item, he sat down and prepared to listen to the whole history of what had happened to them. Tages took up the story again, while Taous added the occasional dramatic detail to highlight it. When they

reached the point in the story when Argynoutis was stabbed in the shoulder, Ptolemaios hastened to assure them of his protection. Apollonios, sitting crosslegged on the floor nearby, added that he too would do all he could to help.

Later, Ptolemaios wrote to his brother, 'My chief concern is to provide a safe harbour for the twins. I worry about nothing else.' Both his natural instincts and the tenets of his religion demanded that he shelter the girls, but he had other motives too, which had more to do with his own advantage. He was not a rich man. He was also single, with no wife and, above all, no children of his own. Three years earlier he had tried and failed to adopt a child. Now fate was dropping this new opportunity into his lap. Tages and Taous could supply his lack of children, and be the support of his old age. (At around forty, Ptolemaios was already elderly in Ancient Egyptian society, where an aristocrat might live to be eighty, but a member of the middle class could look for no longer a span than fifty or sixty, and a peasant only around thirty years.) The twins could turn out to be for him what most children of poorer parents were: the equivalent of a pension. Ptolemaios kept a record of his own dreams, and in at least one of them there is a hint that he may have harboured a sexual desire for Tages, though he never seems to have expressed this openly by word or deed: 'I was walking on the approach to the temple of Serapis with a woman called Tages, a virgin. I spoke to her as follows: "O Tages, are you perhaps perplexed because I have made love to you?" And she replied, "It will be hard in dealing with my sister Taous if they tell her" ...'

Saqqara in 164 BC was a general religious centre, but its principal concern and office still was as a necropolis, the purpose for which it had been founded nearly 3000 years earlier. By the time of the twins, plots could be made available for anyone who could afford one. Nevertheless, securing one's place in the Fields of Iaru was still an expensive business. The priests offered a full funerary package: 60,000 copper drachmae bought one mummification and burial in a fully-furnished tomb (on a ninety-nine-year renewable lease) and care of the dead by a priest forever – as long as annual payments relating to the service were kept up.

As a Greek, Ptolemaios did not save up for an expensive funeral: the Greek religion did not set such great store by the afterlife, or at least not by the preservation of the body for it. However, like everyone professionally involved in the day-to-day life of Saqqara, he knew how to turn his hand to making money out of the death cult. Not earning enough from his profession as an interpreter of dreams, he had started a second career, as a seller of second-hand clothes, and, when his duties in the centre for dreamers permitted, he ran a stall in the business district. People were obliged to sell the effects of a dead relative to pay the expenses of his or her funeral, and clothes were an expensive commodity: a child's new embroidered tunic could cost as much as five hundred copper drachmae, at a time when the monthly wage of a farm labourer was fifty. Thus not only the poor bought their clothes second-hand.

Ptolemaios was not alone in having a second career. The Serapeum attracted hordes of tourists as well as pilgrims, and its atmosphere was often more commercial than spiritual. The temple leased out stalls to increase its already large profits. All around Ptolemaios' pitch were others – either selling clothes as he was, or porridge, or bulrushes used as firelighters, or spices, or beer. Even the full-time professional priests in Saqqara had similar business sidelines. For young girls like the twins there were other ways of earning a living. Just under a kilometre from the Serapeum, beyond the graves of generations of citizens of Memphis, stood the Anubieon, the compound of Anubis, the jackal-headed god of embalming. It was here that the hostels housing the visitors were situated, and here, in the halls of the temples, the temple prostitutes were to be found. They were an innovation borrowed, like so many innovations, from Syria, but the men of Greece and Egypt had quickly taken to the idea. Congress with one of these women, some as young as twelve, could be rationalized on a number of religious lines: one might be association with a goddess of love, such as Hathor, through the medium of her 'representative'; another might be the expiation (for the man) of his

As a town attracting thousands of tourists, especially during the festival seasons, Saqqara provided a thriving trade for prostitutes.

potentially destructive sexual power. Women, or more often young girls, would either sell themselves or be sold to a temple for life, and also enrol any children they might have as temple servants. They would be encouraged to become sexual servants, and, once earning a living, they would pay most of their income to the temple, and be taxed by the Egyptian civil authorities. Above all, prostitution was considered a profession, and did not necessarily attract any stigma, though in a male-dominated society it was not regarded with any particular admiration. Women who knew about the sexual functions of the body, such as midwives, and women who were sexually open, such as prostitutes, were regarded with misgivings by men, as they posed a threat in the misogynists' eyes.

The twins would certainly have visited the Anubieon and could not have failed to notice the girls plying their trade there, perhaps even exchanging half-timid, half-

SEX

The Ancient Egyptians regarded sex as pleasurable and took no shame in it. Most of them were unused to privacy and very used to nakedness: all bodily functions could be performed publicly except in the highest circles, and no doubt were. Interestingly, since people were used to nudity, men were aroused by a woman wearing a wet, clinging, semi-transparent linen dress. A famous erotic papyrus in the Egyptian Museum in Turin shows a cartoon-like sequence of sexual activities between a prostitute and an extraordinary well-endowed middle-aged man. It may well have some, to us obscure, satirical purpose.

Women were allowed to visit the new Apis Bull for the first forty days of his incumbency, as he was a powerful conveyor of fecundity and virility. They would raise their skirts and expose their genitalia to him. When the forty days were over, women were thenceforward forbidden to visit, but the tradition had a long life: worship of Apis lasted into the Christian Era.

There were many words in Ancient Egyptian associated with the sex organs. Among the twenty or so expressions for making love, *nek* was one of the most common. There were several words for the penis, differentiating between ones that had been circumcised and ones that hadn't. Circumcision (as practised on men), though shown occasionally in art, does not seem to have been the rule, however, and it appears to have been rarely practised on women, although the Greek historian and geographer Strabo, writing in about 25 BC, and St Ambrose, writing in the fourth century AD, both allude to it.

Kohl, the black eye-liner still used, which enhances the eyes, was known as the 'pleasure stick', and women wore solid cones of perfumed unguent on their wigs which gave off a pleasant odour as they 'melted' – perhaps in fact they evaporated, or they would have left a mess. Egyptian cosmetics were not cheap, and just as today, their value was enhanced by decanting them into small, decorative glass bottles. They even had brand names: 'Bloom of Youth', 'Elixir of Aphrodite'.

There were also plenty of recipes for love

potions, some revolting, some hard to acquire: 'Take the dandruff from the head of one who has been murdered, barley, the blood of a tic from a black dog, and wine ... give it to the woman you want to love you to drink.'

Incest is often associated with the Ancient Egyptian royal houses, but it was more common in the time of the Ptolemies than during the pharaonic era. In the Middle and New Kingdoms it was the exception rather than the rule, though for dynastic reasons marriage between siblings and even father and daughter did occur. Polygamy, however, was unusual for all but the king.

The god Bes was the protector of anything to

do with a woman's private life, and the goddess Hathor was associated with sexual pleasure, among many other things, as she was a protector goddess, the daughter of Ra, often portrayed as a sacred cow with the disc of the sun between her horns. Although women enjoyed almost equal rights with men throughout long periods of Ancient Egyptian history, matters of sexual fidelity generally favoured the man. It was perfectly in order for an unmarried man to have a mistress, though a concubine could be accorded the same status as a wife by her protector; conversely a married man could take a concubine even if his wife wasn't infertile; and a

sorts of risks is evident from a legal report from the workmen's village of Deir el-Medina, during the Ramesside Period, though the degree of activity detailed here must have been exceptional: 'Paneb raped the citizeness Tuy, when she was the wife of the workman Kenna. He raped the citizeness Hunro, when she was living with Pendua. He raped the citizeness Hunyo when she lived with Hesysunebef. So said his son. And after he had raped Hunro, he raped Webkhet, her daughter; and his son Apahte also raped Webkhet.'

There are many erotic tales and stories, some with a moral tone, others apparently told merely for entertainment. Though homosexuality in either sex was disapproved of by men at least – between men because it seemed unmanly and between women because it seemed unnatural – there seems to have been no formal law against it.

ABOVE: A fragment from the erotic 'Turin Papyrus', now in the Egyptian Museum, Turin, Italy, which dates back to the Nineteenth Dynasty.

ABOVE LEFT: Prostitutes were a source of income for the temples to which they were often attached.

slave girl would be obliged to do her master's bidding in all things. Men did most of the writing and commentary on sex, and predictably enough disapproved of women who showed sexual, or any other, initiative, at least in polite society. Rameses II related cowardice to the female genitalia while Herodotus carried on an ancient tradition by complaining about how hard it was to find a faithful woman, and in 1450 BC the papyrus known as 'The Instructions of Ani' advised:

Go not after a woman, and let her not steal your heart. Beware of a strange woman who is not known in town. Do not look at her, do not know her. She is

a deep pool whose swirling is not known. 'Am I not beautiful?' a woman who is far from her husband tells you every day, when no-one else listens; and then she tightens the rope.

Diodorus Siculus, admittedly writing late, in 40 BC, noted that 'If a man had violated a free, married woman, they stipulated that he be emasculated ... If a man committed adultery with the woman's consent, the laws ordered that the man should receive 1000 blows with the rod, and that the woman should have her nose cut off.' Men rather enjoyed stories in which the woman takes the initiative, but then comes a cropper. That people were quite happy in earlier times to take all curious glances with them, for the girls would for the most part have been no older than Tages and Taous. But the Anubieon was also the legal district, where citizens of Memphis could go in search of redress, and it may be that the girls were there, accompanied by Apollonios, for Ptolemaios could not leave the Serapeum, to seek justice for their father.

But if they went, and it seems more than likely that they did, they found no satisfaction, and meanwhile, more bad tidings were on the way from Memphis. Their father's old housekeeper arrived with the news that Argynoutis was dead. His brother, in accordance with custom, had sent his body home for burial. But there were strict rules in the city that no corpses could be kept there, and in order to avoid the cost of a burial, Nephoris and Philippos had disposed of the body by night in the

desert. They had then sold his clothes and personal effects. In their letter of petition, the twins state that their father died of despair. If they had clung to the hope that their father might yet return to right his and their wrongs, they had to abandon it now. And Ptolemaios couldn't support them any longer – they would have to find work. The halls of the temples of the Anubieon beckoned, and their future looked bleak.

But then, in the Egyptian month of Pharmouthi, on 7 April in the modern calendar, 164 BC, there came news of another death, and this time the news was good. The Apis Bull had died in his temple-compound in Memphis. The bull was at the time the most sacred animal in Egypt, associated with the gods Ptah and Serapis. The death of the bull ushered in a time of national mourning, and it was a rare event, for the bull, whose successor

The sphinx-lined Serapeum *dromos*, or sacred way, connected the Anubieon to the Serapeum where the twins Tages and Taous lived with Ptolemaios.

must now immediately be sought, could live up to twenty-five years. The Apis Bull had to have certain attributes: a black hide, and a white diamond blaze on the forehead. His back had to bear the outline of a vulture, there had to be double-hairs on his tail, and the image of a scarab on the underside of his tongue.

The bull in question had lived for fourteen years, which was about the average span. Its body would now be mummified and buried in the Serapeum in Saqqara. On its death it would become identified with Osiris. The death and funeral enjoyed the same standing as the death of a pharaoh had once had, and the Egyptians focused on the ritual, in the face of their foreign overlords, as an assertion of their nationalism. The Greeks, confident of their hold on power, continued to encourage the cult and even paid it at least lip-service themselves to enhance their status. Ptolemaios was excited by the news, because it meant that after ten years of being cut off from the world, the world would come to him. And there was more good news. As soon as Apollonios, coming from Memphis, had told him of the bull's death, he summoned the twins.

Having roughly explained what was in his mind, Ptolemaios took the twins hastily to the Serapeum and sought an interview with one of the senior priests in charge of the funeral arrangements for the Apis Bull. At the death of the bull, a pair of female twins was appointed to take on the roles of the goddesses Isis (the mother of Apis) and Nephthys, the sister-consorts of Osiris and Set, to mourn for the bull during the seventy days of mummification and mourning leading up to burial, and thereafter devote themselves to his service until the time of the death of his successor. As we know, this period averaged fourteen years but could be as long as twenty-five. Twins were rare in the ancient world, where giving birth successfully to single children was perilous enough; and female twins were even rarer. The Egyptians reared all their children lovingly, regardless of their gender, but in Graeco-Egyptian times among the poorer members of the population, girl-children were sometimes quietly allowed to die: they were an expense to the family and unlike men it was not thought that they could fend for themselves. Greek men

The Egyptian week was ten days long, with a holiday every tenth day; but in addition to that time off, the year was peppered with festivals which were also treated as national holidays.

Epiph	25 June – 24 July
Mesore	25 July – 23 August
	24 – 28 August: Epagomenal
	Days (these were 'additional'
	days inserted to make up the
	full number of days for the year)
Thoth	29 August – 27 September
Phaophi	28 September – 27 October
Hathyr	28 October – 26 November
Choiak	27 November – 26 December
Tybi	27 December – 25 January
Mecheir	26 January – 24 February
Phamenoth	25 February – 26 March
Pharmouthi	27 March – 25 April
Pachon	26 April – 25 May
Payni	26 May – 24 June

generally regarded the presence of many daughters as embarrassing. Even middle-class families sometimes regarded the birth of twin daughters as a misfortune. Tages and Taous were lucky to have come from a wealthy family, and to have had an adoring father. But Ptolemaios knew that his charges were not the only female twins in the area, and that he would have to get in first to secure the job he wanted for them.

He was fortunate. After having been introduced, the priest approved the appointment, and dispatched the girls to a scribe in the legal department in the Anubieion who would draw up the contract of their employment. Once the scribe had signed their contract and had it witnessed, he handed the twins' copy to Tages, rolled and sealed with a mud seal. She placed it carefully in a leather drawstring pouch. The role they had been selected for carried great honour with it, and also guaranteed income, paid from the temple coffers. In addition, they would receive a bonus ration of castor oil during the seventy days of mourning. Castor oil was not an especially precious commodity, but the girls would have been able to trade it for other goods, or sell it for drachmae. Together with their wooden salary tokens, also issued to them by the scribe, they would, with careful management, be able to accumulate some capital for their futures. Never as much as their mother had stolen from them, but enough.

The major drawback of the duty the twins had now undertaken was that until the death of the new bull, which priests were even now seeking throughout the land, Tages and Taous would have to remain chaste. They might be thirty or older before they would be free to find a husband, and by then it would almost certainly be too late. The twins would have to learn and perform long incantations to the god. They would also have to subject themselves to ceremonial tattooing, which would identify them as the representatives of the goddesses. Tattooing was not unusual for women in Ancient Egypt, though it was generally associated with dancers and musicians, who in turn were frequently associated with women of easy virtue.

From Ptolemaios' point of view, the arrangement car-

ried nothing but advantages. By association with the girls, his status would rise, and through them a comfortable income would be secured. He might himself not outlive the new Apis Bull, unless for any reason he died early. It was in his interest for the bull to live as long as possible.

Whatever their private thoughts, ambitions and misgivings may have been, the die was now cast. The twins

had to don drab grey mourning costumes and daub their faces with ash before making what would be a daily walk of a hour or more at dawn and dusk to and from the Temple of the Apis Bull in Memphis, where they would spend the day formally mourning the passing of the god-on-earth. Perhaps it was the thought of returning to her home town, so near and yet so far, given her exclusion from her family, that triggered a dream of reconciliation with her mother that Tages had. She told it to Ptolemaios, who, with professional interest, noted it down, and it is among those of his records that have survived and come down to us:

I saw myself in Memphis. I dreamed that the water had

BELOW: Tages and Taous at the notary's office. As chief mourners of the Apis Bull the twins would be guaranteed an income.

OPPOSITE ABOVE: The twins prepare to mourn the Apis Bull. The ash-covered faces and grey clothes were an outward display of mourning.

BELOW The twins descend into the catacombs below the Serapeum, which contained the mummified bodies of the Apis Bulls.

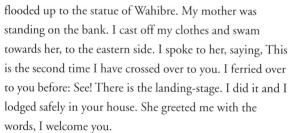

flooded up to the statue of Wahibre. My mother was standing on the bank. I cast off my clothes and swam towards her, to the eastern side. I spoke to her, saying, This is the second time I have crossed over to you. I ferried over to you before: See! There is the landing-stage. I did it and I lodged safely in your house. She greeted me with the words, I welcome you.

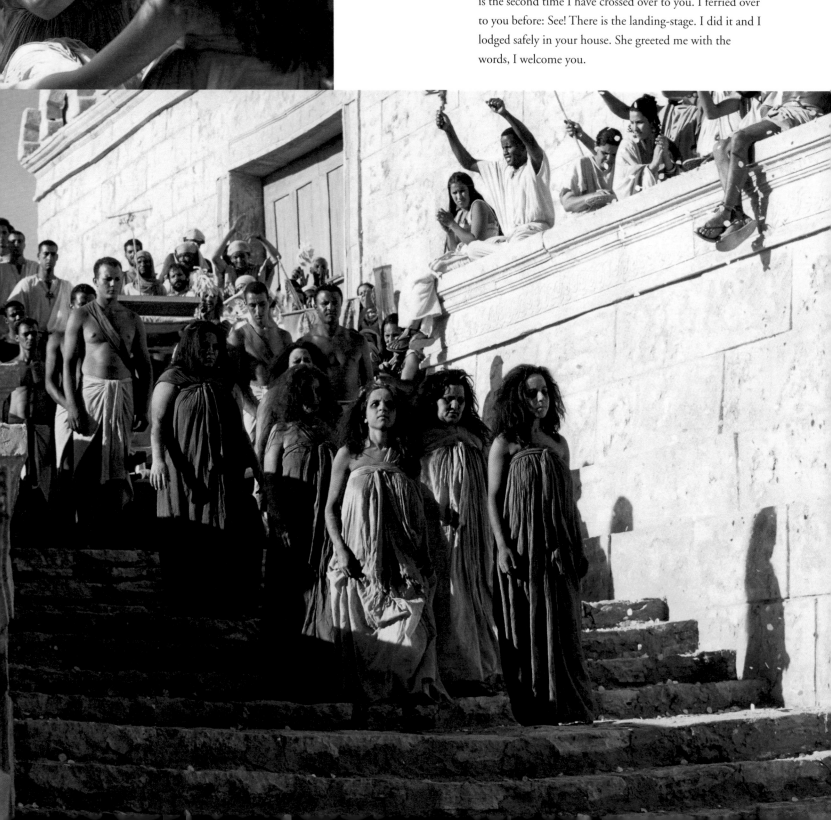

But in reality there was to be no fulfilment of this poignant dream. Nephoris in the meantime was learning Greek – with difficulty – from her son Pakhrates, who had been taught it at school: the sons of wealthy Egyptians were being taught Greek, which was now the language of the administration and of business, as well as of the court. Nephoris had by now sold half her late husband's holdings, reinvesting the proceeds in her own name in land and rental properties.

Not long after the twins had started their daily visits to the embalming-place of the Apis bull, Nephoris' Greek lesson, which she was attending to with increasing impatience, was interrupted by the arrival of two women friends of hers, bringing news. She went out with them and together they joined the crowd of Egyptians, Greeks, Nubians, Syrians and Libyans who had gathered next to the embalming-place, some to mourn the dead bull, and some to enjoy the festival atmosphere. Soon afterwards, a small procession arrived: leading it were the scribe and the Medjay from the Anubieion, the officiating priest from the Serapeum, and Tages and Taous in their robes of mourning, their faces as usual covered with ash, and the kohl make-up round their eyes specially painted to look as if their 'tears' had made it run. They were greeted at the door of the embalming-place by a priest dressed in crisp white linen robes, his whole body clean-shaven in mourning, and ushered in. They did not see their mother, but she saw them, and realized the significance of what she had seen.

The embalming-place was a large tent erected inside one of the chambers of the temple. The twins were led to a shrine which contained a statue of the Apis Bull, garlanded and covered with a decorated linen shroud. There, they poured libations of wine, to the sound of

A priest wearing the mask of Anubis presides over the mummification of the Apis Bull. The Apis Bull was revered as the most sacred animal in Egypt and its death was an occasion for national mourning.

Mummifying the bull. Tools (left) were used to scramble its brain, which was then removed through the nostrils (above left). Organs which were removed from the bull during the process were preserved in natron, a natural salt.

ululations from a group of female professional mourners. As embodiments of Isis and Nephthys, the twins' duty for seventy days was to lead the faithful in mourning.

On an alabaster table within the tent, the body of the bull lay on its side. For the first four days following his death, it had been purified with water and anointed with precious oils. Its hooves were gilded, and it was very fat from years of good living and little exercise beyond servicing the cows which had formed its harem. The floor of the tent was strewn with sand to prevent the feet of the priests and other officiants from touching the unclean ground.

Back home, Nephoris brooded on the good fortune that had befallen her daughters. She knew that their position attracted a healthy income, and devised a plan to extract it from them. It isn't known quite how she did it, but she did employ the persuasive services of her women friends, since as public figures the girls would

have been difficult to approach privately. What is certain from the petition is that Pakhrates, the twins' half-brother, managed to insinuate himself into their good graces. Perhaps they were too ready to forgive him; perhaps they did not suspect his role in the ruin of their father. It is possible that, as they must clearly still have felt vulnerable, he was able to approach them in Memphis, away from Ptolemaios' influence, and to persuade them of his contrition at having let their mother treat them so badly. Tages, who yearned for reconciliation with her mother, may have been easier to persuade than Taous, who was beginning to enjoy the attention that went with her new role. In such a case, Pakhrates may have pretended that he himself had been thrown out by the cold-hearted Nephoris.

Whatever the reason, the twins agreed to take their half-brother back with them to the Serapeum. It was a decision they would live to regret bitterly.

As the day of the burial of the Apis Bull approached, more and more pilgrims flooded into Saqqara. The hostels and boarding houses were full, shopkeepers and stallholders were doing a roaring trade, and while the tame baboons they used as watchdogs kept a careful eye on possible shoplifters, special Medjay would have been drafted in to control petty street-crime, as, along with the crowds, cutpurses and pickpockets were attracted to the festival. Women bought ceramic or wooden phalluses, fertility charms associated with the god, and, as this was an especially auspicious time to bury the dead, queues formed at the desks of the scribes whose job it was to allocate burial plots. The beer-houses would have been full, with wine and fig-liquor too. In the Anubieion, the prostitutes organized rotas for themselves in order to get some rest.

Pakhrates had not been idle either. Having wormed his way entirely into his half-sisters' confidence, he now knew where they stored their wooden payment tokens and their papyrus bills of exchange – their investment for the future.

The mummification process was finally complete, and the embalmers had put the finishing touches to the bull's carcass in the tent reserved for this work, the so-called 'House of Beauty'. The animal had been transformed into something resembling life, assembled on a huge litter, in a sphinx-like posture, wearing a gold bull-mask, with gilded horns and hooves. When all was ready, the litter was borne aloft by a contingent of hefty priests, and carried out of the Temple of Apis on the first stage of the journey to Saqqara, westward along the so-called Serapeum Way.

When the procession emerged from the temple, the crowd went wild, especially the women, for whom the bull as a symbol of fertility had a special significance. Infertility was regarded with distaste and barren women

The twins, as part of the burial cortège, are carried in a procession of mourning.

eagerly sought the god's intercession. Extravagantly robed and crowned, the twins surveyed the crowd as they lurched and swayed through it, dizzy even if there had been no excitement, no clouds of incense, no loud drumming or ululation to make their heads swim. Slowly, to the accompaniment of incantations from the priests, the dead god and his entourage made their way eastwards.

Long before they arrived, Pakhrates had reached Ptolemaios' quarters off the all-but deserted *dromos*, entered the twins' room and completed his task.

At length the cortège reached Saqqara and entered the avenue leading to the Serapeum. All was prepared at the entrance to the mortuary temple of the Apis Bulls and the crowd waiting there, Ptolemaios and Apollonios among them, fell silent. The twins were supposed to behave with all the distant dignity of goddesses.

The litter was borne into a colourfully painted tent made of sewn hides. This was the Tent of Purification and here a priest wearing the grey jackal-mask of Wepwawet – the god of Opening the Ways – performed one of the final rituals, the Opening of the Mouth, which was supposed by magic to breathe life back into the god. The twins stood to one side as, holding a special ceremonial adze, the priest touched the mouth of the bull. The twins then stepped forward to breathe into it.

Once the rite had been completed, the cortège continued to the catacombs, where the dead Apis Bulls lay at rest in massive stone sarcophagi. Here, at the entrance, two *Muu* dancers performed the special dance which symbolized the crossing of the threshold between this life and the next. Then the bull was carried by torchlight along the corridor between the basalt tombs until he came to the sarcophagus that had been made ready for him, and was lowered into his last resting-place by a system of ropes and poles: the pulley was unknown to the Ancient Egyptians. Once the massive lid had been

The funerary procession of the Apis Bull.
The bull is carried through Memphis on its way
to Saqqara one mile away to the west.

replaced, the procession withdrew, and priests sealed the doors of the catacombs. They would not be reopened until the death of the next Apis Bull.

As evening fell, and returning home at last, exhausted but excited, it occurred to Tages and Taous that they had not seen Pakhrates since that morning before dawn when he had accompanied them to Memphis. They called out for him, and alerted Ptolemaios and Apollonios. Finally Tages took up the pottery vessel where they had stored

their wealth. It was empty. There was no doubt about who was the author of this treachery.

They had to continue their work, however, and so they continued to be paid – at least Pakhrates and Nephoris would get nothing more out of them. It was not until the following year that Ptolemaios presented their petition to the King and his Consort.

To King Ptolemy and Queen Kleopatra his sister. Greetings from Tages and Taous, twins who perform ritual service in

Muu dancers in their conical hats lead the funeral procession.

A priest wearing a
headdress representing
Anubis, one of
the principal gods
of the dead, prepares
to receive the body
of the Apis Bull ready
for embalming.

the Great Serapeum ... Being wronged on many counts by our mother Nephoris ... we flee for refuge to you, that we may obtain justice. Our mother left our father for Philippos, a Greek soldier, and she treacherously egged him on to kill him ... We beg you to send our petition to the local officials so that they do not pay [to our mother] either the oil that belongs to us or anything else of ours. Compel her also to return whatever [there is due to us] of our father's she holds illegally so that we are helped through you. May you prosper.

The reason for the delay in the petition is unknown, and their hope that Nephoris would still not have exchanged any of the tokens or bills-of-exchange seems optimistic. In any case, despite their status as servants of the Apis Bull, their petition appears to have been largely forgotten, though it appears that King Ptolemy VIII Euergetes II did order an official called Sarapion to look into the matter in 162 BC. They received neither their inheritance nor full restitution of the salary that had been stolen from them.

Ptolemaios lived on in the Serapeum as an interpreter of dreams. His surviving letters show him to have become increasingly wretched at his confined life, but he was apparently never released from his temple contract.

We hear no more of the twins, and cannot tell for how long they served the dead god. But we do know that Apollonios survived long enough at least to fall in love with Tages and perhaps have an affair with her. He followed his brother into the Serapeum at first, but later joined the army. In a letter to Ptolemaios four years later, which has survived, he wrote: 'I am sick with worry over Tages. What is to become of us?' Had she broken her vow of chastity and had that been found out by the temple authorities? We shall probably never know her ultimate fate, nor that of any of the protagonists of this story. We may perhaps hope, however that, despite all their travails, the ending for Tages and Apollonios at least was a happy one.

The mummified Apis Bull, wearing a gold mask and with gilded horns and hooves, is lowered into its vast basalt sarcophagus at the Serapeum in Saqqara.

SOURCES
FOR THE
STORY OF
'THE TWINS'

The source for this chapter is extremely rare in the literature of Ancient Egypt in that it tells a story in which children play central roles. It also describes the domestic impact of Greek immigrants (of superior standing) on local society in the late days of the civilization of Ancient Egypt.

The source comes from a cache of over one hundred papyri found in a single jar in Saqqara by locals in 1820. The Egyptians who found the hoard spilt it between them in order to sell it off piecemeal to ardent collectors, with the result that the papyri are now scattered throughout the museums and learned institutions of Europe. Those which principally concern us are now in the Louvre and the Bibliothèque Nationale in Paris, and in the Hermitage, St Petersburg. A large part of the collection concerns Ptolemaios and his family.

Alongside the poignant family drama described in a copy of a petition sent to the pharaoh, Ptolemaios' letters provide a vivid picture of temple life at Saqqara, while his dream records give a fascinating insight into Egyptian attitudes towards dreams and their interpretation. The story forms part of the collection gathered for scholarly purposes and published in Volume One of Ulrich Wilcken's magisterial *Urkunden der Ptolemaerzeit*.

Ptolemaios, the middle-aged man whose letters and papers (in Greek) tell the story, was of Macedonian origin, though born in Egypt. He had, at around the age of thirty, become a *katochos*, or 'recluse', in the Serapeum at Saqqara. He may have turned to this life through poverty or from religious conviction, but in accepting it he also had to accept that never more could he leave the temple confines, and indeed Ptolemaios does seem to have lived out his life in a cell within the shrine of the Syrian goddess Astarte, next to the Serapeum. Certainly he was still there when his correspondence comes to an end in 152 BC, and we can infer that he was born sometime before 200 BC.

The sources reveal that the twin girls Ptolemaios adopts, and on whose behalf he petitions the pharaoh (a tradition widely practised in Ancient Egypt), were not the only ones whose cause he took up. He also wrote to the palace on behalf of his brothers in around 160 BC, whom he alleges were being maltreated in some way. He wrote again on behalf of another girl, Heracleia, whom he adopted, but who, in 164 BC, seems to have been taken from him by force by one Zoilos and 'handed … over to one of the soldiers from Memphis'. Family concerns, debts and mortgages, make up the subject matter of a good deal of his remaining correspondence, revealing a life beset with worldly stress.

Apollonios was the younger brother of Ptolemaios and acted as his secretary as well as his link with the outside world. Their relationship was sometimes strained. Apollonios' handwriting was better, but from his style and spelling it may be inferred that he spoke Greek with an Egyptian accent. By the time of the story, their father is dead and Ptolemaios is head of the family. Apollonios defers to him and refers to him as 'father'. In view of the age difference they may in fact have been half-brothers, and it is possible that Apollonios' mother was Egyptian, though there is no hard evidence for this. Apollonios complains frequently of being picked on by Egyptians on account of his Greek origin, and even of being beaten up. He appears to have continued to live a volatile life, ultimately getting an army posting, which may have been unpaid since he also earned money as a police informer.

The twins of the story throw themselves, according to Ptolemaios' papers, on his mercy in late 165 BC or early 164 BC. The death of the sacred and deified Apis Bull in early April 164 BC led to the twins' advancement as the priestesses of the new 'god' – the 'successor' bull – as the deity had to be attended by twin virgin girls, and they, as the story reveals, were rare in Ancient Egypt.

The source for the twins' story is their petition, a letter from Ptolemaios to Apollonios, a dream by one of the twins, a dream by Ptolemaios and a reference to Tages in a letter from Apollonios. The archive gives us an unusually full account of a dramatic human story. The tale is further enriched by Apollonios' own writings, which deal with his dreams and his own possible aspirations towards at least one of the twins. And added to this are the reports by Ptolemaios of the dreams of the twins themselves, all of which, woven together, form an irresistible pattern.

One of the letters found in a pot in Saqqara in 1820, this papyrus, now in the Louvre, tells the story of the twins. It is a petition from the twins, written by Ptolemaios, asking for the help of the pharaoh.

GLOSSARY

AKHET: Summer or inundation; the first of the three seasons of the Ancient Egyptian year, running between June and October.

AMDUAT: 'The Book of What Is In The Underworld'; ancient royal funerary texts describing the hereafter and the journey of the sun through the night, as well as offering advice on how to behave during the journey from death to the afterlife.

AMULET: Magical jewels made in specific designs and having specific names. Worn by the living to protect themselves against evil spirits, and also placed inside mummy wrappings. From the Arabic, *hamulet*, 'what is portable'. Two of the best-known amulets are the *ankh* and the *wedjat*, or 'Eye of Horus'.

Ankh, a common type of amulet.

BOOK OF THE DEAD: Called by the Ancient Egyptians 'The Book of Going Forth by Day', this was a guide, developed in various forms over centuries, to how to manage the journey to the Fields of IARU, the Ancient Egyptian paradise.

CANOPIC JARS: The four jars in which various internal organs were stored and preserved during the process of mummification. The heart, which the Ancient Egyptians believed was the centre of all intelligence, had to remain with the body, as did the kidneys, perhaps because they were difficult to access. The canopic jars, which conventionally had lids depicting guardian deities, contained: the liver, guarded by human-headed Imsety; the lungs, guarded by baboon-headed Hapy; the stomach, guarded by jackal-headed Duamutef; and the guts, guarded by hawk-headed Qebehsenuef. They are called 'Canopic' jars because originally they were confused with human-headed jars associated with the cult of the god Osiris at the Ancient Egyptian port of Canopus.

CARTONNAGE: Stiff material made of layers of linen or papyrus stiffened with plaster. Usually decorated and gilded, it was used to make mummy masks and inner caskets.

CARTOUCHE: A near-oval with a straight line at one of the short ends, in which the two principal names of a pharaoh were enclosed in HIEROGLYPHIC writing. The French name comes from Napoleonic soldiers stationed in Egypt, for whom the shape recalled that of the cartridges they used.

A cartouche from the Temple of Rameses III, Abu Simbel.

CATARACTS: The six series of rapids along the Upper Nile, which in ancient times generally prevented the passage of boats up them, so they often had to be carried past them overland.

DECANS: Ancient Egyptians divided the day-time and the night-time into twelve 'hours' each; however, the 'hours' of day and night varied in length according to the time of year. Thus in winter, the twelve night-time 'hours' were relatively longer than the twelve day-time 'hours'; in summer, they were relatively shorter. The divisions came to be known as 'decans'.

DEMOTIC: A fluent, cursive form of Ancient Egyptian writing – close to handwriting – which developed from the formal, antique HIEROGLYPHIC form and was much used towards the end of the Empire for secular documents.

DESHRET: The Pharaonic Red Crown of Lower (or northern) Egypt, which is to say, the Delta area from Memphis to the coast.

DIVINE ADORATRICE: The highest religious office open to a woman. The incumbent was 'God's Wife of Amun' at Thebes in the south in the Third Intermediate Period. Thebes was an important religious and political centre, a rival to Memphis and at certain periods replacing it as the centre of power. The appointment was often political, the pharaoh appointing one of his relatives to the post in order to keep an eye on the powerful priesthood based at Thebes. Theoretically at least, the post demanded celibacy of its incumbent.

DJED: One of the common amulets, in the form of a pillar.

DYNASTY: A system of divisions of the chronology of Ancient Egypt introduced by Manetho (fl. 305–285 BC), a priest and historian who compiled a record of the kings of his country from the beginning. The divisions are generally ordered by family groupings; but it will be noted that some dynasties overlap each other, and indeed run contemporaneously, especially where there were parallel rulers in the north and south of the country, or when outsiders intervened and set up their own kingdoms.

ENNEAD: Called in Ancient Egyptian *pesedjet*, an ancient group of nine (sometimes more) gods of the earliest generations of divine beings. The chief centre of their cult was Heliopolis. The creator-god was Atum; his children were Shu, the air, and his sister-wife Tefnut, moisture. They gave birth to Geb (the god of the earth) and Nut (the goddess of the sky), who in turn produced the two gods, Osiris and Set, and the two goddesses Isis and Nephthys.

HEB-SED: A festival to mark the thirtieth anniversary of a pharaoh's accession to the throne. Thereafter the festival was celebrated more frequently, at the discretion of the pharaoh.

HEDJET: The Pharaonic White Crown of Upper (southern) Egypt, which is to say the region south of Memphis to the southernmost borders of the Empire (which varied with time).

HIERATIC: A fluent form of HIEROGLYPHIC writing which evolved as early as the Old Kingdom and is less informally cursive than DEMOTIC.

HIEROGLYPHIC: Writing most popularly associated with Ancient Egypt. More than 600 different signs have been identified to date. Used throughout the Empire and virtually unchanged in 3500 years, hieroglyphs adorned the temples, and formed the language of sacred texts.

HYKSOS: (*Hekaw Khaswt* – 'rulers of foreign lands'.) Invaders from what are now Palestine and Syria, who arrived in Egypt towards the end of the Middle Kingdom and reigned during the Second Intermediate Period. They are credited by some scholars with the introduction of the chariot and the curved (*khepesh*) sword, as well as, possibly, the composite bow, and the horse, which had special applications in warfare.

IARU: (The Fields of Iaru – 'The Field of Reeds'.) A paradise after death for Ancient Egyptians, where there would be massive harvests of enormous crops. SHABTIS would work in the fields for the deceased, allowing them to reap the benefits without suffering the drudgery.

LOTUS: This is the water-lily (*seshen*) which was the emblem of Upper Egypt. There were two main kinds of lotus originally, the white and the blue; the blue had the greater fragrance and is the flower which takes precedence in the symbolism. The lotus also symbolized rebirth.

LOWER EGYPT: The Nile flows northwards. Thus, Lower Egypt is the northern part of the country, north of modern Cairo and ancient Memphis, covered by the Delta.

MASTABA: A tomb, often of mud-brick, which appeared early and continued in use throughout the Old Kingdom, especially for the aristocracy and high officials. Its rectangular design

Lotus flowers depicted in the tomb of Sennufer at Thebes. Eighteenth Dynasty.

resembled a bench, hence *mastaba* means 'bench' in modern Arabic.

MATET BOAT: The first six hours of the day, from dawn until noon.

MUMMY: The preserved body of a corpse which is, after the pyramids, the most famous image of Ancient Egypt. The word derives from the Persian/Arabic for bitumen, *mum/mumia*. This comes from a mistaken apprehension in the earliest times of historical interest in mummies, when the black resins used for preservation were confused with pitch, which was held to have medicinal properties. Francis I of France (AD 1494–1547) always carried a packet of powdered mummy-and-rhubarb with him as a general cure-all.

NEMES: A type of headcloth which frequently appears in depictions of pharaohs.

NOME: Greek word for the Ancient Egyptian *sepat*. The country was divided into forty-two administrative districts (the number varied from time to time) each bearing this name and governed by a *nomarch*.

OBELISK: A slender four-sided stone column topped with a pyramidion, or small pyramid. This column, used either commemoratively or as a boundary marker, is frequently also associated with temples. It represents the ancient *benben* stone, a kind of conical obelisk symbolizing the primal mound which rose from the primal waters at the beginning of creation. The word 'obelisk' derives from the Greek for a skewer, reflecting the patronizing attitude of Greek immigrants to Egypt at a late stage in the Empire's history.

OGDOAD: An alternative grouping of primal deities to the ENNEAD, this time eight in number, based on a cosmogony held in Hermopolis Magna. The Ogdoad comprises four frog-gods 'married' to four snake-goddesses, each pair representing aspects of the primal chaos from which life and order emerged. They were: Nun and his 'wife' Naunet (the primal waters), Heh and Hauhet (the infinity of space), Amun and Amaunet (that which is hidden) and Kek and Kauket (darkness).

OPET: An annual festival which took place at Thebes from the Eighteenth Dynasty onwards, in the second month of the season of AKHET, and lasting between fourteen and twenty-eight days. During it, images of the gods were paraded between Karnak and Luxor.

OSTRACA: (Singular: ostracon). Pottery or stone shards used as sketch pads or notebooks, and a valuable source of information, especially about the lives of ordinary Ancient Egyptians.

PAPYRUS: The plant that represents Lower Egypt, though long since extinct there. Its stems, once harvested, could be used in rope-making or to build small skiffs for temporary use; but above all papyrus – the word derives from a root which signifies 'of the king' and is itself the root of our word 'paper' – could be made into writing paper that was both durable and practical in use. Its discovery and the attendant birth of literacy on a large scale in human culture has given us a wealth of information on how the Ancient Egyptians lived.

PERET: The 'Season of Coming-Forth', when the crops grew and were harvested. The Ancient Egyptian autumn, which ran from October to mid-February.

PHARAOH: The word is the Greek form of the Ancient Egyptian *per-aa*, which means 'Great House', signifying the palace rather than the king. It came to be applied to the king himself only from the time of the New Kingdom.

PSCHENT: The double-crown, combining the Red Crown of Lower Egypt and the White Crown of Upper Egypt and worn by rulers who governed the unified 'Two Lands'.

PUNT: A land to the south-east of Egypt, probably on the coast, in the region of modern Eritrea. Punt – from *Pwenet*, the 'land of the god' – was rich in exotic goods, from hardwoods, ivory and fragrances to gold, slaves and wild animals such as cheetahs and the sacred dog-headed baboon.

PYLON: From the Greek word for a gate, this signifies a monumental temple gateway.

PYRAMID: The massive funerary monument, consisting of four triangular sides meeting at a point, of the early kings of Egypt, notably those of the Fourth Dynasty. The word derives from colloquial Greek, variously translated as 'cheesecake' or 'wheatcake' – a mocking term used by later Greek immigrants because the shape reminded them of these comestibles.

ROYAL NAMES: Kings after the Fourth Dynasty had five formal names: the Horus, by which he was proclaimed a god; the Two Ladies, designating him king of both Upper and Lower Egypt; the Golden Horus, an additional honorific; the Throne Name and the Son of Ra name, the name by which he or (very occasionally) she was known popularly. The Throne and Son of Ra names were usually enclosed in a CARTOUCHE.

SARCOPHAGUS: Large rectangular box-like container, of wood or stone, which contained the MUMMY. The word derives from a Greek one meaning 'flesh-eater' – reflecting an early belief that certain stone used to contain a body actually consumed or annihilated its contents.

SCARAB: The dung-beetle who rolled a ball of its dung which contained its eggs. The ball represented the sun, the young beetles emerging from the ball seemed to indicate the spontaneous emergence of life. The *Scarabaeus* beetle was also one of the few creatures active when the sun was at its zenith. As the sun-god was the principal deity, it is small wonder that the scarab was always a powerful symbol.

SEQTET BOAT: The second six hours of day, from noon until nightfall.

SERDAB: An Arabic word variously translated to mean 'corridor' or 'cellar'; in Ancient Egyptian funerary architecture it denotes a chamber in a *mastaba* tomb, entirely enclosed, in which one or more statues of the deceased were placed. There would be two 'eye-holes' in one wall, facing the statue, through which it could be observed, and through which attendant priests could blow incense.

SHABTI: Small mummiform statues buried with royal or noble corpses. The *shabti* would, through magic, perform any tedious or disagreeable tasks in the afterlife. The word derives from the Ancient Egyptian *ushabti*, meaning 'answerer'. They were the servants and farm-labourers of the Fields of IARU.

SHEMU: Spring, or the 'Season of Drought'; the third season of the Ancient Egyptian year, running from mid-February until the end of May.

SOPDET: Sirius or the Dog Star. The rising of the star in mid-June, after dropping below the horizon for seventy days, marked the beginning of the Ancient Egyptian agricultural year, as it coincided with the beginning of the rise in the level of the Nile.

SPHINX: The Greek word denotes 'strangler', but the derivation may be from the Ancient Egyptian *shesep ankh*, meaning 'living image'. After the pyramid, probably the best-known image of Ancient Egypt. The human-headed lion (though there are variations) imbues the late king with the strength and force of the 'king of beasts'.

STELA: Marker of wood or stone which can act as a designator of a boundary, and/or as a record of some great event, personal achievement, or quasi-tombstone.

UPPER EGYPT: The southern part of the country, through which the Nile flows before it fans out into the Delta.

URAEUS: Possibly deriving from a Greek term, meaning 'she who rears up'. This cobra-about-to-strike decorated the front of the royal crown, often together with the head of a vulture. The vulture and the cobra, known as the 'Two Ladies', symbolized Upper and Lower Egypt respectively, and were embodied in two goddesses, Nekhbet and Wadjet.

VIZIER: The Ottoman term 'vizier' is commonly used today to translate the Ancient Egyptian *tjaty*, which is thought to have been a similar administrative post. The rank is that of chief district administrator, where the 'district', from the Eighteenth Dynasty onwards, was that of Upper or Lower Egypt. Earlier, however, the post reflected the chancellorship of the whole country.

Shabti found in the royal tomb of Tutankhamun.

CHRONOLOGY

All dates are BC (most dates are approximate).

5000: Trade between Northern Egypt and Palestine.
Late-Neolithic culture in Mesopotamia.

4500: Trade between Southern Egypt and Kush
(Nubia). Standing stones erected at Nabta Playa.

3500: First cities in Southern Mesopotamia.
Basket-coffin burials existing in Egypt.

3400: Writing developed in Sumeria.

3150: Earliest texts created for royal tombs at
Abydos.

3000: First towns of consequence in Southern
Egypt. Sumerian culture in the ascendancy
in Southern Mesopotamia. Pot-burials
existing in Egypt.

2900: Mud-brick royal funerary enclosures
at Abydos.

2800: *Gilgamesh* poems written in Sumeria – among
the very earliest known works of literature.

2630: Step Pyramid of King Djoser constructed
at Saqqara by his architect and vizier, Imhotep.
This was the first great pyramid.

2560: Construction of the Great Pyramid of Khufu
at Giza. The 'companion' smaller pyramids of
his successors Khafra and Menkaura followed
in about 2530 and 2500 respectively. Stone
and wooden sarcophagi. Corpse bandaged up.

2350: King Urukagina of Lagash in Sumeria
introduces first-known system of laws.

2250–2240: Harkhuf, Governor of Aswan,
leads expeditions to Kush.

2055: Middle Kingdom begins – the golden age
of Ancient Egyptian literature. Cartonnage
mummy-cases existing.

1840: Red Sea port built at Sawu.

1765: Hamurabi is King of Babylon.

1560: Kush becomes a unified kingdom.

1540: King Ahmose attacks Avaris.

1490: Valley of the Kings (known as 'The Great
Place') and the workmen's village at Deir el-
Medina founded. Tuthmosis I campaigns
against Mitanni (modern-day Syria).

1460: Queen Hatshepsur's expedition to the
land of Punt. Construction of her mortuary
temple at Deir el-Bahri.

1457: Tuthmosis III
defeats rebel Syrian princes
at the Battle of Megiddo
(*see* Chapter 6, p.111)
in Palestine.

1453: Tuthmosis III
marches on Qadesh.

1447: Tuthmosis III marches on Mitanni.

1441: Campaigns of Tuthmosis III in Southern
Palestine.

1400: Egyptian town and fort established at Napata
in the far south.

1385: Egypt exploits gold mines at Ibhet
and Ikhuyta in Nubia.

1340: Akhenaten founds a new royal capital,
Akhetaten (modern el-Amarna) to the north
of Thebes. Theban priesthood deprived of their
power and all gods subjugated to the Aten,
a deity associated with the sun and its
life-giving heat.

1323: Horemheb ascends the Egyptian throne.
Restores gods and general status quo. Last king
of Eighteenth Dynasty.

1300: Great Hypostyle Hall built at Karnak.

1279: Rameses II ascends the throne.

1274: Rameses II fights the Hittite king Muwatallis
at Qadesh. Both sides claim victory.

1259: Peace treaty between Egypt and
the Hittites, to face jointly the growing
threat posed by Assyria.

1250: Temple of Rameses II built at Abu Simbel.

1210, 1180–1175: Libyan incursions repulsed. Around
1177 BC incursion from the north by the 'sea
peoples' repulsed.

1185: Collapse of Hittite
Empire. Fall of Troy.

1115: Extensive investigations
into tomb robberies
(*see* Chapter 7, p.147)
at the Valley of the Kings.

950: Solomon builds the temple in Jerusalem.

900: Homer writes the *Iliad* and the *Odyssey*.

776: First Olympic Games.

750: Beginning of the rise of the Greek States.

674–664: War with Assyria.

663: The Assyrians sack Thebes.

656–513: The events resulting
from the murder in the
temple (*see* Chapter 8,
p.181) at Teudjoi unfold.

616: Egyptian campaigns
against Babylon.

600: Nekau II instigates plans for a canal
at the Red Sea isthmus.

587: Nebuchadrezar of Babylon takes Jerusalem.

525: Egypt defeated by Persia. Growing popularity
of animal cults and interest in magic.

490: Persia defeated by the Greek States at
Marathon.

450: The historian and writer Herodotus visits
Egypt. His account of the country in his *Histories*
remains a valuable source of information.

332: From this date onwards construction begins,
in traditional form, of some of Egypt's greatest
temples (Dendera, Edfu, Kom Ombo, Philae, etc.).

305: Accession of the Ptolemies.

164: The twin's tale
(*see* Chapter 9, p.209)
unfolds at Memphis
and Saqqara.

48: Queen Kleopatra VII
attempts to maintain
Egyptian independence of Rome, negotiating on
a political and personal level first with Julius
Caesar and then with Marcus Antonius.
In 48 BC Caesar, trapped in Alexandria by
Kleopatra's main adversary, Potheinos, set on fire
the ships in the harbour to prevent the enemy
from using them. The fire raged out of control,
spreading to the docks and finally to the great
library of Alexandria, where 400,000 papyrus
rolls were destroyed.

30: Egypt becomes a province of Rome.

PRINCIPAL DEITIES

Over their 3500-year history, the Ancient Egyptians worshipped a great number of gods and goddesses. Some of them were restricted to cities or localities, while others waxed and waned in importance with time. Certain gods were duplicates of the same 'idea'.

AMUN: Chief god of Thebes, the southern capital. Represented as a man, and associated with the supreme sun-god, RA. Animals dedicated to him were the ram and the goose.

ANUBIS: Jackal- or dog-headed god of embalming, and the protector of the mummy from the forces of evil during the night. Jackals roamed the Western Desert, where the dead were believed to dwell. Jackals also dug up corpses. Their adoption into the persona of a protector-god reflects an Ancient Egyptian tenet that a potential enemy may be disarmed by turning it into a 'friend'. Crocodiles, scorpions, hippos and (sometimes) snakes were treated similarly.

APIS: An aspect of PTAH as a bull. A real bull was selected, which had to have specific physical characteristics, and kept in luxurious confinement at Memphis. When it died, it was buried with great pomp at Saqqara. The cult was known as early as the First Dynasty, and was very popular in the Late Period.

APOPHIS: Great serpent demon of the night, representing the powers of darkness and evil. Apophis attacked the sun at dawn and dusk, and at those times of day the sky was stained red with the blood of the serpent, wounded in the battle.

ATEN: The God of the sun's energy, represented as the sun's disk whose rays ended in protecting hands.

ATUM: In some cosmogonies, the ur-god or quasi-chaos from which all things were created and who created the first generation of gods. He is associated with the primal mound, which emerged from the primal waters at the beginning of creation.

BA-NEB-DJEDET: Goat-god (of fertility) worshipped at Mendes, and usually represented as a ram.

BASTET: Goddess in the form of a cat, principally worshipped at Bubastis in the Delta. Originally inspired by a wildcat that lived in the region. Cats were domesticated by the Eleventh Dynasty and came to be universally revered.

BES: A grotesque dwarf with leonine attributes who protected the household from demons. Also associated with sex and childbirth.

GEB: The God of the Earth, represented as a man.

HAPY: The God of the Nile, especially in flood. A man whose woman's breasts represented fecundity.

HATHOR: The Goddess of love, music and dance. Often represented as a cow, or a human whose head is surmounted by a cow's horns and the sun's disk, she was also the suckler and protectress of the king.

HEKET: Frog-goddess associated with childbirth.

HORUS: One of the oldest and most popular gods. Horus was a defender of good against evil, the hawk-headed son of ISIS and OSIRIS, and therefore a member of the most important trinity in Ancient Egyptian theology. He was also associated with the sun. There were many manifestations of this god.

IMHOTEP: King Djoser's architect and chief minister's fame lived on after him and he was deified 2000 years after his death, a most unusual and signal honour. He came to be associated with healing and medicine and was associated by the Greeks with Aesculapius.

ISIS: The divine mother; wife and sister of OSIRIS.

KHEPRI: A primal god (sometimes seen as the creator-god) manifested as a scarab beetle.

KHNUM: Ram-headed god of Elephantine.

KHONS: God of the moon; the son of AMUN.

MAAT: Goddess of law, truth and world harmony. Her emblem was the feather, which she wore on top of her head.

MIN: The God of sexual fertility, always shown with a large erect phallus.

MUT: Wife of AMUN, originally a vulture-goddess, though also sometimes represented as lioness-headed.

NEITH: Ancient goddess of war. She was worshipped by a cult at Saïs in the Delta.

NEKHBET: The Vulture-goddess of Upper Egypt. The lotus and the White Crown were associated with this southern region.

NEPHTHYS: The sister of ISIS, and the wife of SET.

NUT: The Goddess of the sky and the sister-wife of GEB.

OSIRIS: The God of the underworld and of resurrection. The afterlife was of great importance to the Ancient Egyptians.

PTAH: Ancient god whose cult was centred at Memphis. Shown as a wrapped mummy, he may originally have been a god of craftsmen, but by the age of the pyramids he had become a creator-god. Later associated with two gods of death and the afterlife, OSIRIS and SOKAR.

RA: Principal sun-god.

SEKHMET: Lioness-headed goddess of destruction, a defender of the gods against evil and associated with healing; but also dangerous when uncontrolled.

SELKET: Protector-goddess of both the living and the dead, taking the form of a scorpion.

SERAPIS: A late-introduced god (under Ptolemy I) who was a composite of OSIRIS and APIS. The cult of Serapis spread throughout the Greek and Roman worlds, where the god also acquired the attributes of Aesculapius, Bacchus and Zeus.

SET: The God of storms and violence; brother and murderer of OSIRIS. Although sometimes regarded as a protector-god, Set was roughly equivalent to Satan. In the dualistic world-view of Ancient Egypt, Set resolved into the antithesis of Osiris: Osiris meant vegetation and cultivation, Set meant desert; Osiris meant the Nile, Set meant the wild and unpredictable sea. The animal associated with Set may have been dog- or horse-like: it has not been identified, but it is unlikely to have been a mythical creature since all other cultic animals were real.

SOBEK: The Crocodile god of Kom Ombo. Crocodile-worship was widespread.

SOKAR: Memphite god of the dead, who lent his name to Saqqara, the great necropolis near Memphis.

TAWERET: Hippopotamus-goddess endowed with human arms and legs and sometimes wearing a crocodile headdress and cloak or fused with a crocodile. A powerful goddess of childbirth.

THOTH: The god of time, also associated with writing: usually ibis-headed, he sometimes takes the form of a baboon.

WADJET: The Cobra-goddess of Lower Egypt, the northern of the 'Two Lands'. The papyrus was associated with this region, as was the Red Crown.

DYNASTIES

Although the scheme used by modern scholars is still that constructed by Manetho around 300 BC, and follows his divisions into 'dynasties' which roughly equate with, for example, the Plantagenets, Tudors and Stuarts in British history, there is now a refinement by which the dynasties are grouped into periods of homogeneous political and geographical-social themes. Much in Egyptology, where perhaps seventy-five per cent of data is still undiscovered, remains under discussion, however, and before the time that historical records that can be trusted began, around 700 BC, margins of question in dating can run to over 100 years in some cases. The following list of dynasties derives broadly from Shaw and Nicholson, but readers should not be surprised to find divergences in other books, where much earlier dates are often ascribed. The same *caveat* applies to the Chronology (*see* p. 247).

Kings had five names (*see* Glossary, p. 244), of which only one is usually given here. In most of the early cases, the throne name has been used. From the Middle Kingdom onwards, the popular name is generally used, the criterion being simply to adopt the name by which any given king is best known today. Names in round brackets in the Dynasty list are English translations of the Ancient Egyptian. Dates against kings' names refer to regnal years. All dates prior to about 700 BC should be regarded as approximate; if designated *circa*, the ascribed date is especially tenuous.

PRE-DYNASTIC PERIOD: 5500–3000 BC

Badarian	5500–4000
Naqada I (Amratian)	4000–3500
Naqada II (Gerzean)	3500–3150
Naqada III	3150–3000

ARCHAIC PERIOD (EARLY DYNASTIES)

Zekhen [='Scorpion']	pre-3100

'Scorpion' is one of the few very early kings to be documented, remembered in a large ceremonial mace-head as well as on shards of pottery. He ruled from Hierakonpolis (Nekhen) in the south, one of the earliest town-foundations, and from there his descendants possibly unified the greater part of the country.

1ST DYNASTY: 3100–2890 BC

Narmer [= Menes]	*c.* 3100
Aha ('Fighter')	*c.* 3100
Djer ('Stockade')	*c.* 3000
Djet ('Cobra')	*c.* 2980
Den ('Killer')	*c.* 2950
[Queen Merneith	*c.* 2950]

Daughter of Djer, wife of Djet, mother of Den. Possibly reigned as regent during Den's minority.

Anedjib	*c.* 2925
Semerkhet	*c.* 2900
Qa'a	*c.* 2890

2ND DYNASTY: 2890–2686 BC

Hetepsekhemwy	*c.* 2890
Raneb	dates uncertain
Nynetjer	dates uncertain
Weneg	dates uncertain
Sened	dates uncertain
Peribsen	*c.* 2700
Neferkasokar	*c.* 2700
Khasekhemwy	*c.* 2686

OLD KINGDOM

3RD DYNASTY: 2686–2613 BC

Sanakht	2686–2667
Djoser	2667–2648
Sekhemkhet	2648–2640
Khaba	2640–2637
Nebkare	*c.* 2637
Huni	*c.* 2637–2613

4TH DYNASTY: 2613–2498 BC

Sneferu	2613–2589
Khufu (alt: Cheops)	2589–2566
Djedefra	2566–2558
Khafra (alt: Chephren)	2558–2532
Menkaura (alt: Mycerinos)	2532–2503
Shepsekaf	2503–2498

5TH DYNASTY: 2494–2345 BC

Userkaf	2494–2487
Sahura	2487–2475
Neferirkara	2475–2455
Shepseskara	2455–2448
Raneferef	2448–2445
Nyuserra	2445–2421
Menkhauhor	2421–2414
Djedkara	2414–2375
Unas	2375–2345

6TH DYNASTY: 2345–2181 BC

Teti	2345–2323
Userkara	2323–2321
Pepy I	2321–2287
Merenra	2287–2278
Pepy II	2278–2184

Pepy II came to the throne as a child (of six years old, Manetho tells us), and his reign of 94 years is the longest known.

Queen Nitiqret	2184–2181

FIRST INTERMEDIATE PERIOD

7TH AND 8TH DYNASTIES: c. 2181–2125 BC

These consisted of a large number of short-lived 'mini-kings' based at Memphis whose dates are uncertain. Among the names identified are:

Netjerkare
Menkare
Neferkare I (?)
Neferkare II
Djedkare
Neferkare III
Merenhor
Nikare
Neferkare IV
Neferkahor
Neferkare V
Neferkamin
Qakare
Wadjkare
Neferkauhor
Neferirkare

9TH AND 10TH DYNASTIES: c. 2160–2025 BC

The Ninth Dynasty was founded at Herakleopolis (Heneneswe) by Meryibra, and the Tenth Dynasty continued there. Some overlap between these and the preceding (local) dynasties will be noticed. The following names have been identified; dates are uncertain:

Meryibra
Neferkare
Wahkare
Nebkaure
Merykare

11TH DYNASTY: c. 2125–2055 BC

This first phase of the Dynasty was centred in Thebes. The second phase, which ushered in the Middle Kingdom Period, saw the unification of the whole land under one king again. Further overlap with the preceding dynasties will be noticed.

Mentuhotep I	c. 2125
Intef I	2125–2112
Intef II	2112–2063
Intef III	2063–2055

MIDDLE KINGDOM

11TH DYNASTY: 2055–1985 BC

Mentuhotep II	2055–2004
Mentuhotep III	2004–1992
Mentuhotep IV	1992–1985

12TH DYNASTY: 1985–1795 BC

The overlapping dates of some of the kings in this period probably reflect periods when the successor reigned in tandem with the occupant – a kind of handover term which ensured stability.

Amenemhat I	1985–1955
Senusret (alt: Sesostris) I	1965–1920
Amenemhat II	1922–1878
Senusret II	1880–1874
Senusret III	1874–1855
Amenemhat III	1855–1808
Amenemhat IV	1808–1799
Queen Sobekneferu	1799–1795

13TH AND 14TH DYNASTIES: c.1750–1650 BC

As the Middle Kingdom declined, Ancient Egypt entered a new dark age. The country became divided again, and the obscure kinglets of the Thirteenth and Fourteenth Dynasties probably ruled contemporaneously from different power centres – more than one or even two kinglets may well have been ruling in different places at the same time. The throne seldom passed from father to son or relative to relative, and the seventy-odd rulers of the Thirteenth Dynasty held power on average for about two-and-a-half years each. Thirteenth Dynasty rulers operated from Memphis or Itjtawy but the Fourteenth Dynasty is still shrouded in mystery. Most dates are uncertain.

Hor	
Khendjer	
Sobekhotep III	
Neferhotep I	c. 1730–1720
Sihathor	
Sobekhotep IV	

Some sources state that the last three were brothers.

SECOND INTERMEDIATE PERIOD

15TH DYNASTY: 1650–1550 BC

This was the first Hyksos dynasty, ruling from Itjtawy and without control of the whole country. The Hyksos infiltrated from the north-east, and preferred to stay in northern Egypt. The last kings of the Thirteenth and Fourteenth Dynasties were probably under their sway. Note the 'foreign' names of the rulers.

Salitis	dates uncertain
Khyan	c. 1600
Apepi	c. 1555
Khamudi	dates uncertain

16TH DYNASTY: 1650–1550 BC

Composed of minor Hyksos kinglets, contemporaneously ruling their own fiefdom.

17TH DYNASTY: 1650–1550 BC

A contemporaneous dynasty of Egyptian rulers based in Thebes (Waset), the chief town of the south. 'Isolated and impoverished', as one commentator has it, but full of indomitable spirit. From this power base the Hyksos were eventually driven out (or, according to some sources, left peacefully). Most dates are uncertain. The following lists only the principal rulers:

Rehotep	
Djehuty	
Mentuhotep VII (?)	
Nebiriau I	
Nubkheperra Intef VI	
Senakhtenra Taa I	
Seqenenra Taa II	c. 1560
Kamose	1555–1550

NEW KINGDOM

18TH DYNASTY: 1550–1295 BC

One of the greatest periods of Ancient Egypt. The second half of the Eighteenth Dynasty, from Tuthmosis III, through to the first reigns of the Nineteenth Dynasty could arguably be described as the golden age of the Empire. Overlapping dates indicate co-regencies.

Ahmose	1550–1525
Amenhotep I	1525–1504
Tuthmosis I	1504–1492
Tuthmosis II	1492–1479
Tuthmosis III	1479–1425
Queen Hatshepsut	1473–1458
Amenhotep II	1427–1400
Tuthmosis IV	1400–1390
Amenhotep III	1390–1352
Amenhotep IV (Akhenaten)	1352–1336
Smenkhkara	1338–1336
Tutankhamun	1336–1327
Ay	1327–1323
Horemheb	1323–1295

19TH DYNASTY: 1295–1186 BC

Rameses I	1295–1294
Sety I	1294–1279
Rameses II ('The Great')	1279–1213
Merenptah	1213–1203
Amenmessu	1203–1200
Sety II	1200–1194
Saptah	1194–1188
Tausret	1188–1186

20TH DYNASTY: 1186–1069 BC

Sethnakhte	1186–1184
Rameses III	1184–1153
Rameses IV	1153–1147
Rameses V	1147–1143
Rameses VI	1143–1136
Rameses VII	1136–1129
Rameses VIII	1129–1126
Rameses IX	1126–1108
Rameses X	1108–1099
Rameses XI	1099–1069

THIRD INTERMEDIATE PERIOD

21ST DYNASTY: 1069–945 BC

Egypt ceased to be a great power after the reign of Rameses III. A long, slow decline followed. The seven kings of the Twenty-first Dynasty ruled from Tanis in the Eastern Delta, and were active only in the north. The dynasty is described as 'Tanite'.

Smendes	1069–1043
Amenemnisu	1043–1039
Psusennes I	1039–991
Amenemope	993–984
Osorkon ('The Elder')	984–978
Siamun	978–959
Psusennes II	959–945

22ND DYNASTY: 945–715 BC

A dynasty of ethnic Libyan kings (Libyans had been settling in Egypt throughout the Twenty-first Dynasty) who made their base at Bubastis (Per-Bastet, modern Zagazig), to the south-west of Tanis.

Sheshonq I	945–924
Osorkon I	924–889
[Sheshonq II	c. 890
Died within a year of co-regency with his father, Osorkon I.]	
Takelot I	889–874
Osorkon II	874–850
Takelot II	850–825
Sheshonq III	c. 825–798
Sheshonq IV	c. 798–773
Pimay	773–767
Sheshonq V	767–730
Osorkon IV	730–715

23RD DYNASTY: 818–715 BC

A partially contemporaneous regime of Libyan kings based in Tanis, Herakleopolis Magna, Hermopolis Magna and Leontopolis. Three principal rulers emerge from this dynasty.

Pedubastis I	818–793
Seshsonq	c. 780
Osorkon III	777–749

24TH DYNASTY: c. 727–715 BC

A short-lived dynasty contemporaneous with the end of the Twenty-second. Its founder was a Libyan prince of Saïs in the Western Delta. The dynasty was overwhelmed by Kushite (Nubian) invaders from the south. There is great disagreement here as to names and dates. Two kings, tentatively identifed as father and son, are given. Dates are uncertain.

Tefnakhte
Bakenrenef

LATE PERIOD

25TH DYNASTY ('KUSHITE'): 747–656 BC

Power returned to the south under the Nubian founder of this dynasty, Piankhy (or 'Piy'). Note that there is a wide overlap in dates, since Piankhy was already ruling in the south. His brother Shabaqo may be regarded as the true founder of the dynasty.

Piankhy	747–716
Shabaqo	716–702
Shabitqo	702–690
Taharqo	690–664
Tanutamani	664–656

26TH DYNASTY ('SAÏTE'): 664–525 BC

The Assyrians conquered Egypt from the north in 671 BC and appointed a prince of Saïs in the Western Delta as vassal ruler. His name was Nekau and it is likely that he was killed in battle with the last of the Kushite rulers, Tanutamani. The true founder of the dynasty was his son, Psamtek I, who with his father had undergone a period of Assyrian indoctrination. Under him, the land of Egypt was in due course once again unified.

Nekau I	672–664
Psamtek I	664–610
Nekau II	610–595
Psamtek II	595–589
Apries	589–570
Ahmose II	570–526
Psamtek III	526–525

27TH DYNASTY: 525–404 BC

Persia, expanding aggressively west and south, conquered Egypt and deposed Psamtek III. The country was then ruled by Persian governors (*satraps*) while the Persian Emperor was Pharaoh *in absentia*. Apart from Darius I, the Persians ruled with a heavy hand.

Cambyses	525–522

Darius I	522–486
Xerxes I	486–465
Artaxerxes I	465–424
Darius II	424–405
Artaxerxes II	405–359

28TH DYNASTY: 404–399 BC

This king was a one-man dynasty. He was Amyrtaios, a prince of Saïs who, following in his eponymous grandfather's footsteps, led a revolt against the oppressive Persian regime after the death of Darius II, and had himself proclaimed king. He won popular acclaim, but details of his life, rule and death are still unclear.

Amyrtaios	404–399

29TH DYNASTY: 399–393 BC

The Persians were finally driven out, and the Twenty-ninth and Thirtieth Dynasties saw a resumption of Saïte power.

Nepherites I	399–393
Hakor	393–380
Nepherites II	c. 380

30TH DYNASTY: 380–343 BC

Nectanebo I	380–362
Teos	362–360
Nectanebo II	360–343

31ST DYNASTY: 343–332 BC

This 'dynasty' saw the return of the Persians, who invaded again brutally after several aggressive attempts during the Thirtieth Dynasty.

Artaxerxes III	343–338
Arses	338–336
Darius III	336–332

PTOLEMAIC PERIOD

The Persian dominion was short-lived, swept aside by the triumphant armies of Alexander the Great, who ushered in a short period of chaotic rule. He was succeeded as 'pharaoh' by his simple-minded half-brother Philip (they shared their father), who was subsequently murdered on the orders of Alexander's mother. Philip was succeeded by Alexander's son, who was himself subsequently murdered (in 311 BC), though represented as ruler until 305.

THE MACEDONIANS: 332–305 BC

Alexander the Great	332–323
Philip Arrhidaeus	323–317
Alexander IV	317–305

THE PTOLEMAIC DYNASTY: 305–30 BC

Ptolemy I was a boon-companion of Alexander the Great and one of his principal generals. On Alexander's death the empire was divided up between his chief officers and Ptolemy took Egypt. A sort of regeneration of Egypt followed and the dynasty, though often deeply flawed and corrupt, featuring perverts to make the Borgias blush, somehow maintained the integrity of the country until it was finally swept away by the 'modern' might of Imperial Rome. Overlaps in regnal years reflect the vicissitudes of this troubled period.

Ptolemy I Soter I	305–285
Ptolemy II Philadelphus	285–246
Ptolemy III Euergetes I	246–221
Ptolemy IV Philopator	221–205
Ptolemy V Epiphanes	205–180
Ptolemy VI Philometor	180–145
Ptolemy VII Neos Philopator	145
Ptolemy VIII Euergetes II	170–116
Ptolemy IX Soter II	116–107
Ptolemy X Alexander I	107–88
Ptolemy IX Soter II (restored)	88–80
Ptolemy XI Alexander II	80
Ptolemy XII Neos Dionysius	80–51
Queen Kleopatra VII Arsinoe	51–30
Ptolemy XIII	51–47
Ptolemy XIV	47–44
Ptolemy XV Caesarion	44–30

This concludes the dynasties of Ancient Egypt. In 30 BC the future Roman Emperor Augustus assumed the kingship of Egypt, which remained under Roman control until AD 395.

379–395: Reign of the Emperor Theodosius I – 'The Great' – who converted to Christianity in 380 after an illness and four years later ordered the closure of the Egyptian temples. He subsequently sanctioned the persecution of the 'pagans' and the destruction of their places of worship, and these moves were endorsed by his successor, Valentinian II. The Christians were all too happy to carry out his wishes.

There followed a period of Byzantine rule, until the Arab conquest of 640. In 1517 Egypt became part of the Ottoman Empire. From 1882 to 1922 the country was controlled by the British. It was an independent kingdom again from 1922 to 1953, and since then has been a republic.

BIBLIOGRAPHY

Adkins, Lesley and Roy: *The Keys of Egypt*. HarperCollins, London, 2000

Aldred, Cyril: *Akhenaten*. Thames & Hudson, London, 1988

Andrews, Carol: *Ancient Egyptian Jewellery*. British Museum Publications, London, 1990

Bagnall, Roger: *Egypt in Late Antiquity*. Princeton University Press, Princeton, 1993

Bagnall, Roger and Frier, B.: *The Demography of Roman Egypt*. Cambridge University Press, Cambridge, 1994

Bowman, A.: *Egypt After the Pharaohs*. University of California Press, Berkeley, 1990

Cambridge Ancient History: Cambridge University Press, Cambridge: several different volumes consulted, under different editors, with contributions by various scholars.

Chaveau, M.: *Egypt in the Age of Cleopatra*. Cornell University Press, Ithaca, 2000

Cohen, E.: *Athenian Economy and Society: A Banking Perspective*. Princeton University Press, Princeton, 1992

David, Rosalie: *The Ancient Egyptians*. Sussex Academic Press, Brighton, 1998 (revised edition)

Davies, W. V.: *Egyptian Hieroglyphs*. British Museum Publications, London, 1987

Darby, W., Ghalioungui, P., and Grivetti, L.: *Food – The Gift of Osiris*. Academic Press, London, 1977

Depauw, M.: *A Companion to Demotic Studies*. Fondation Egyptologique Reine Elisabeth, Brussels, 1997

Ellis, S.: *Graeco-Roman Egypt*. Shire Publications, Princes Risborough, 1992

El-Mahdy, Christine: *Mummies, Myth and Magic*. Thames & Hudson, London, 1989

Freed, Rita E., Markowitz, Yvonne J. and D'Auria, Sue H. (eds): *Pharaohs of the Sun*. Thames & Hudson, London, 1999

Freud, Sigmund: *Moses and Monotheism*. Vintage, New York. Orig. publn. 1939

Garrison, D.: *Sexual Culture in Ancient Greece*. University of Oklahoma Press, Norman, 2000

Gill, Anton: *City of Dreams*. Bloomsbury, London, 1994

Gurney, O. R.: *The Hittites*. Penguin, Harmondsworth, 1952

Goudriaan, K.: *Ethnicity in Ptolemaic Egypt*. J. C. Gieben, Amsterdam, 1988

Green, P.: *Alexander to Actium: The Hellenistic Age*. Thames & Hudson, London, 1990

Hazzard, R. A.: *Imagination of a Monarchy: Studies in Ptolemaic Propaganda*. University of Toronto Press, Toronto, 2000

Herodotus: *The Histories* (trl. Aubrey de Sélincourt). Penguin, Harmondsworth, 1954

Hölbl, Günther (trl. Tina Saavedra): *A History of the Ptolemaic Empire*. Routledge, London, 2001

Hornung, Erik (trl Elizabeth Bredeck): *Idea into Image – Ideas on Ancient Egyptian Thought*. Timken, New York, 1992

Houlihan, Patrick: *The Animal World of the Pharaohs*. Thames & Hudson, London, 1996

Houlihan, Patrick: *Wit and Humour in Ancient Egypt*. Rubicon, London, 2001

Houston, Mary G. and Hornblower, Florence S.: *Ancient Egyptian Costume*. Dar Al-Fergiani, Cairo, n.d.

Ikram, Salima and Dodson, Aidan: *The Mummy in Ancient Egypt*. Thames & Hudson, London, 1998

James, T. G. H.: *An Introduction to Ancient Egypt*. British Museum Publications, London, 1979

James, T. G. H.: *Pharaoh's People*. Oxford University Press, London, 1985

Janssen, Rosalind M. and Jac. J.: *Growing Up in Ancient Egypt*. Rubicon, London, 1990

Josephus: *The Jewish War and Other Selections* (trl. H. St. J. Thackeray and Ralph Marcus; ed. Moses I. Finley). NEL, 1966

Karageorghis, V.: *Kition*. Thames & Hudson, London, 1976

Kemp, Barry J.: *Ancient Egypt*. Routledge, London, 1989

Kitchen, K. A.: *Pharaoh Triumphant [a life of Rameses II]*. Aris and Phillips, 1982

Lambelet, K.: *How to Read Hieroglyphs*. Lehnert and Landrock, Cairo, 1974

Lauer, Jean-Philippe: *Saqqara: the Royal Cemetery of Memphis*. Thames & Hudson, London, 1976

Lewis, N.: *The Interpretation of Dreams and Portents*. Sameil Stevens Hakkert and Co., Toronto, 1976

Lichtheim, Miriam: *Demotic Ostraca from Medinet Habu*. Chicago University Press, Chicago, 1957

Lichtheim, Miriam: *Ancient Egyptian Literature, Vol. III: The Late Period*. University of California Press, Berkeley, 1980

Lurker, Manfred (trl. Barbara Cummings): *The Gods and Symbols of Ancient Egypt*. Thames & Hudson, London, 1980

Macdowell, Andrea: *Village Life in Ancient Egypt*. Oxford University Press, London, 1999

Manley, Bill: *The Penguin Historical Atlas of Ancient Egypt*. Penguin, Harmonsworth, 1996

Manniche, Lise: *Sexual Life in Ancient Egypt*. Kegan Paul International, London, 1987

Montet, Pierre (trl A. R. Maxwell-Hyslop and Margaret S. Drower): *Everyday Life in Ancient Egypt*. Edward Arnold, London, 1958

Montserrat, Dominic: *Sex and Society in Graeco-Roman Egypt*. Kegan Paul International, London, 1996

Montserrat, Dominic: *Akhenaten*. Routledge, London, 2000

Moorey, P. R. S.: *Ancient Egypt*. Ashmolean Museum, Oxford, 1988

Nunn, John F.: *Ancient Egyptian Medicine*. British Museum Publications, London, 1996

Parkinson, R. B.: *Voices from Ancient Egypt*. British Museum Publications, London, 1991

Parkinson, Richard: *Cracking Codes*. British Museum Publications, London, 1999

Partridge, Robert: *Transport in Ancient Egypt*. Rubicon, London, 1996

Peet, Thomas Eric: *Great Tomb Robberies of the XXth Dynasty*. Clarendon, Oxford, 1930

Pinch, Geraldine: *Magic in Ancient Egypt*. British Museum Publications, London, 1994

Pliny the Younger: Letters (trl. Betty Radice). Penguin, Harmondsworth, 1963

Plutarch: Makers of Rome (trl. Ian Scott-Kilvert). Penguin, Harmondsworth, 1965

Pomeroy, S. B.: *Women in Hellenistic Egypt – from Alexander to Cleopatra*. Schocken Books, New York, 1984

Quirke, Stephen: *Ancient Egyptian Religion*. Dover, New York, 1990

Ray, J.: *Reflections of Osiris – Lives from Ancient Egypt*. Profile, London, 2001

Redford, Donald B.: *Egypt, Canaan and Israel in Ancient Times*. Princeton University Press, Princeton, 1992

Redford, Donald B. (ed.): *Oxford Encyclopaedia of Ancient Egypt*. Oxford University Press, Oxford, 2001

Rice, Michael: *Who's Who in Ancient Egypt*. Routledge, London, 1999

Roberts, Alison: *Hathor Rising*. Northgate, Totnes, 1995

Robins, Gay: *Women in Ancient Egypt*. British Museum Publications, London, 1993

Romer, John: *Romer's Egypt*. Michael Joseph/Rainbird, London, 1982

Romer, John: *Ancient Lives*. Guild, London, 1984

Rowlandson, J.: *Women and Society in Greek and Roman Egypt*. Cambridge University Press, Cambridge, 1998

Sauneron, Serge (trl. David Lorton): *The Priests of Ancient Egypt*. Cornell University Press, Ithaca and London, 2000

Seton-Williams, M. V.: *Egyptian Legends and Stories*. Rubicon, London, 1988

Shaw, Ian: *Egyptian Warfare and Weapons*. Shire Publications, Princes Risborough, 1991

Shaw, Ian and Nicholson, Paul: *British Museum Dictionary of Ancient Egypt*. British Museum Publications, London, 1995

Shipley, G.: *The Greek World After Alexander*. Routledge, London, 2000

Spencer, A. J.: *Death in Ancient Egypt*. Penguin, Harmondsworth, 1982

Staatliche Museen Preussischer Kulturbestiz: Aegyptisches Museum Berlin. Belser AG, Stuttgart and Zurich, 1980

Stead, Miriam: *Egyptian Life*. British Museum Publications, London, 1986

Strouhal, Eugen: *Life in Ancient Egypt*. Cambridge University Press, Cambridge, 1992

Taylor, J.: *Death and the Afterlife in Ancient Egypt*. British Museum Publications, London, 2001

Thompson, Dorothy: *Memphis Under the Ptolemies*. Princeton University Press, Princeton, 1988

Treasures of Tutankhamun. Exhibition catalogue. British Museum/Rainbird, 1972

Wallis Budge, E. A.: *Egyptian Magic*. Arkana edition, London, 1988

Wallis Budge, E. A.: *The Book of the Dead*. Arkana edition, London, 1989

Watterson, Barbara: *The Gods of Ancient Egypt*. Batsford, London, 1984

Watterson, Barbara: *The Egyptians*. Blackwell, Oxford, 1997

Wilkinson, Richard H.: *Reading Egyptian Art*. Thames & Hudson, London, 1992

Wilkinson, Richard H.: *The Complete Temples of Ancient Egypt*. Thames & Hudson, London, 2000

Wilson, Hilary: *Egyptian Food and Drink*. Shire Publications, Princes Risborough, 1988

INDEX

PICTURE CREDITS

While every effort has been made to trace
the owners of copyright material reproduced
herein, the publishers would like to apologize
for any omissions and will be pleased to
incorporate missing acknowledgements
in any future editions.

Ancient Art & Architecture Collection: 16,
21, 39, 40, 43, 47 (top right), 48, 49, 58
(below), 62, 78, 82, 83, 84, 85, 86, 93, 94,
96, 97, 100, 101, 102, 104, 106, 107, 174,
192, 244, 245, 246

The British Museum: 24, 41, 44, 45, 46,
47(below, left), 58 (below, centre), 79, 88, 98,
99, 151, 179

Hardlines: (Maps) 15, 61

Graham Harrison: 20, 57, 112

The John Rylands University Library
of Manchester: 68, 207

Musée du Louvre: 242

Petrie Museum of Egyptian Archaeology,
University College London: 214

Soprintendenza Al Museo Delle Antichità
Egizie-Torino (Italy): 227

All other photographs:
© Wall to Wall (Egypt) Ltd 2003,
photographer Giles Keyte